ADVENTIST PIONEER PLACES

New York & New England

ADVENTIST
PIONEER
PLACES

New York & New England

Merlin D. Burt

 REVIEW AND HERALD®
PUBLISHING ASSOCIATION

Since 1861 | www.reviewandherald.com

This book was
Copyedited by James Cavil
Interior designed by Katy Wolfer
Cover designed by Bryan Gray
Vector illustrations by Katy Wolfer and Nathan Hellman

PRINTED IN U.S.A.

15 14 13 12 11   5 4 3 2 1

Library of Congress Cataloging-in-Publication Data
Burt, Merlin D.
  Adventist pioneer places : New York and New England / Merlin D. Burt.
      p. cm.
  Includes index.
  1. Seventh-day Adventists—New York (State)—History. 2. Historic sites—New York (State)—Guidebooks. 3. New York (State)—Guidebooks. 4. Seventh-day Adventists—New England—History. 5. Historic sites—New England—Guidebooks. 6. New England—Guidebooks.
  I. Title.
  BX6153.3.N7B87 2011
  286.7'74—dc22
                        2011003392
  ISBN 978-0-8280-2568-3

Dedicated

to

the many Seventh-day Adventist Theological
Seminary students and spouses who have over the
years attended the Adventist History Study Tour
of New York and New England. Their enthusiasm,
pursuit of knowledge, and spiritual focus have
inspired me to develop this tour guide book.

Table of Contents

Preface

Seventh-day Adventists have an incredible heritage of faith. In some ways they are unique among Protestant Christians. They see themselves as a movement of prophecy connected to the events described in Daniel 2 and 7-9 and Revelation 12-14. Adventists are a people who love Jesus and look for His soon return in the clouds of glory. The Second Coming is a tangible hope repeatedly emphasized in the Bible.

They also cherish the Sabbath because it memorializes God's six-day creation of the world, Jesus' finished work on the cross, and righteousness by faith. The Sabbath has further end-time importance because it calls us back to worship the Creator and Redeemer. This book is written from a faith perspective. The stories of this book are directly linked to a cherished biblical faith and a living experience with God.

I am glad that you have decided to visit some of the significant Adventist historical sites in New York and New England. Both personal visits and a guided Adventist heritage tour can be a very rewarding experience. It brings to life the stories of God's leading in the past and provides new perspectives on how God can work in our lives today.

First Samuel 4-7 tells the story of how God delivered Israel when they were spiritually backslidden from Him and were challenged by a most dangerous enemy. It begins with a terrible defeat when the ark of the covenant was captured by the Philistines and concludes with the establishment of a memorial stone named Ebenezer after their deliverance by a mighty act of God (1 Samuel 7:12). The word *Ebenezer* means "stone of help." This monumental stone reminded the children of Israel how God had delivered them from their enemies. In many ways the historical sites and the stories of God's leading described in this book are Ebenezers for those who are the spiritual descendants of the early Advent movement. They point to the mighty acts of God in the lives of people who, though weak and fallible, were used by God in remarkable ways to establish the Seventh-day Adventist Church that today circles the globe and includes many millions of people.

Every effort has been made to make this guidebook as historically accurate as possible. Nearly every site described has been historically researched and confirmed. Those who have read previous Adventist tour guide books will find that some sites are omitted. In most cases this is because research has shown that the site was incorrect. Fortunately, research has also led to the discovery of many new sites.

GPS coordinates and maps are provided for most of the sites in this book. Some locations require further directions, and where needed, this has been provided. It is also useful to have a modern road map available. Adventist history sites are sometimes located at remote locations; at other times they are in the midst of large cities. For nearly all the sites described in this book there are modern pictures of the location.

Many of the sites described in this book are privately owned. Some of the various owners have at times opened their homes to tour groups and showed an interest in the history of their property. I would request that when visiting at historical sites, visitors respect the privacy of the owners.

Earlier editions of this book were published on a very limited basis for graduate study tours at the Seventh-day Adventist Theological Seminary at Andrews University. I wish to express appreciation to Katy Wolfer for her excellent work in layout and design. Her skill in designing maps was particularly helpful. Nathan Hellman assisted her in some aspects of creating maps. Also, I am grateful to Stan Hickerson, Jerry Moon, James R. Nix, Tim Poirier, and Brian Strayer for reading the manuscript and suggesting improvements and editorial corrections. Stan Hickerson and Jim Nix were valuable partners in research trips to confirm historical locations and information. Denis Kaiser, my graduate assistant, helped with verifying quotes and in other ways. I would further thank the various curators, librarians, and archivists who provided assistance at various institutions and organizations. Thanks are due to Barbara M. Rimkunas of the Exeter Historical Society, Edouard L. Desrochers of the Phillips Exeter Academy, Nicholas Noyes of the Maine Historical Society, and the New Bedford Whaling Museum. Appreciation is also due to Andrews University and the Ellen G. White Estate for providing time and support for the development of this book. Many of the photographs in this volume were taken by capable former seminary students who attended previous tours, and by others who shared their talents. Jerry Moon has been a faithful tour guide partner and has contributed in many ways. Finally, I would express appreciation to JoAlyce Waugh and others at the Review and Herald. Some information in this book is drawn from the White Estate publication *In the Footprints of the Pioneers,* which has been used for many years as a tour guide book.

I pray that this book will not only satisfy your intellectual curiosity but also be a real spiritual blessing. Ellen G. White, one of the three key founders of the Seventh-day Adventist Church, wrote words that are often quoted as Adventists think about heritage. "In reviewing our past history, having traveled over every step of advance to our present standing, I can say, Praise God! As I see what God has wrought, I am filled with astonishment and with confidence in Christ as Leader. We have nothing to fear for the future, except as we shall forget the way the Lord has led us, and His teaching in our past history. We are now a strong people, if we will put our trust in the Lord; for we are handling the mighty truths of the Word of God. We have everything to be thankful for" (*General Conference Daily Bulletin,* Jan. 29, 30, 1893, p. 24; see also *Life Sketches,* p. 196).

Merlin D. Burt
Center for Adventist Research
White Estate Branch Office
Andrews University

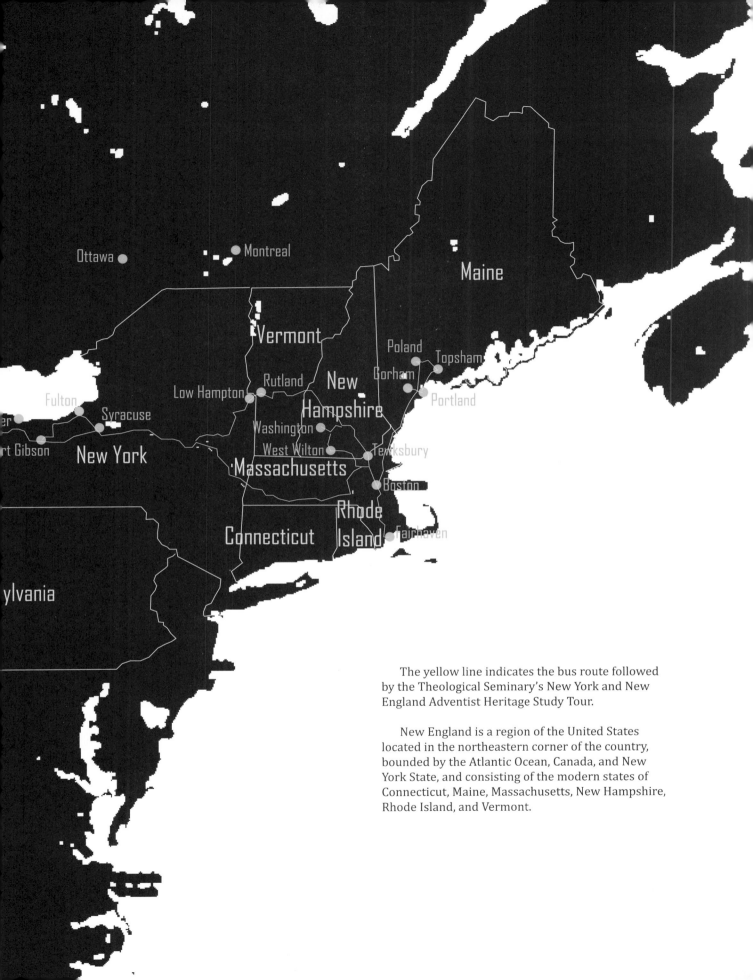

The yellow line indicates the bus route followed by the Theological Seminary's New York and New England Adventist Heritage Study Tour.

New England is a region of the United States located in the northeastern corner of the country, bounded by the Atlantic Ocean, Canada, and New York State, and consisting of the modern states of Connecticut, Maine, Massachusetts, New Hampshire, Rhode Island, and Vermont.

Locations

Maine

Cape Elizabeth

Portland Head Lighthouse
1000 Shore Road
Cape Elizabeth, Maine
N 43°37.359'
W 070°12.628'

East Sullivan

William Foy grave
Birch Tree Cemetery
near 185 Tunk Lake Road
N 44°51.346'
W 068°14.548'

Site of William Foy home
near 1013 Tunk Lake Road
N 44°33.306'
W 068°06.233'

Gorham

Ellen G. White historic marker
corner of Fort Hill Road and
      Valley View Drive
Gorham, Maine
N 43°42.084'
W 070°27.331'

Harmon home (1846-1853)
243 Fort Hill Road
Gorham, Maine
N 43°41.755'
W 070°27.138'

North Street Cemetery
Fort Hill Road
Gorham, Maine
N 43°43.483'
W 070°29.003'

Robert Harmon, Jr., grave
Fort Hill Cemetery
Gorham, Maine
N 43°41.917'
W 070°27.259'

Palmyra

Deacon John White home
110 Warren Hill Road
Palmyra, Maine
N 44°85.459'
W 069°36.988'

Paris Hill

Charles Andrews home
450 Paris Hill Road
Paris Hill, Maine
N 44°15.496'
W 070°30.012'

Cyprian Stevens home
Hooper Ledge Road
Paris Hill, Maine
N 44°14.651'
W 070°30.035'

Edward Andrews home
455 Paris Hill Road
Paris Hill, Maine
N 44°15.496'
W 070°30.012'

Hillside Cemetery
Paris Hill Road
Paris Hill, Maine
N 44°25.160'
W 070°49.890'

Review and Herald site
Academy Road
Paris Hill, Maine
N 44°25.866'
W 070°50.067'

Poland

Foss home (1840-1849)
on Strout Road
Poland, Maine
N 44°03.405'
W 070°24.643'

Harmon home (1829-1833)
4510 Jackson Street
Poland, Maine
N 44°02.860'
W 070°23.893'

Portland

Bracket Street School
155 Bracket Street
Portland, Maine
N 43°39.048'
W 070°15.992'

Chestnut Street
Methodist Church
15 Chestnut Street
Portland, Maine
N 43°39.568'
W 070°15.472'

Deering Oaks Park
Park Avenue and Forest Avenue
N 43°39.503'
W 070°16.480'

Longfellow's home
489 Congress Street
N 43°39.395'
W 070°15.615'

Site of baptizing shore (approximate)
near Longfellow's boyhood home on
    the corner of Fore and Hancock
N 43°39.717'
W 070°14.859'

Site of Beethoven Hall
N 43°39.422'
W 070°15.600'

Site of Casco Street Christian Church
N 43°39.392'
W 070°15.750'

Site of Harmon home (1833-1846)
(currently a school play area)
Spruce Street
Portland, Maine
N 43°39.023'
W 070°15.962'

Topsham

Stockbridge Howland home
7 Elm Street
Topsham, Maine
N 43°55.567'
W 069°57.770'

Massachusetts

Boston

Quincy Market
Quincy Market Colonnade
Boston, Massachusetts
N 42°21.36'
W 071°3.18'

Fairhaven

Joseph Bates' boyhood home
(Meadow Farm)
191 Main Street
Fairhaven, Massachusetts
(774) 328-8882
Hours: (call for hours)
N 41°38.777'
W 070°54.504'

Joseph Bates home on Mulberry Street
19 Mulberry Street
Fairhaven, Massachusetts
N 41°38.470'
W 070°54.063'

Bunker home
209 Main Street
Fairhaven, Massachusetts
N 41°38.867'
W 070°54.536'

Fairhaven Academy
45 Center Street
Fairhaven, Massachusetts
N 41°38.606'
W 070°54.409'

Fairhaven Bridge
N 41°38.426'
W 70°54.470'

Washington Street Christian Church
32 Washington Street
Fairhaven, Massachusetts
N 41°38.243'
W 070°54.212'

Haverhill

Hazen Foss grave
Elmwood Cemetery
96 Salem Street
Haverhill, Massachusetts
N 42°45.914'
W 71°04.178'

North Lancaster

J. N. Andrews home
1444 Main Street
North Lancaster, Massachusetts
N 42°28.323'
W 071°40.860'

South Lancaster

Founder's Hall
Atlantic Union College
338 Main Street
South Lancaster, Massachusetts
N 42°26.737'
W 071°41.114'

Sturbridge

Old Sturbridge Village
1 Old Sturbridge Village Road
Sturbridge, Massachusetts
N 42°06.467'
W 072°05.933'

New Hampshire

East Kingston

Site of East Kingston camp meeting
45 Sandborn Road
East Kingston Township, New
Hampshire
N 42°56.167'
W 071°00.025'

Exeter

Phillips Exeter Academy
53 Front Street
Exeter, New Hampshire
N 42°58.772'
W 070°57.013'

Site of Exeter camp meeting
80 Newfields Road
Exeter, New Hampshire
N 43°01.037'
W 070°56.471'

New Ipswich

Leonard Hastings farm
Boynton Hill Road
New Ipswich, New Hampshire
N 42°46.720'
W 071°52.272'

Leonard and Elvira Hastings graves
Central Cemetery
New Hampshire 123A
New Ipswich, New Hampshire
N 42°44.999'
W 071°51.318'

Washington

Cyrus Farnsworth home
8 Millen Pond Road
Washington, New Hampshire
N 43°09.779'
W 072°07.655'

Historic marker
Washington, New Hampshire
N 43°10.408'
W 072°05.581'

Washington, New Hampshire, church
N 43°09.206'
W 072°07.587'

Wilton Center (West Wilton)

Annie Smith grave
South Yard Cemetery
Isaac Fry Highway
Wilton, New Hampshire
(exact location in cemetery)
N 42°49.663'
W 071°46.313'

Smith Tavern
West End Highway
Wilton, New Hampshire
N 42°49.844'
W 071°48.330'

South Yard Cemetery
Isaac Fry Highway
Wilton, New Hampshire
N 42°82.461'
W 071°46.354'

New York

Clifton Springs (Port Gibson)

Hiram Edson farm
780 Field Street
Clifton Springs, New York
N 43°00.028'
W 077°08.511'

Rochester

Mount Hope Cemetery
1133 Mount Hope Avenue
Rochester, New York
N 43°07.773'
W 077°36.950'

Site of White home
491 Mount Hope Avenue
Rochester, New York
N 43°08.421'
W 077°36.820'

Site of White home
228/230 Monroe Avenue
Rochester, New York
N 43°09.001'
W 077°35.968'

Site of Orton home
120 S. Union Street
Rochester, New York
N 43°09.036'
W 077°35.968'

Site of Andrews home
964 E. Main Street
Rochester, New York
N 43°09.709'
 077°35.171'

Site of Lamson home
59 Prince Street
Rochester, New York
N 43°09.611'
W 077°35.367'

Site of *Advent Review* office
31/33 South Saint Paul
Rochester, New York
N 43°09.341'
W 077°36.496'

Fulton (Roosevelt)

Roosevelt church
4456 State Route 49
Fulton, New York
N 43°18.481'
W 076°15.325'

Alexander Ross grave
Roosevelt Cemetery
near Roosevelt church
State Route 49
Fulton, New York
N 43°18.465'
W 076°15.313'

Hiram Edson grave
Roosevelt Cemetery
near Roosevelt church
State Route 49
Fulton, New York
N 43°18.444'
W 076°15.273'

Volney

David Arnold barn
27 Mount Pleasant-Palermo Road
    (County Road 45)
Volney, New York
N 43°23.135'
W 076°22.430'

West Monroe

Frederick Wheeler grave
2746 State Route 49
West Monroe Township, New York
N 43°17.092'
W 076°06.248'

Site of Frederick Wheeler home
Wheeler Road
West Monroe, New York
N 43°26.799'
W 076°05.494'

Whitehall (Low Hampton)

William Miller farm and chapel
1614 County Route 11
Whitehall, New York
(518) 282-9617
Hours: (call for hours)
N 43°59.484'
W 073°31.093'

Vermont

Vernon

Rachel Oaks Preston grave
Tyler Cemetery
Vernon, Vermont
N 42°44.095'
W 072°29.833'

Rachel Oaks Preston home
630 Pond Road
Vernon, Vermont
N 42°44.831'
W 072°30.672'

You can get directions to these locations using an online direction generator. We suggest Google Maps.

To enter coordinates into Google Maps, enter the following coordinates:

41 degrees 05.625 minutes North

90 degrees 12.500 minutes West

as:

41 05.625 - 90 12.500 or 41.05625 -90.12500

ADVENTIST PIONEER PLACES

MAINE

Palmyra

East Sullivan

Paris Hill

Poland

Augusta

Topsham

Gorham

Portland

East Kingston

Merlin D. Burt 2009

Paris Hill, Maine

William Foy grave
GPS: N 44°51.346' W 068°14.548'

Merlin D. Burt 2010

William Foy grave in East Sullivan, Maine

East Sullivan, Maine

William Ellis Foy (1818-1893) was a Black Freewill Baptist preacher who experienced two visions in Boston, Massachusetts, during 1842, plus other subsequent visions. The visions convinced him of the soon coming of Jesus, and eventually he traveled to various places to share them. Ellen White believed that Foy's visions were a true manifestation of the prophetic gift. She interacted with him and his first wife during 1845 and probably before the 1844 disappointment. Foy should not be confused with Hazen Foss, who also received visions before the October 1844 expectation in Poland, Maine. Foss refused to share his vision then and indicated to Ellen White that his gift was removed. Foss believed he was a lost man and abandoned religion. Foy, on the other hand, was faithful to his calling.

Ellen White remembered Foy being present on one occasion when she told an audience about her visions. This led to an interview with Foy. Ellen White recollected:

> I had an interview with him. He wanted to see me, and I talked with him a little. They had appointed for me to speak that night, and I did not know that he was there. I did not know at first that he was there. While I was talking I heard a shout, and he is a great, tall man, and the roof was rather low, and he jumped right up and down, and oh, he praised the Lord, praised the Lord. It was just what he had seen, just what he had seen. But they extolled him so I think it hurt him, and I do not know what became of him.[1]

For further recollections, see the chapter on Portland, Maine.

Family History of William Foy

Foy was born a free Black near Augusta, Maine, to Joseph and Elizabeth (Betsy) Foy. He married Ann about 1835, and they had at least one daughter, Amelia, who is listed in census records. Ann died at some point between 1845 and 1850. In the 1850 census Foy is listed as living in New Bedford, Massachusetts, with Amelia and his mother, Betsy. Under the heading "occupation" he is listed as a Freewill Baptist minister.

Foy married Caroline T. Griffin, of Gardiner, Maine, daughter of Reuben and Fanny Griffin in Augusta, on September 24, 1851.[2] They had two children. Their son, Orrin, was born about 1852, lived until after 1920, and had a number of children. He lived for a time on an island off Schoodic Point in Maine and then moved to Milbridge, where he was a fisherman and laborer.[3] After Caroline's death the 1860 Federal Census indicates that William Foy served as a Freewill Baptist minister in Burnham, Waldo County, Maine. Robert Potter, a local Maine researcher, cites a source that recollected that following the Civil War Foy "organized a 'Christian Church' of 25 members at Otter Creek, Mount Desert, Maine."[4]

In 1868 Foy purchased property for $10 consisting of 64 square rods on the north side of the public road from William Johnson in Plantation No. 7. The next year he bought another small plot across the road for $5.[5] Thus began his connection with Sullivan, Maine, where he remained for the rest of his life. Foy married Percintia W. Rose in Bangor, Maine, on July 5, 1873.[6] In 1875 he deeded his property to Percintia, perhaps to help her avoid probate.[7] He passed away on November 9, 1893, and is buried in the Birch Tree Cemetery. Buried with him are his daughter Laura and his last wife, Percintia, who died in 1908.

William Foy, the Millerite Movement, and Sharing His Visions

Though most of the principal leaders of the Millerite movement, including William Miller, rejected the possibility of modern prophetic revelation, there were people who claimed God spoke to them through a vision or a dream. Some Millerites who had these manifestations were clearly fanatical, but others seem to have experienced legitimate divine revelation.

Foy received his first vision on Southack Street in Boston on January 18, 1842. It lasted for about two and a half hours. "I was immediately seized as in the agonies of death," he wrote, "and my breath left me; and it appeared to me that I was a spirit separate from this body. I then beheld one arrayed in white raiment."[8] His second vision occurred on May Street, also in Boston, two weeks later on February 4, 1842. "I heard a voice, as it were, in the spirit, speaking unto me," he recalled. "I immediately fell to the floor and knew nothing about this body, until twelve hours and a half had passed away, as I was afterwards informed." In this vision he saw the judgment bar of God and "innumerable multitudes" gathered before it.[9]

Foy was converted in 1835 through the preaching of Elder Silas Curtis. Curtis was a prominent minister of

the Freewill Baptist Church in Augusta, Maine, where Foy lived during his early Christian experience.[10] Foy described what happened:

Christians directed me to the Lamb of God that taketh away the sins of the world. I then began to pray earnestly to God to pardon my sins; but the more I prayed the more I beheld the sinfulness of my heart; and for many days I feared there was no mercy for me; but was led to see that it would have been justice in God to have cut me off and sent me where hope or mercy could not have reached me. I then became willing to give up all; and in that moment Christ appeared the one altogether lovely, and the chiefest among ten thousands, and spake the life-giving word to my soul. I then rejoiced in the God of my salvation; while all things around me appeared new, shining forth with the glory of God.[11]

Foy was reluctant to share his visions. "I was disobedient," he wrote, "settling upon this point for an excuse, that my guide did not command me so to do; and I thereby brought darkness, and death, upon my soul." He indicated that to avoid personally sharing his first vision, he had an "account of it printed" that he said was "a very imperfect sketch." His second vision occurred while he was struggling with the "duty" to share his vision. He was at an evening meeting in a "large congregation" on May Street in Boston.[12] A more

Site of William Foy home
GPS: N 44°33.306' W 068°06.233'

N
W E
S

Merlin D. Burt 2010

Site of William Foy's home in East Sullivan, Maine

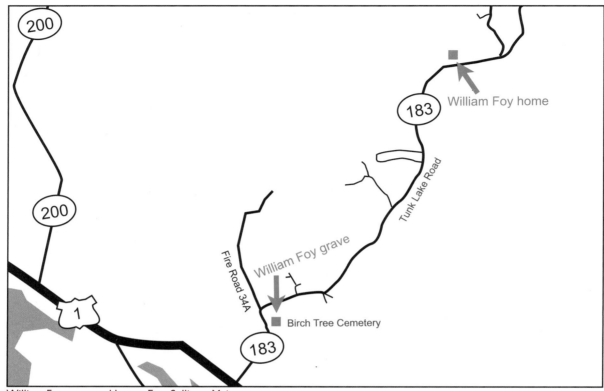

William Foy grave and home, East Sullivan, Maine

complete description of the setting of his second vision is given.

> In the last part of the evening, the house being much crowded, I gave my seat to a friend who had been standing through the evening. While I was thus standing, I began to reflect on my disobedience; and while thus engaged, suddenly I heard a voice, as it were, in the spirit, speaking unto me. I immediately fell to the floor, and knew nothing about this body, until twelve hours and a half had passed away, as I was afterwards informed.[13]

After this second vision, which may have disrupted the meeting, he waited three more days before he "revealed them [his visions] in a public manner."

His reluctance is understandable. He wrote of the reasons.

> The message was so different—and the manner in which the command was given, so different from any I had ever heard of, and knowing the prejudice among the people against those of my color, it became very crossing. These questions were continually arising. Why should these things be given to me, to bear to the world, and not to the learned or to one of a different condition from myself?[14]

He first shared his visions at the Methodist church on Broomfield Street on February 7, 1842, to a congregation that "sat in perfect stillness." This led to other appointments, and he traveled for three months speaking to "crowded houses." He then did manual labor for three more months to support his family. After this he resumed his preaching work. In 1845 he wrote that he had "traveled from place to place, and suffered some persecution."[15]

The tract of Foy's first two visions was published in 1845. There are two notations about Foy in public papers of Portland, Maine, during 1844. A newspaper advertisement indicated that Foy was holding meetings at the Casco Street Christian Church during February 1844.[16] About the same time, the Portland *Tribune* described an unnamed Black man, probably Foy, who had "dreams and prognostications."[17]

Ellen White indicated that Foy had four visions. She recollected one occasion that may have been a vision. She wrote: "He was in a large congregation, very large.

He fell right to the floor. I do not know what they were doing in there, whether they were listening to preaching or not. But at any rate he fell to the floor. I do not know how long he was [down]—about three quarters of an hour, I think—and he had all these [visions] before I had them."[18]

Henry Cummings, a botanic physician in Boston, and Foy's wife Ann described his condition in vision:

> I was present with our brother at the time of his visions. I examined him, but could not find any appearance of life, except around the heart.[19] [Henry Cummings]

> The first appearance of life I saw in him was the raising of his right hand. He then arose upon his knees, and made signs for water, which was given him. He dipped his hand into it, and wet his forehead, and his speech immediately came to him.[20] [Ann Foy]

J. N. Loughborough described Foy as an "eloquent speaker" who "was preparing to take holy orders as an Episcopal minister." Census records all show Foy as being a Freewill Baptist minister, but Loughborough writes that when Foy spoke, "he always wore the clergyman's robe, such as the ministers of that church [Episcopal] wear in their services."[21]

The Center for Adventist Research at Andrews University holds an original of Foy's 24-page tract and reprinted it to make it available and further enhance understanding and appreciation of Millerite Adventism, of Adventist Black heritage, and American popular religious experience during the nineteenth century.

Sites Related to William Foy

To reach the Birch Tree Cemetery, go .9 miles on Route 183 (also known as Tunk Lake Road). Turn right on to the driveway for house number 185. The cemetery is not visible from the road. Go up the driveway just over the knoll by a mobile home on the left. Birch Tree Cemetery is directly in front of you. The grave is in the back right corner of the small cemetery.

To visit the site of Foy's home, continue on route 183 about 4 miles beyond the cemetery to just beyond 1013 Tunk Lake Road on the right. The site is just up the hill a half mile beyond the former railroad crossing and the end of Route 183. All that remains of the

William Foy's stone-lined well in East Sullivan, Maine

cabin are some fallen boards and a rock-lined well. Just back from the site is a white home set off from the road where Foy is thought to have lived for a time near the end of his life.

Notes

[1] Ellen G. White, *Manuscript Releases* (Washington, D.C.: Ellen G. White Estate, 1993), vol. 17, p. 96.

[2] Marriage notices from the *Maine Farmer* 1833-1852, p. 143, cited from an unpublished paper by Robert L. Potter titled "William Ellis Foy" (n.p., n.d.).

[3] *Ibid.*; Robert L. Potter, "Citizen of Sullivan: William Ellis Foy" (n.p., n.d.).

[4] *Ibid.*

[5] *Hancock County Registry of Deeds,* vol. 133, p. 11; vol. 281, p. 212.

[6] Ruth Gray, ed., *Marriage Returns of Penobscot County Prior to 1892* (Camden, Maine: Picton Press, 1994), p. 587, cited from Potter, "William Ellis Foy."

[7] *Hancock County Registry of Deeds,* vol. 153, p. 120.

[8] William E. Foy, *The Christian Experience of William E. Foy Together With the Two Visions He Received in the Months of January and February 1842* (Portland, Maine: J. and C. H. Pearson, 1845), p. 9.

[9] *Ibid.,* p. 16.

[10] Delbert W. Baker, *The Unknown Prophet* (Washington, D.C.: Review and Herald, 1987), pp. 45-48.

[11] Foy, p. 7.

[12] *Ibid.,* p. 15.

[13] *Ibid.,* p. 16.

[14] *Ibid.,* p. 21.

[15] *Ibid.,* pp. 22, 23. For a detailed description of the content of each of Foy's visions, see Baker, pp. 87-124.

[16] William Ellis Foy, "Notice," Portland *Advertiser*, Feb. 27, 1844, p. 2.

[17] "When Will Wonders Cease?" Portland *Tribune*, Feb. 10, 1844, p. 351.

[18] White, *Manuscript Releases*, vol. 17, pp. 95, 96.

[19] Foy, *Christian Experience*, p. 24.

[20] *Ibid.*

[21] J. N. Loughborough, *The Great Second Advent Movement: Its Rise and Progress* (Washington, D.C.: Review and Herald, 1905), pp. 145, 146.

Ellen White (1827-1915)

Gorham, Maine

Gorham, Maine

Gorham, Maine, is the birthplace of Ellen G. White. During her childhood her father, Robert Harmon, alternated between farming in Gorham and Poland and operating a hat shop in Portland. The family moved from Gorham to Portland about the time of her birth in 1827. In 1829 they relocated to Poland, Maine, and about 1833 they returned to Portland. For the remainder of Ellen's childhood the Harmon family lived in Portland. Soon after James and Ellen White's marriage on August 30, 1846, Robert and Eunice Harmon purchased a farm on Fort Hill Road in Gorham. For a little more than a year following their marriage, the Whites lived with Ellen's parents. Their first son, Henry Nichols White, was born here on August 26, 1847. Though Ellen's parents shared many aspects of faith with their daughter and son-in-law, they did not at first accept the Sabbath. This produced tension during the time the two families lived together.

Other Harmon family connections to Gorham include Robert, Jr., who lived and died with his parents on Fort Hill Road. Ellen's twin sister, Elizabeth Bangs, married a native of Gorham and settled for the remainder of her life near where she was born.

Robert and Eunice Harmon had a total of eight children divided into an older and younger group. The older ones included Carolyn, Harriet, and John. The younger were Mary, Sarah, Robert, Elizabeth, and Ellen. By the time the twins, Elizabeth and Ellen, were born, the three oldest children were already in their teens or nearly so. Hence the older children were grown and married before the Millerite movement reached Maine, and so they were not closely connected to the events described in this guidebook.

The order of the chapter sections is based on the route one would likely drive if leaving downtown Gorham and driving north on Fort Hill Road.

1846-1853 Harmon Home

This home is located at 243 Fort Hill Road before Phinney Street intersects on the east side of the road. It is presumed that this is the original structure occupied by the Harmon family, though with some modifications. The yard has flagstones from a large barn and other structures.

Robert Harmon purchased this farm on September 16, 1846, and sold it on November 3, 1853. James and Ellen White were married on August 30, 1846, and lived with Ellen's parents in this home for more than a year. On August 26, 1847, while the Whites were living in Gorham, their first child, Henry Nichols, was born. While James White lived with his in-laws it

1846 Harmon home in Gorham, Maine

Harmon home (1846-1853)
GPS: N 43°41.755' W 070°27.138'

was expected that he would provide help on the farm. Robert Harmon, Sr., was nearing retirement age, and young James was tall and strong. But James believed he needed to travel and preach. When he was home, there were difficulties with the Sabbath. The Harmons, who were not yet Sabbathkeepers, could not understand why James would not work on Saturday. Since Robert kept Sunday as the Sabbath, it meant there was no help from young James on the weekends. In October of 1847, realizing that it was not good to be dependent upon Ellen's parents, the Whites moved to Topsham, Maine. They "commenced housekeeping with borrowed furniture" in a part of Stockbridge Howland's home. To avoid dependency upon the Howland family, James White worked hauling stone on the railroad, but was not paid his wages faithfully. [1]

Grave of Robert Harmon, Jr.

Robert Harmon, Jr., grave
GPS: N 43°41.917' W 070°27.259'

Grave of Robert Harmon, Jr.

Ellen White's older brother Robert F. Harmon (1825-1853) is buried in the little Fort Hill Cemetery just north of his parents' home on Fort Hill Road. In March 1840 Robert, Jr., attended William Miller's lectures in the Casco Street Christian Church in Portland, Maine. He was converted at the meetings and was soon baptized, joining the Chestnut Street Methodist Church, where his parents were members. Ellen White remembered attending class meetings with her brother. On one occasion he testified to the soon coming of Jesus, and a "heavenly light" was upon his "usually pale countenance." [2] It seems that Robert, like Ellen, was somewhat introverted. Ellen White spoke of him as having a "meek way" and being timid. [3] Ellen White was emotionally close to her twin sister and also to her brother. She confided her feelings with him, and they, together with their parents, were expelled in 1843 from the Methodist Church for believing the Millerite doctrine.

Sometime after 1844 Robert gave up his belief in the soon coming of Jesus. He rejoined the Methodist Church in 1852. Sadly, he contracted tuberculosis and passed away on February 5, 1853, following an eight-month illness. He was only 26 years old. During the last months of his life James and Ellen White traveled from Rochester, New York, to visit him. They shared Bible studies with Robert and spent time in conversation and prayer. This resulted in his readopting a belief in the soon coming of Jesus. He then asked to have his name removed from the Methodist Church record book. The minister visited him before his death and remarked to Eunice Harmon, "That is a triumphant soul." Frederick Wheeler, who happened to be in Maine at the time of Robert's death, conducted the funeral.

Gorham historic marker

Ellen G. White historic marker
GPS: N 43°42.084' W 070°27.331'

Gorham Historical Society Marker on Fort Hill Road

In 1983 a historical marker was placed in front of what was then believed to be the site of Ellen White's birth. The original location of the marker was across Fort Hill Road, north of the cross street. The then owners of the property were opposed to the marker, so it was moved to its present location. Since that time records have revealed that Robert Harmon never owned the property at the traditional location for Ellen White's birth. Thus the marker indicates in a general way that Ellen G. White was born in Gorham, Maine. The location has a beautiful view overlooking the valley where she was born. The dirt road across Fort Hill Road used to be part of Buck Road, which continued down to North Street and the area where Robert Harmon's 1827 farm was located. On Buck Road is the home of Elizabeth Bangs, twin sister of Ellen White. About 1857 the

North Street Cemetery
GPS: N 43°43.483' W 070°29.003'

North Street Cemetery, Gorham, Maine

Bangses moved to what is today 288 Buck Road. They lived there until Elizabeth's death in 1891.

Gravestones of Reuben and Elizabeth Bangs

Elizabeth Bangs' grave

Buried in the North Street Cemetery are Ellen White's twin sister, Elizabeth, nicknamed "Lizzie," her husband, Reuben Bangs, and Eva, a baby daughter who died when she was about 6 weeks old.

Ellen White and her twin sister remained emotionally close throughout their lives. As children, Ellen seems to have been the more dominant of the two. While playing together in Deering Oaks Park near their home in Portland, Lizzie would sometimes ask for help over fallen trees. She would say to Ellen, "Help over log." Of course Ellen would help her. She remarked years later to a nurse, Delia Walker-Lovell, "I have been helping [people] over logs ever since."[4]

In 1849 Lizzie married Reuben Bangs, who operated a general store. They had three children, Clarence, Bertha, and Eva. Reuben was an inactive Quaker, and Lizzie was from a Methodist background. Both showed little interest in religious things. In 1874 Ellen White

observed that there were "no prayers" in her sister's home.[5] She also observed, "Her sympathies are with us, yet she takes no open stand."[6] Throughout her life Ellen White sought to influence her sister spiritually and to help bring her to conversion. Two examples illustrate the intensity of Ellen's efforts.

Gravestone of Eva Adalaide Bangs (1851)

The Bangses lost their infant child Eva in 1858. A poem was composed and published in the *Youth's Instructor*. Also Ellen White wrote a touching appeal to her sister:

Our fondest hopes are often blighted here. Our loved ones are torn from us by death. We close their eyes and habit them for the tomb, and lay them away from our sight. But hope bears our spirits up. We are not parted forever, but shall meet the loved ones who sleep in Jesus. They shall come again from the land of the enemy. The Life-giver is coming. Myriads of holy angels escort Him on His way. He bursts the bands of death, breaks the fetters of the tomb, the precious captives come forth in health and immortal beauty.

As the little infants come forth immortal from their dusty beds, they immediately wing their way to their mother's arms. They meet again nevermore to part. But many of the little ones have no mother there. We listen in vain for the rapturous song of triumph from the mother. The angels receive the motherless infants and conduct them to the tree of life. Jesus places the golden ring of light, the crown upon their little heads. God grant that the dear mother of "Eva" may be there, that her little wings may be folded upon the glad bosom of her mother.[7]

It is hard to imagine a more compelling appeal to a grieving mother. How Lizzie responded is not known, but clearly Ellen White remained concerned about her sister's spiritual welfare.

During the last years of Lizzie's life she suffered from crippling arthritis. In 1880 Ellen White arranged for Lizzie to go the Battle Creek Sanitarium for treatments. Apparently they did little or no good, and she continued to suffer. During the last four years of her life

Ellen White (standing) and twin sister, Elizabeth Bangs (1878)

Courtesy of the Ellen G. White Estate

Lizzie was bedridden. One of Ellen White's most touching and spiritually compelling letters is written to her sister the year she died. It was never published and was intended to be personal. It reveals Ellen's love for Jesus and spiritual longing for her sister. She wrote:

I love to speak of Jesus and His matchless love and my whole soul is in this work. I have not one doubt of the love of God and His care and His mercy and ability to save to the utmost all who come unto Him. . . . Don't you believe on Jesus, Lizzie? Do you not believe He is your Saviour? That He has evidenced His love for you in giving His own precious life that you might be saved? All that is required of you is to take Jesus as your own precious Saviour. I pray most earnestly that the Lord Jesus shall reveal Himself to you and to Reuben. . . .

Dear sister, it is no wonderful thing that you have to do. You feel poor, suffering, and afflicted, and Jesus invites all of this class to come to Him. . . . Friends may feel sorrowful, but they cannot save you. Your physician cannot save you. But there is One who died that you might live through eternal ages. Just believe that Jesus will hear your confession, receive your penitence, and forgive every sin and make you children of God. . . . Will you give yourself in trusting faith to Jesus? I long to take you in my arms and lay you on the bosom of Jesus Christ. . . . With Jesus as your blessed Friend you need not fear to die, for it will be to you like closing your eyes here and opening them in heaven. Then we shall meet nevermore to part.[8]

Like her appeal at the death of Eva, it is not known how Lizzie responded to this appeal. We sometimes wonder what sets a person on a lifelong path of spiritual indifference. Too often there are no definitive answers. There is an experience that may have influenced Lizzie to turn away from religion. The Harmon family was expelled from the Methodist Church in 1843 for their belief in the soon coming of Jesus. Ellen was accepted as a member on probation to the Chestnut Street Methodist Church on September 20, 1841, and was approved for baptism on May 23, 1842. John Hobart baptized her in Casco Bay on June 26, 1842. Hobart was moved to a new location because of his Millerite sympathies, and the new pastor, William Farrington, was commissioned to deal with the Millerite "problem." The Chestnut Street Methodist Church records reveal that Elizabeth

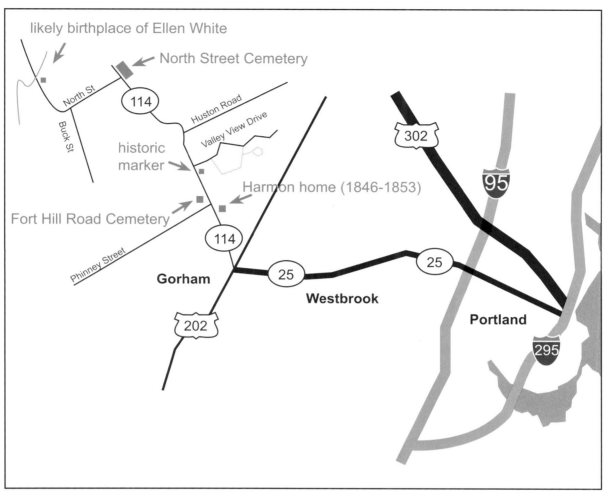

likely birthplace of Ellen White

North Street Cemetery

North St

Buck St

114

Huston Road

Valley View Drive

historic marker

Harmon home (1846-1853)

Fort Hill Road Cemetery

Phinney Street

114

Gorham

302

95

25

25

Westbrook

Portland

202

295

Adventist historic sites, Gorham, Maine

Katy Wolfer 2008

Remnant of road off of Fort Hill Road that goes down toward the likely birthplace of Ellen Harmon

Harmon was voted for probation on October 31, 1842. There is no further mention of her name. In February 1843 the pastor formed the first of several committees to expel the Harmons from membership. It is not hard to understand why Elizabeth was never voted for full membership and baptism. One can only wonder what effect this experience had on Lizzie. Did she become disillusioned with organized religion? Did she equate the actions of the Methodist Church with God?

Ellen White's Likely Place of Birth

Deed records show that Robert Harmon purchased the 35-acre "homestead farm" of Isaac Sawyer on October 21, 1826. He then sold it on September 3, 1827, to Zebulon Whitney. It is unclear just where the Harmon family lived between 1827 and 1829, but it is presumed that they were in Portland. In January 1828 Robert Harmon entered an agreement to buy a home on Jefferson Street in Portland, but the deal fell through.

Given that the Harmon home was sold in September 1827 and that the accepted date for Ellen White's birth is November 26, 1827, it is possible that Ellen was born some place other than the Sawyer homestead. It is also possible that the Harmons continued to live at the farm for a few months until the twins were born. A more radical idea would be that the date of Ellen White's birth was earlier than what is traditionally believed. Robert Harmon, Sr., was not always clear on dates, and Ellen White herself expressed some question about whether she was born in 1826 or 1827.[9] In any case, the Sawyer homestead is located off North Street about a quarter of a mile west beyond Buck Street. The Harmon homesite is located on the right just before the bridge over a stream. When the property was discovered in 1994, the foundation was all that remained. The home was of typical early-nineteenth-century style. It contained a central brick fireplace, and the dimensions of the foundation were about 35 feet by 30 feet. Various flagstones showed that there was a barn to the west of the home and perhaps other outbuildings. Soon after the ruins were discovered, the property owners filled in the foundation and covered part of it with a new driveway. With typical Yankee efficiency the various flagstones were reused to help construct a small bridge in another part of Gorham.

There was a schoolhouse back up North Street toward Buck Road on the same side of the road as the Sawyer homestead, where it may be presumed that the older Harmon children were students. Nothing remains of this early school.

Notes

[1] Ellen G. White, *Christian Experience and Teachings of Ellen G. White* (Mountain View, Calif.: Pacific Press, 1922), p. 114.

[2] *Ibid.*, p. 35.

[3] *Ibid.*, p. 38.

[4] Arthur L. White, *Ellen G. White: The Early Years, 1827-1862* (Washington, D.C.: Review and Herald, 1985), vol. 1, pp. 20, 21

[5] Ellen G. White to James White, Sept. 10, 1874 (letter 51, 1874) (Silver Spring, Md.: Ellen G. White Estate).

[6] Ellen G. White to Edson and Emma White, Sept. 1874, (letter 50b, 1874) (Silver Spring, Md.: Ellen G. White Estate).

[7] Ellen G. White, "Bereavement," *Youth's Instructor*, April 1858, p. 29.

[8] Ellen G. White to Elizabeth Bangs, Feb. 21, 1891 (letter 61, 1891) (Silver Spring, Md.: Ellen G. White Estate).

[9] Ellen G. White to Mary P. Foss, Sept. 30, 1907 (letter 308, 1907) (Silver Spring, Md.: Ellen G. White Estate).

Likely birthplace of Ellen White
GPS: N 43°71.984' W 070°49.987'

Robert Harmon (1786-1866)

Courtesy of the Center for Adventist Research

Deacon John White home
GPS: N 44°85.459' W 069°36.988'

Home of Deacon John White and birthplace of James White, Palmyra, Maine

Palmyra, Maine

James White, a principal founder of the Seventh-day Adventist Church, is linked to Palmyra, Maine. It was here that he was born, grew to adulthood, and became a Christian minister and Millerite preacher. His father, John White (1785-1871), was an early settler in Palmyra. He settled his homestead in 1806 and personally cleared the land and farmed the rocky Maine soil. James White wrote that his father possessed "great physical strength, and activity of body and mind. With his own hands he cleared the heavy timber from his land. This revealed stones in the soil, which his own hands removed and placed into [a] stone fence, to prepare the way for the plow." Then for more than 50 years he worked the land until it was "literally worn out."[1]

Until 1820 the territory that became the state of Maine was a part of Massachusetts. On June 12, 1800, John Warren of Boston purchased some 28,800 acres that comprised the region of Palmyra. The deed stipulated that he would settle a specified number of families in the town during the first five years, which he did. In 1800 the first settler to purchase land from Warren is said to have been Daniel Gale. Gale's son-in-law, David

Jewett, an attorney, settled near Gale about the same time. Jewitt's daughter Elizabeth (1788-1871), or Betsey, as she was known, married John White, probably in 1809.[2]

John White first joined the Congregational Church in February 1808, then the Baptist Church, and finally the Christian Church. The latter was a loose fellowship of churches called the Christian Connexion. John White served as a deacon for 50 years, 10 years with the Baptists and 40 years with the Christian Connexion.

James White was born on August 4, 1821, the fifth of nine children. Deprived of an education until the age of 16 because of a problem with his eyesight, he redeemed the time by overexertion. At the age of 19 James went to school rather than devote his life to farming. He entered an academy in St. Albans, Maine, and during that first three-month term applied himself to study as much as 18 hours a day. He continued his studies for another term at a Methodist academy and took natural philosophy, algebra, and Latin. He spent a total of 29 weeks in formal schooling and gained a certificate

Deacon John White (1785-1871)

Betsey White (1788-1871)

to teach. W. C. White, in a paper he wrote about his father, aptly called him "the man who couldn't wait."[3]

In 1842 James White's mother, Betsey, became interested in William Miller's teachings about the second coming of Jesus. John joined his wife in this belief. Betsey also influenced her son, James, to consider the Millerite message. After attending Millerite camp meetings during the summer and early fall of 1842, James White determined to become a preacher. He first gave lectures in four towns surrounding Palmyra. By doing this, he was able to add sermons to his limited repertoire. He then traveled to Burnham and helped a teacher who had lost an eye. For one week he taught school in the morning and lectured in the evening. White says of this week, "At this place I began to feel the burden of the work, the condition of the people, and love for precious souls." At the close of his lectures, 60 arose for prayers. He didn't know what to do. He wrote, "My little pond of thought, in the course of seven lectures, had run out."[4] Twenty-two-year-old James called for help from his older brother, John, who had been a minister for five years.

To assist his preaching work, Father John Harmon lent James White a horse, and a fellow Christian minister, Moses Polley, gave James a "saddle with both pads torn off, and several pieces of an old bridle."[5] After

repairing these, the young preacher determined to travel south through the winter of 1842-1843, preaching wherever he could. He had little money or warm clothing, but was fired with a zeal and a conviction that he must share with others about the soon coming of Jesus. In this way he traveled south down to the coast of Maine, preaching wherever he was welcomed.

James White in Augusta, Maine

Perhaps the most remarkable story from this preaching tour occurred in Augusta, Maine. He arrived in January 1843 during the dead of winter. Thinly clad but gaining experience, he was given an opportunity to speak in a schoolhouse. Universalists were opposed to the Second Advent doctrine. They believed everyone would be saved. Millerites taught that the wicked would be destroyed when Jesus returned.

James White spoke to a crowded schoolhouse audience. At the close of a meeting a Universalist minister attempted to have his colleague (a prominent editor) address the audience. James refused to stay, and left with all but about 25 people. This angered the Universalists. The next evening as James came to the meeting he saw about 300 men standing around the school, which had all the windows open. Determined to meet the challenge, he moved forward into the building, which was filled mostly with frightened women. Meeting him at the desk was the Universalist minister to whom he had previously denied a hearing. While James usually chose to kneel when he prayed, on this occasion he remained standing. According to White this was because (1) there was no room to kneel and (2) he feared the Universalist would strike him. While he was praying, a snowball whistled by his head and struck the ceiling behind him. After prayer he read from 2 Peter 3 regarding the burning day of the Lord. Because of the shouting outside, he could be heard by only a few near the front. Snowballs and debris kept hitting the wall and ceiling behind him. As a result, he and his Bible were wet. James White recalled:

> That was no time for logic, so I closed my Bible and entered into a description of the terrors of the day of God, and the awful end of the ungodly. These opened before me wonderfully. Language and power of voice seemed to be given me for the occasion. I was nearly lost to all around me, while the naked glare of the fires of the day of God seemed to light up the field of slaughter of the ungodly men before me. I cried, "Repent and be converted, that your sins may be blotted out, or you will drink of the wrath of God. Repent, and call on God for mercy and pardon. Turn to Christ and get ready for His coming, or in a little from this, on rocks and mountains you will call in vain. You scoff now, but you will pray then."[6]

The mob quieted down. The previous evening James White had had a spike thrown at him that had hit his forehead and fallen on his Bible. At the time he put it in his pocket. Continuing, White wrote:

> Inexpressible pity and love for the crowd came over me, and as I was pointing sinners to the Lamb of God, with tears, I held up the spike, saying, "Some poor sinner cast this spike at me last evening. God pity him. The worst wish I have for him is that he was this moment as happy as I am. Why should I resent his insult when my Master had them driven through His hands," and at the moment raising my arms and placing my hands upon the ceiling behind me, in the position of Christ on the cross.[7]

The results were remarkable. The Spirit of God was moving on hearts. Some shrieked, and a general groan was heard. "Hark! Hark!" cried a score of voices. It became very quiet. In tears James White called for sinners to turn to God. He spoke of the love of God, the sacrifice of Christ, his undying pity for vile sinners. He then spoke of the coming of Jesus to save all who would seek him just then. "More than a hundred were in tears."[8] They arose when he gave the invitation. He closed with prayer, gathered his dampened Bible and chart, and walked out. As he left, an impressive person locked arms with him to protect him. But soon the "man" disappeared. James White believed it was an angel.

As James White traveled from place to place he was able to inspire people not only with his preaching but also through his singing. He remarked that often the "first words they heard from me were in singing,

> *'You will see your Lord a coming,*
>
> *You will see your Lord a coming,*
>
> *You will see your Lord a coming,*
>
> *In a few more days,*
>
> *While a band of music,*
>
> *While a band of music,*
>
> *While a band of music,*
>
> *Shall be chanting through the air.'"*

Describing its impact, he wrote:

> The reader certainly cannot see poetic merit in the repetition of these simple lines. And if he has never heard the sweet melody to which they were attached, he will be at a loss to see how one voice could employ them so as to hold nearly a thousand persons in almost breathless silence. But it is a fact that there was in those days a power in what was called Advent singing, such as was felt in no other.[9]

In April 1843 James White returned to Palmyra riding his "poor, chest-foundered horse," "much worn by the labors of the winter."[10] Following this successful winter of lecturing and some further speaking appointments, he was ordained to the ministry, by the "hands of ministers of the Christian denomination,"[11] in Palmyra.

Thus Palmyra was where he became settled on the Second Advent message, and received the call to gospel ministry. His parents' home was his base of operation until his marriage in 1846.

After 1844 James White became the organizational leader and a principal founder of Sabbatarian Adventism and the Seventh-day Adventist Church. He died at 60 years of age on August 6, 1881, and is buried in Oak Hill Cemetery in the White family plot in Battle Creek, Michigan.

Deacon John White and his wife, Betsey, continued to live in Palmyra until about 1857, when they moved to Columbus, Ohio, presumably to live with their eldest son, John. In March 1859 they purchased "a small 16 by 21 foot one-story cabin with loft" located across the street from the home of James and Ellen White in Battle Creek.[12] There in his retirement Deacon John worked as a cobbler. It was also there in 1860 that he and his wife became Sabbathkeepers. Both passed away in Battle Creek and were buried in the White family plot in Oak Hill Cemetery.

Directions:

Take I-95 north from Augusta to Exit 157 (Newport/Dexter). Turn left and proceed over the Interstate Highway less than .5 mile to Highway 2. Turn left and proceed four miles through Palmyra to Highway 151. Turn right and proceed north a half mile. You will pass a cemetery on the right and a long building on the left. Just beyond this building on the left is the John White

home. The original barn is now gone. Local tradition says that James White was born in the front part of the house closest to the road.

Notes

[1] James White, *Life Incidents* (Battle Creek, Mich.: Seventh-day Adventist Pub. Assn., 1868), p. 10.

[2] *Palmyra, Maine, 200th Anniversary Bicentennial: 1807-2007*, 2nd ed. (Palmyra, Maine: Penobscot Press, 2007), pp. 1, 2; James R. Nix, "John and Betsey (Jewett) White," in *Palmyra, Maine, 200th Anniversary Bicentennial*, p. 145. Most of the unique information in this chapter on John and Betsey White comes from the detailed and carefully researched article by James R. Nix.

[3] W. C. White, "Sketches and Memories of James and Ellen White: 'The Man Who Couldn't Wait'" (Silver Spring, Md.: Ellen G. White Estate).

[4] James White, p. 74.

[5] *Ibid.*, p. 73.

[6] *Ibid.*, pp. 77, 78.

[7] *Ibid.*, p. 78.

[8] *Ibid.*

[9] *Ibid.*, p. 94.

[10] *Ibid.*, p. 96.

[11] *Ibid.*, p. 104.

[12] Nix, in *Palmyra, Maine, 200th Anniversary*, pp. 146, 147.

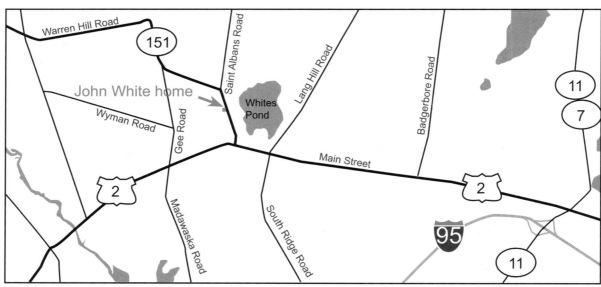

White home, Palmyra, Maine

James White (1821-1881)

Hillside Cemetery, Paris Hill, Maine

Merlin D. Burt 2010

Paris Hill, Maine

Paris Hill, Maine

About 13 miles from Poland is Paris Hill. Like many other towns in New England, Paris Hill was part of an area with other similarly named towns nearby. There is South Paris and West Paris, and of course Paris Hill, which was the county seat for a time and still has the historic courthouse square close to the Adventist sites. Paris Hill has a spectacular sweeping view from its long ridge. There are stately white buildings and a golf course with a country club that are located at this peaceful and sedate setting. The atmosphere feels almost nineteenth century.

On this hill lived the Andrews family, the Stowell family, and the Stevens family. The Edward Andrews home is part of what is now the country club building. His son, John N. Andrews, who grew up in this home, was one of the important pioneers of the Seventh-day Adventist Church.

The Andrews family was one of the most prominent in Paris Hill. John Nevins Andrews (1829-1883) was the first official Seventh-day Adventist overseas foreign missionary and the namesake of Andrews University. Charles Andrews (1814-1852), an uncle to John, became a lawyer and politician. He was first a state

representative from 1839 to 1843 and served as speaker during 1842. In 1845 he became clerk of courts for

William (1838-1878) and John Andrews (1829-1883)

Courtesy of the Center for Adventist Research

18

Oxford County, Maine, and in 1851 became a member of Congress. His political career was cut short when he died of tuberculosis on April 30, 1852.[1]

In September 1848 Charles Andrews built a comfortable home for his wife. It still stands on Paris Hill almost directly across from the site of the Edward Andrews home. The Maine Historical Society has the diaries and papers of Persis Sibley Andrews, wife of Charles. The diaries give interesting insights into the Andrews family and the Millerite movement in Paris Hill.

Down the hill beyond the cemetery and off Paris Hill Road on Hooper Ledge Road is the comfortable and beautifully situated home of Cyprian Stevens. The Stevenses had five daughters. At one point an early Adventist quipped that Cyprian and his wife served God's cause by providing spouses for church workers. Angeline Stevens became the beloved wife of J. N. Andrews and Harriet Stevens married Uriah Smith.

There is an important early seventh-day Sabbath story from Paris Hill. In the spring of 1845 T. M. Preble's tract on the Sabbath was sent to Lewis B. Stowell. This tract, reprinted from the Portland, Maine, Adventist paper *Hope of Israel,* advocated the seventh day, or Saturday, as the Sabbath of the Bible. Stowell set the tract aside, but his 15-year-old daughter Marian picked it up and read it. Convinced that the Sabbath was biblical, she decided to keep it. Soon her brother Oswald and J. N. Andrews (also 15 years old) joined her, as did their parents. In Paris Hill it was the teenagers who spiritually led the way to observe the fourth commandment. Young Oswald later became an apprentice printer in the Review and Herald office in Rochester, New York. He continued to work with the office after it relocated to Battle Creek, Michigan, in 1855.

Lewis Stowell sent a letter and $10 to the Seventh Day Baptist minister in Hopkinton, Rhode Island, to obtain some materials on the Sabbath. Soon Seventh Day Baptist tracts were delivered, and a small community of Sabbathkeeping Adventists that included the Stowell, Andrews, and Stevens families was formed.[2]

Paris Hill is also the birthplace of the *Review and Herald*, still published today as the *Adventist Review*. The *Review and Herald* is not to be confused with the

Advent Review. James White published the *Advent Review* between August and November 1850. Though titled similarly, it is a different publication. The first number of the *Review and Herald* was printed in November 1850 and continued through June 1851. The paper then moved to Saratoga Springs, New York; Rochester, New York; and Battle Creek, Michigan.

By 1856 the Andrews and Stevens families relocated to the state of Iowa, and Paris Hill, Maine, became a memory of the early beginnings and struggles of Sabbatarian Adventism.

Fanaticism in Paris Hill

Soon after the 1844 disappointment some people from the eastern part of Maine were teaching, among other things, that people should cut off their hair and not eat anything grown that year. Some even practiced creeping on the ground as a sign of humility. Fanaticism can range from extreme literalism to extreme spiritualizing (as was the case with some Boston fanatics). Often fanatical ideas were bizarre and defy categorization.

During 1845 fanaticism was particularly strong in Paris Hill. Ellen Harmon went there to address some of the confusing problems. She was told in vision to reprove Jesse Stevens. Stevens, who had been a Methodist minister, was advocating that it was a sin to work and taught that humility meant crawling on the ground and washing feet. One time he was crawling around town and got in front of a coach, and the driver plied him with his whip. The Stevens family and others who refused to work were at times provided food by the Stowell family. Harmon rebuked Stevens for going contrary to the Lord "in abstaining from labor, and urging his errors upon others." He rejected the visions and went his strange way. His story ended sadly when he hanged himself with his own bedclothes. Marian

Congressman Charles Andrews' home, Paris, Maine

Merlin D. Burt 2009

Stowell, a young girl living in Paris at the time, shared their experience with Ellen White:

Soon fanaticism of the rankest kind came again among us. This time I stood alone. Several fanatics came from the eastern part of the State. Dorinda Baker and Miss Blaisdell were among them. Miss Baker would feign sickness. The church would pray, and she would claim to be healed, and then closing her eyes, would pretend to be in vision. She was at our house over two months, then visited the home of John Howe of Norway, feigning her visions and sickness, according to my opinion. Mother [Laura Stowell] would say, "How can you doubt, when the Lord shows her so many good things about you?" I replied, "It is only another one of her tricks to win me over." Soon after [October] 22 . . . , 1844, a young girl by the name of Mary Hamlin of Waterford staid at our house over three months, was often in vision, she would warn me of my danger, which had been shown her of the Lord. [Brother] J. N. [Andrews] tried hard to show me I was in

the wrong. Yet I stood firm through it all. These early experiences have had a tendency to keep a close watch of Satan's many tricks to lead us astray. You [Ellen White] were shown that this Miss Baker was acting the hypocrite[;] both her sickness and her visions were only made by her to deceive.[3]

Ellen White told a humorous story about one of these false prophets, perhaps Dorinda Baker or Mary Hamlin. "One woman—she was holy, tall, dignified. . . . The poor woman did not know what spirit she was of. 'But, Sister Howland,' said I, as though I was whispering, 'get a pitcher of cold water, good cold water, and throw it right in her face; that will bring her out of it the quickest of anything you can do.' She [Howland] started to get the water, but before she got there, [Baker or Hamlin] had come out."[4]

Some others included a man named Hewitt. He advocated that one should eat nothing but sugar. He also acted the part of a stern Old Testament prophet. Ellen White tried to show him that he was being inappropriate. He finally came out of it all right.

Hillside Cemetery
GPS: N 44°25.160' W 070°49.890'

Merlin D. Burt 2008

Graves of Charles and Persis Andrews

While we do not know exactly where it occurred, there is a story told by Ellen White of a man who came to her in meeting saying, "The Lord tells me, Sister White, that I must wash your feet." Ellen responded, "The Lord tells me that you have no business with my feet at all. When my feet are washed it will be by a sister, not by any man." The man then began to cry. Said Ellen, "I wouldn't use up my strength in that way, because it doesn't make any more impression on me than the barking of a dog, not a bit."[5]

These and other fanatical ideas, together with a national antipathy to Millerites and concern that Millerites would require support from the local town, produced strong negative feeling in Paris Hill and the state of Maine. This led to various Adventists having their property and personal relationships placed under the control of court-appointed trustees. This sometimes led to legal injustice. The story of Cyprian Stevens is particularly tragic. Following a petition from the selectmen of Paris, Maine, to the probate judge, Cyprian was declared insane. According to the April 8, 1845, court transcript, he was judged as wasting and lessening his estate to "expose himself, and family to want." He was separated from his family and prohibited from even seeing his children.

The trustee purchased Cyprian's personal property, held the money in trust, and then charged fees for managing the estate. By January 1846 the value of Cyprian's personal property was exhausted. The trustee then sought to sell the remaining real estate to pay the mounting debts caused by the court-appointed guardianship. In March 1846 the probate judge authorized the sale of the Stevens home. Thus the very result the court sought to avoid was caused by the expenses of court.

This was too much for the citizens of Paris Hill. Twenty-five people signed a petition that Cyprian Stevens have his property and rights restored. On April 14, 1846, Stevens was decreed sane and freed from guardianship. The court, however, upheld the fees charged by the trustee. Cyprian Stevens found it necessary to mortgage his home to redeem his personal property and pay the trustee fees. In July 1847 Stevens sold his home and paid the mortgage note. Ironically, Stevens was forced to sell his home, not because of his Millerite beliefs, but because of the legal actions taken against him by the town and county.[6]

Edward (-1865) and Sarah Andrews (1803-1899)

Notes

[1] "Charles Andrews," *Biographical Directory of the United States Congress, 1774-Present* (http://bioguide.congress.gov, Sept. 30, 2008); William David Barry and Stephanie Philbrick, "From the Collections: The Persis Sibley Andrews Black Diaries," *Maine History*, Winter 2001-2002, pp. 333-336.

[2] Marion C. Stowell Crawford, "A Letter From a Veteran Worker," *Southern Watchman*, Apr. 25, 1905, p. 278.

[3] Marion C. Stowell Crawford to Ellen G. White, Oct. 9, 1908 (Silver Spring, Md.: Ellen G. White Estate).

[4] Interview: Ellen G. White with C. C. Crisler (circa 1906) (manuscript 131a, 1906) (Silver Spring, Md.: Ellen G. White Estate).

[5] *Ibid.*

[6] Information on Cyprian Stevens is drawn from Probate Record, drawer 93, Oxford County Probate Court, South Paris, Maine, and county property records.

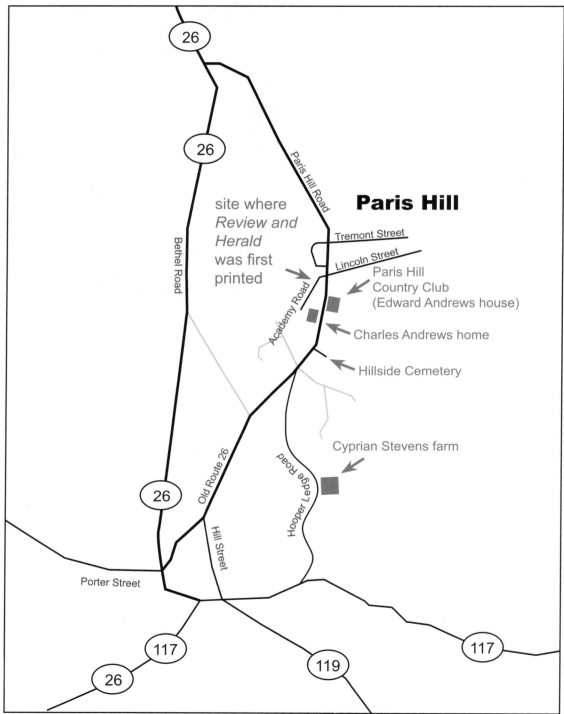

26

26

Paris Hill Road

site where
*Review and
Herald*
was first
printed

Paris Hill

Bethel Road

Tremont Street

Lincoln Street

Academy Road

Paris Hill
Country Club
(Edward Andrews house)

Charles Andrews home

Hillside Cemetery

Cyprian Stevens farm

26

Old Route 26

Hooper Ledge Road

Hill Street

Porter Street

117

119

117

26

Adventist historic sites, Paris Hill, Maine

Merlin D. Burt 2008

Hillside Cemetery

Merlin D. Burt 2008

Gravestones of Charles and Persis Andrews

Merlin D. Burt 2008

Edward Andrews home, Paris Hill, Maine

Merlin D. Burt 2008

Cyprian Stevens farm, Paris Hill, Maine

Foss home
GPS: N 44°03.405' W 070°24.643'

Samuel and Mary Foss home, Poland, Maine

Poland, Maine

Poland, Maine, is significant for Adventist history largely because of Ellen White and her family's connection. Robert and Eunice Harmon and their family lived in Poland for about four years while Ellen White was a young child. Two of Ellen White's older sisters also lived in Poland—Harriet McCann and Mary Foss. Several significant stories are connected with the homes of Mary Foss and Captain John Megquier. The most significant story is about Ellen's conflict with Joseph Turner, a prominent Millerite minister in Maine.

Three interesting details about Poland, Maine, are worth noting. In Poland Spring, a community connected to Poland, there are deep aquifers of exceptionally pure and refreshing water. It is the source of the most popular bottled water brand in New England—Poland Spring Water. On the road to Poland is the Sabbath Day Lake Shaker community. The Shaker faith is all but extinct, but the settlement is maintained and their history is explained. During the nineteenth century there was a large and famous spa resort in Poland Spring. It was established in 1876 atop Ricker's Hill and had a magnificent view of the White Mountains. Though not in any way connected to the Seventh-day Adventist Church, it was a popular destination for the same type of people who frequented Battle Creek Sanitarium. In its heyday the Poland Spring Resort could accommodate 450 guests. The depression of the 1930s and World War II brought an end to the era of grand hotels. The huge building remained vacant for many years and finally burned in 1975.

Harmon Home in Poland, Maine

Ellen Harmon and her family lived at 4510 Jackson Street, in Poland, Maine, between 1829 and about 1833. On August 7, 1829, the Harmons purchased from William Smith a home and barn situated on about 100 acres.[1] Ellen's earliest memories must have been of this place. The Harmon farm was identified in 1994. The home has since been moved to a new foundation, and the original barn has been replaced. The story of Bossy the cow, which has been passed down in the White family, probably occurred at the creek to the southeast side of the home. Arthur White, in his biography of his grandmother Ellen White, recalled wht happened:

One evening as she went to the pasture gate to bring the cow to the shed for milking, the bossy that usually was there waiting for her was nowhere in sight. Ellen went down through the woods, frequently calling the cow. Not until she had reached a little brook in the valley below did she hear a response. To her dismay she found the cow in the middle of the stream, with all four feet stuck in the mud. Immediately Ellen set about devising a plan to get the cow unstuck. Picking some luscious grass nearby, she reached out to the cow, who was grateful for something to eat. After repeating this several times, Ellen offered the cow another generous handful of grass, but this time held it just a little beyond her reach. Then with her free hand grasping the nearest horn Ellen

Harmon home (1829-1833)
GPS: N 44°02.860' W 070°23.893'

4510 Jackson Street
Poland, Maine

Robert Harmon home, Poland, Maine

urged, "Come, Bossy," and moved the grass away. The cow, fearful of losing the promised morsel, put forth extraordinary effort to break loose from the mud. Soon Ellen and cow were making their way back to home and shed.[2]

Samuel and Mary Foss Home

On several occasions Ellen White visited her sister Mary Foss in Poland, Maine. The Foss home is still standing and is known as the Mannis Hill Farm. It is located at the end of Strout Road. The present owners, Byron W. Strout and his wife, have an appreciation of the history of their home. The construction is a typical early-nineteenth-century New England rural farm home. It is small, with a central fireplace. Entering the home by the front door, visitors must turn either right into the parlor or left into the "great room" and back kitchen area. There was also a small room off the parlor at the back of the house and a few smaller rooms connected to the kitchen area. Upstairs there were two more rooms, though only one was finished.[3] The home was owned by Samuel Foss between 1840 and 1849. After Foss sold the home to William M. Boothby, it passed to the Strout family, who have owned it ever since.

The Foss home does not have a regular street address. To visit the home, take Route 26 north from Interstate 495. Just past Middle Range Pond, go left on Skellinger Road. Turn right at Jackson Road. Stay on Jackson until it dead-ends at White Oak Hills Road and turn left. The first street to the right is Strout Road. Take Strout until it appears to dead-end before going down the hill. The house and barn on the right belonged to the Foss family.

First Traveling Work

Ellen's first out-of-town trip to share her vision was in January 1845. Samuel Foss, her sister Mary's husband, arrived in Portland to invite his sister-in-law to come to Poland. The Adventists there wanted to hear the account of her vision.[4] Poland is about 30 miles from Portland, and one can imagine Ellen huddled in Samuel's small Portland sleigh, covered with wool blankets and buffalo robes.[5] After resting a few days in her sister's home, she traveled the three miles to Megquier Hill—probably to the home of John Megquier. John and Hannah Megquier had three daughters and were known for their caring hospitality. At Hannah's death in 1874 the following was written:

> When we first visited [Brother Megquier's] peaceful home upon the hillside, and the loving family gathered around the old hearth-stone, there was Sister [Megquier's] sainted mother, with her Bible in her hand, [Brother and Sister Megquier], as loving and true as Zechariah and Elizabeth, with their three daughters, enjoying the sweetness of holy sympathy, and all feasting upon the richest blessings of life—the love of God.[6]

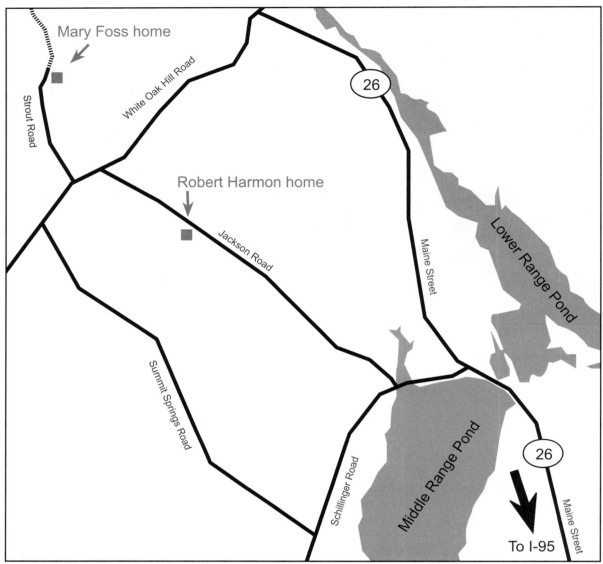

Adventist historic sites, Poland, Maine

The Megquier home is no longer standing, though the site has been located.

Miraculous Sharing of the Vision

J. N. Loughborough described Ellen Harmon's state of health during the time following her first vision. "For a number of weeks she had scarcely been able to speak above a whisper; one physician had decided that her trouble was dropsical consumption. He said her right lung was decayed, and the left one considerably diseased, and that her heart was affected. . . . It was with great difficulty that she could breathe when lying down. At night she obtained rest only by being bolstered up in

the bed in an almost sitting posture. Frequent spells of coughing and hemorrhages from the lungs had greatly reduced her physical strength."[7] When she rose to speak she struggled to make herself heard. After about five minutes the soreness and obstruction left her throat, and she spoke freely for two hours. When the message was finished, she was again hoarse. To her and the others present this was a sign that the Lord was with her and had helped her to testify. Otis Nichols, writing to William Miller from Dorchester, Massachusetts, on April 20, 1846, says of this experience:

> At the time she first went out to deliver her message (Jan 1845) [*sic*] she was scarcely able to walk across the room and

Samuel Foss (1817-1888)

Mary P. Foss (1821-1912)

could not speak with an audible voice, but had perfect faith in God and was carried in this state a few miles to deliver her message and when she arose to speak her voice was nearly gone, but God fulfilled his word: gave her strength of body and a clear loud audible voice to talk nearly two hours with tremendous power and effect on the people and without fatigue of body, and from that time for many weeks she continued to travel day and night talking almost every day until she had visited most of the advent bands in Maine and the easterly part of New Hampshire.[8]

Talking to Hazen Foss

Hazen Foss's story is described in the section on Haverhill, Massachusetts. But the important events that connect Foss to Ellen White occurred in Poland, Maine. Foss heard the description of her vision from another room, probably at Megquier's home. Loughborough's explanation follows:

> About three months from the time he [Foss] failed to recall his vision, he heard from an adjoining room a vision related by another [Ellen Harmon]. The meeting was held in a dwelling-house where he was. He was urged to come into the meeting, but refused to do so. He said the vision was as near like that shown him as two persons

could relate the same thing. . . . On getting a view of the person afterward, he said, "That is the instrument on whom the Lord has laid the burden."[9]

It was probably at the home of Samuel (Hazen's brother) and Mary Foss that Ellen spoke with Hazen Foss. One can imagine them sitting together in the parlor or kitchen area in the Foss's simple home. Their talk made a great impression on young Ellen. Hazen warned her not to refuse to share her vision. She recollected in quotation form what Hazen Foss had told her in that meeting:

> Ellen, I want to speak with you. The Lord gave me a message to bear to His people, and I refused after being told the consequences. I was proud; I was unreconciled to the disappointment. I murmured against God, and wished myself dead. Then I felt a strange feeling come over me. I shall be henceforth as one dead to spiritual things. I heard you talk last night. I believe the visions are taken from me, and given to you. Do not refuse to obey God, for it will be at the peril of your soul. I am a lost man. You are chosen of God; be faithful in doing your work, and the crown I might have had, you will receive.[10]

It may have been Hazen Foss's misconception about the close of probation on October 22, 1844, that caused his despair. In any event he never showed an interest in religious matters, and according to his sister-in-law

Mary, he died "an infidel."[11] Soon after her remarkable visit to Poland, Ellen embarked on a more extended trip through northeast Maine, followed by another trip into New Hampshire and Vermont.

Joseph Turner: Ellen's Nemesis

During the first months of 1845 Joseph Turner tried to bring Ellen Harmon under his control. Initially he was very supportive of her visions. He asked her to travel with him in his handsome buggy. But Ellen said no. The story of her conflict with Turner is one of several that lend veracity to her prophetic claim. Here is the story.

While Ellen Harmon was away from home traveling, the fanaticism in Portland grew worse. At Grantham, Vermont, she received a vision telling her to confront Turner's fanaticism head-on. Ellen was fearful of the task, but upon returning to Portland, she attended a meeting conducted by Turner in Elizabeth Haines' home. During the meeting she was taken off in vision. As was often the case, she began to speak in vision. Turner told those attending that this was from the Lord. But then a frown came to Ellen Harmon's face. She said

Hazen Foss (1819-1893)

Courtesy of the Ellen G. White Estate

that he was not keeping the commandments of God but transgressing them by giving attention to another woman. With this revelation Turner became agitated. He said that the first part of the vision was from the Lord, but that the second was a kind of mesmerism from someone in the room. Once Ellen Harmon came out of vision, she felt uncomfortable and slipped out of the room.

As she was leaving, a woman in the house asked Ellen to speak to one of her two daughters who was under the influence of Turner. Agreeing, Ellen went upstairs and spoke with the girl. "I told her what her dangers were, to have no intercourse [interaction] with him [Turner] in speech, or to see him alone. He would mesmerize her if she did. . . . [Said I], 'If he has not ruined you, he will, and now, do not have a word of conversation with him, because he will mesmerize you.' It was hypnotism, but we did not know then what it was." Ellen White went on to describe Turner's methods, "He could take a child and set it on his hand, and so mesmerize the child that it would stay there if he took his hand away. I never saw that done, but that is what he said he could do."[12]

Following this interview, Ellen went to see Joseph Turner's wife. Ellen wrote, "She looked most discouraged. She was a beautiful-looking woman. I put my arms around her back, and [she] cried like a baby." Said she, "Sister Ellen, my heart is breaking." As the two of them wept, Mrs. Turner told how her husband had been spending much of his time with Sarah Jordan, sometimes even entire nights in the Turner home. Ellen explained to Mrs. Turner that he was practicing hypnotic techniques on her. He "was hovering right over her all the time." As a result, this young woman thought she had had visions in which she had been instructed that she must go with him and speak publicly. Because Mrs. Turner could not accept that this was from the Lord, Joseph had told his own wife that she was lost. Ellen Harmon's message for Mrs. Turner must have been a help and encouragement.[13]

The Harmon Family Refuses to Let Turner Hold Meetings in Their Home

There was an additional stress on Ellen and her parents caused by Turner. The Harmon home in Portland had on occasion been used for meetings. But Robert and Eunice Harmon had become so disgusted with Turner's fanaticism that they had closed their home and gone to their daughter's home in Poland. Turner had become very upset about this. As soon as Ellen Harmon returned from Vermont and New Hampshire, he told her that her father was lost. The only reason he offered was that Robert Harmon would not give him the use of his home. Ellen's older sister Sarah remained in Portland to care for Ellen. She had a key to the house, and Turner sent word that she should open the house for a meeting. "Well," Sarah said, "Ellen, I have no idea of being put in that man's power. I shall lock the door, and shall go off, and we will go to the neighbors that they know nothing about."[14] Ellen and Sarah soon went to Poland to be with their parents, who were probably staying at the Foss home. This is likely because Mary was a Millerite believer and her older sister Harriet was not.

Poland, Maine: Meeting Joseph Turner's Mesmerism

After arriving in Poland, Ellen became very ill. Her family prayed for her, and Ellen was immediately in vision. She was told to go to the Advent meeting and confront Turner. Though she was terrified, she was assured that God would send as many angels as she needed for protection. With this promise she and her family went to the meeting. She described the experience thus: "We went and found quite a large gathering of the brethren and sisters. . . . J. T. [Joseph Turner] was there. He had boasted that he understood the art of mesmerism, and that he could mesmerize me; that he could prevent me from having a vision, or telling a vision in his presence."[15] As the meetings continued, he tried to

Sarah B. Harmon Belden (1822-1868)

Courtesy of the Ellen G. White Estate

take hypnotic control of Ellen. She vividly described her reaction.

> He had his eyes looking right out through his fingers, and his eyes looked like snake's eyes, evil. I turned and looked right around, I raised both hands, and [cried out], "Another angel, Lord, another angel." The Spirit and power of God came upon me, and I was taken off in vision right there.[16]

There was nothing Turner could do, and his influence was weakened. After the Harmons left, some asked why he had not stopped Ellen from having a vision. His response was "Oh, some of you would have her talk." Ellen White wrote, "With strong confidence, rejoicing in God, we returned to my sister's."[17]

Notes

[1] *Cumberland County Deed Records*, book 119, p. 257.

[2] Arthur L. White, *Ellen G. White: The Early Years, 1827-1862*, vol. 1, p. 20.

[3] This information is based on a site visit made by the author in October 1994; at the time it was determined to be the Foss home.

[4] Weather was severe in early January 1845. A major storm shut down meetings in Portland on January 2. See "Leader's Attendance Records," Chestnut Street Methodist Church, Portland, Maine.

[5] Ellen G. White, *Life Sketches* (Mountain View, Calif.: Pacific Press, 1915), p. 72; *Life Sketches* (Battle Creek, Mich.: Steam Press, 1888), pp. 195-197.

[6] Jesse Gay, "Megguire [*sic*]," *World's Crisis*, Jan. 6, 1875.

[7] J. N. Loughborough, *Rise and Progress of the Seventh-day Adventists* (Battle Creek, Mich.: General Conference Assn., 1892), p. 92.

[8] Otis Nichols to William Miller, Apr. 20, 1846, pp. 2, 3 (Berrien Springs, Mich.: Center for Adventist Research, Andrews University).

[9] J. N. Loughborough, *The Great Second Advent Movement: Its Rise and Progress*, p. 183.

[10] Ellen G. White to Mary Foss, Dec. 22, 1890, (letter 37, 1890) (Silver Spring Md.: Ellen G. White Estate). See also Tim Poirier, "The Visions of William E. Foy and Hazen L. Foss" (Silver Spring Md.: Ellen G. White Estate).

[11] Mary P. Foss to Ellen G. White, Apr. 1, 1894 (Silver Spring, Md.: Ellen G. White Estate).

[12] See Ellen G. White, *Spiritual Gifts* (Battle Creek, Mich.: James White, 1860), p. 49; see also Ellen G. White, "Life Sketches Manuscript" (Silver Spring, Md.: Ellen G. White Estate).

[13] Interview: Ellen G. White with C. C. Crisler, Aug. 13, 1906 (manuscript 131, 1906) (Silver Spring, Md.: Ellen G. White Estate).

[14] The information for this section was taken from Ellen G. White, *Spiritual Gifts*, vol. 2, pp. 49-52; manuscript 1, 1845, and manuscript 131, 1906 (Silver Spring, Md.: Ellen G. White Estate).

[15] Ellen G. White, *Spiritual Gifts*, vol. 2, p. 62.

[16] Interview: Ellen G. White with C. C. Crisler, Aug. 13, 1906 (manuscript 131, 1906).

[17] Ellen G. White, *Spiritual Gifts*, vol. 2, p. 63.

Portland Head Lighthouse
GPS: N 43°37.359' W 070°12.628'

Dragos Profir 2006

Portland Head Lighthouse, Cape Elizabeth, Maine

Portland, Maine

Portland was the center of Ellen White's early Christian experience. Here she and her family believed in the soon coming of Jesus after hearing William Miller preach at the Casco Street Christian Church. Here she was converted and joined the Chestnut Street Methodist Church. Here she was disappointed when Jesus did not come in 1844. In Elizabeth Haines' home in Portland she received her first vision and reluctantly shared it. It was in Portland that she first met her future husband—James White. It was from here that she wrote her first letters to the *Day-Star* describing her visions, and here also was published her first broadside. It was also in Portland that she was severely injured, at age 9, when an older classmate threw a stone that hit her in the face.

Downtown Portland is situated on a water-ringed peninsula with many islands and lighthouses extending into the bay. There are beautiful views of the bay at various places, but particularly from the northeast end of the peninsula.

When Maine was separated from Massachusetts in 1820, Portland became its capital. The city retained this position until 1832, when the seat of government was moved to Augusta. Portland and Casco Bay have always been important for the commerce and industry of Maine and the United States. During the early nineteenth century Maine businessmen owned 20 percent of the merchant fleet of the United States, and by 1855 a third of the merchant ships were built in Maine.[1] A principal state export was lumber from the rich old-growth New England forests. Still a favorite tourist destination is the Portland Head Lighthouse. Completed in 1791 during George Washington's presidency, it is the oldest lighthouse on the bay.

Henry Wadsworth Longfellow is a beloved Portland poet. His home on Congress Street is now part of the Maine Historical Society. The society has an excellent bookstore, museum, and research facility. Not far from the Longfellow home is the Portland Public Library, with its heritage room of early publications on Portland and the state of Maine. In 1866 there was a devastating fire that destroyed much of central Portland, including many sites related to the Millerite movement. Fortunately the 1866 fire did not destroy Longfellow's home. There is no evidence that Ellen Harmon ever visited the Longfellow home, though both she and Longfellow liked to visit the Portland Head Lighthouse. On the south end of Congress Street a monument to Longfellow is prominently displayed.

As one drives through downtown Portland it is important to realize that much of the area was destroyed in the great fire of 1866. Though some 1830s buildings on the

Longfellow home—Maine Historical Society

south side remain, nearly every important Adventist-related structure is now gone. The only original Adventist-related building in Portland is the Brackett Street School, where Ellen Harmon was a student—located to the southwest of the 1866 fire.

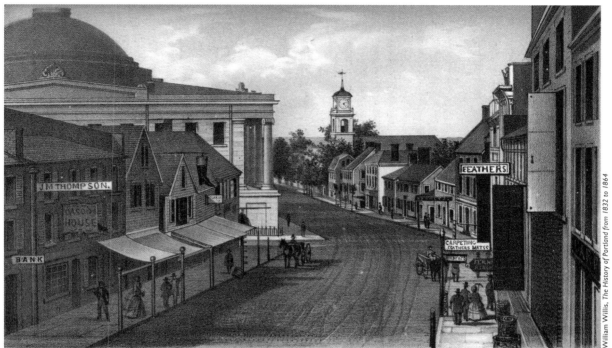

Middle Street, Portland, Maine (1844)

Deering Oaks Park

During the first half of the nineteenth century the large trees and hillside beauty of the Deering property made it a recreational destination for local residents. In 1879 Nathaniel and Henry Deering and other property owners donated land to the city of Portland for a park. The park continued to grow, until in 1922 it totaled nearly 54 acres. The present park is located just below the hill on which old Portland is located. The original property continued up the hill closer to the home of Robert and Eunice Harmon. The Harmon children, including the twins Ellen and Elizabeth, often played in these woods. Ellen White recollected: "I have spent many pleasant hours in the woods at that place."[2]

In 1909 Ellen White returned to her hometown to attend a camp meeting in Deering Oaks Park. She also took a tour of the city.[3] When she arrived on the train at Woodfords Station, her nephew, Clarence S. Bangs, son of her twin sister Elizabeth, conveyed her the short distance to the camp in the park. On Sabbath morning, July 3, 1909, she spoke in the main tent, "giving lessons from the experiences of Israel."[4] It was a great joy for Ellen White to return and once again "bear her mes-

sage" to the people of Portland. Today there is still a Seventh-day Adventist church in Portland.

Elizabeth Haines and Ellen White's First Vision

It was in Elizabeth Haines' home that Ellen White received her first prophetic vision. Haines opened her home to teenage Ellen Harmon at various times during her injury-induced illness. Elizabeth Haines was listed as a delegate with Orinda Haines to the third Millerite General Conference that was held in Portland, Maine, during October 1841.[5] About the time of the 1844 disappointment physicians diagnosed Ellen Harmon as having tuberculosis. Because her chronic illness was exhausting her mother, Eunice Harmon, Haines agreed to care for the young girl for a few days or weeks at a time. It was thus that Ellen happened to be at the Haines home when she received her first vision in December 1844.[6]

Other significant visions occurred during 1845 in the Haines home. There Ellen received a vision that rebuked Joseph Turner for using mesmerism. In the spring of 1845 it was probably in the Haines home that Ellen had her "new earth" vision that inspired William Hyde to write a poem entitled "The Better Land," now a hymn named "We Have Heard." Put to music, using a popular tune of the day, "Carrier Dove," it has appeared

Deering Oaks Park
GPS: N 43°39.503' W 070°16.480'

in Seventh-day Adventist hymnals down to the present. It remains the earliest Seventh-day Adventist hymn directly related to the movement.

At some point after Ellen's new earth vision, Haines again cared for Ellen in her home. It was a protracted bout of illness that resulted in Ellen having mental confusion. In an attempt to discredit Ellen, Joseph Turner and those associated with him extracted a signed statement by Haines concerning comments made by Ellen during her delirium. Haines later tearfully apologized to Ellen that her name was ever attached to the document.[7] In 1858 J. N. Loughborough, in company with James and Ellen White, visited Haines in Portland. Though not a Sabbathkeeper, she willingly gave her name as a reference that Ellen White had not been a part of the fanaticism after 1844.

Unfortunately, little is known about Elizabeth Haines. For many years New England Adventist tours visited the traditional site where it was believed that she lived. But research has shown that the location is incorrect. Perhaps more information on Haines will yet come to light.

Spruce Street Harmon Home

The Harmon family moved from Poland, Maine, back to Portland about 1833, resulting in Robert Harmon being listed in the *1834 Portland Directory*. He bought their Spruce Street home on September 16, 1836. It is possible that his family lived for a time in the home on a lease or rental basis. Their home was originally located on the southeast corner of Spruce and Clark. Spruce Street was moved closer to Spring Street, and today the site is located on the northeast side of Clark Street opposite Spruce Street in the play area of a public school. The Harmons lived in this home until 1846. Robert Harmon then sold his home and moved again to Gorham, Maine.

Much history occurred in the Spruce Street home. It is likely that Ellen and Elizabeth traveled back and forth the short distance to the Brackett Street School beginning perhaps in 1832 or 1833. It was probably during 1836 or 1837, while living at this home, that Ellen Harmon was injured when an older schoolmate thoughtlessly threw a rock at her. Ellen Harmon was living in this home when she and her family became believers in the Second Advent message. It was here that she told

Middle Street, Portland, Maine (1863)

Middle Street, Portland, Maine (1863)

Portland, Maine, after the great fire of 1866

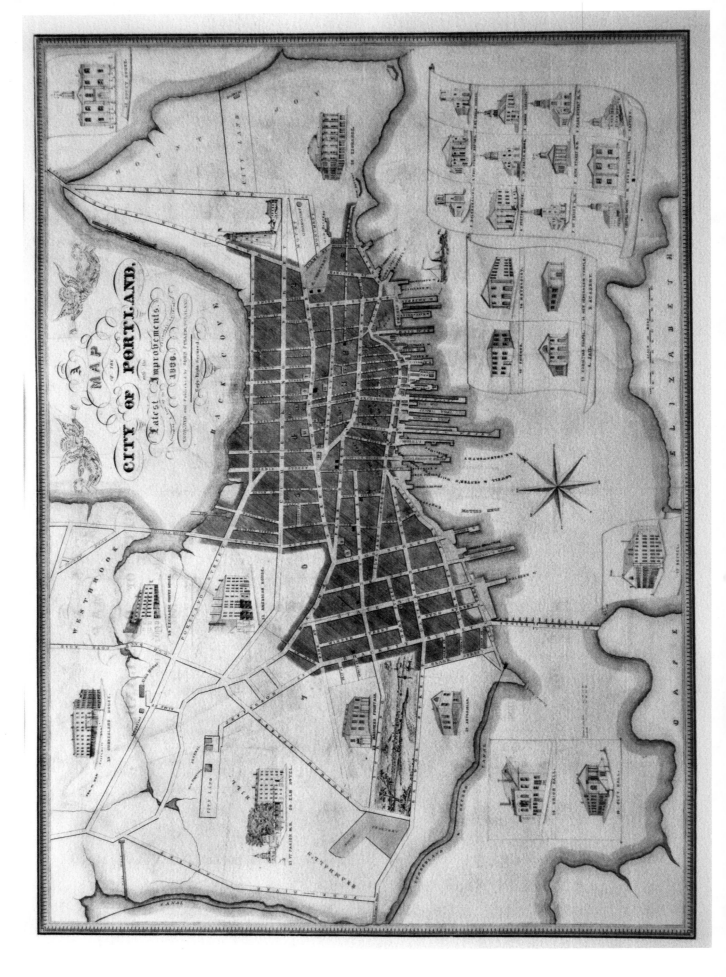

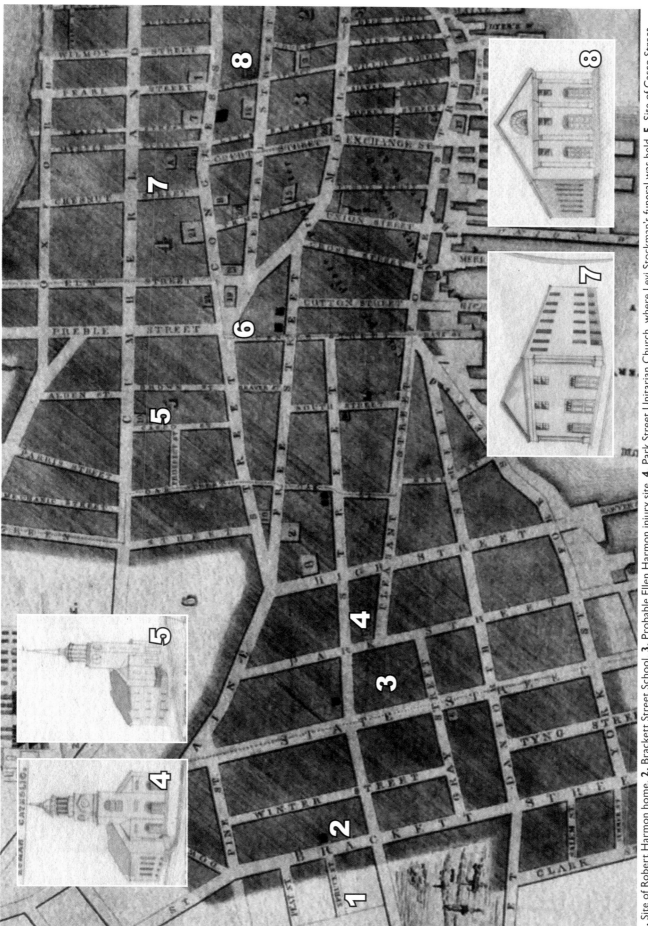

1. Site of Robert Harmon home. 2. Brackett Street School. 3. Probable Ellen Harmon injury site. 4. Park Street Unitarian Church, where Levi Stockman's funeral was held. 5. Site of Casco Street Christian Church. 6. Site of Beethoven Hall. 7. Site of Chestnut Street Methodist Church. 8. Site of Christian chapel where Ellen Harmon first gave her testimony.

Brackett Street School, where Ellen Harmon likely attended

the group of Adventists living in Portland about her first vision. Many other meetings occurred in this home.

Brackett Street School

Ellen Harmon presumably received her earliest formal education in a wooden schoolhouse on Brackett Street just one block east of her home. She was a good student and soon advanced in reading. She recalled: "Many times I was called down stairs to the primary room to read their lesson to the little children." One day in midlife Ellen White was traveling on the train, and a woman overheard her reading to her husband and asked, "Aren't you Ellen Harmon?"

She responded, "Yes, but how did *you* know me?"

The woman replied, "Why, . . . I knew you by your voice. I attended school on [Brackett] Street in Portland, and you used to come and read our lessons to us. We could understand them better when you read than when any one else did."[8]

The Brackett Street School was a wooden structure first erected in 1828.[9] It was replaced with a new brick building in 1836—about the time Ellen probably

Brackett Street School
GPS: N 43°39.048' W 070°15.992'

Building formerly used as Brackett Street School

received her facial injury.[10] This brick building was destroyed by fire in 1852, but was rebuilt and enlarged with the addition of a third story using some of the old brick walls.[11] Thus most of Ellen White's formal education was in the older wooden school, though it is thought that she attended the brick schoolhouse irregularly after her accident.

It was Ellen White's great desire to gain an education and perhaps become a teacher. But her injuries affected her equilibrium and vision, thus preventing her from making academic progress. She attempted to continue her education until about 1839, when she made a final effort to attend a "female seminary." Her fragile health collapsed, and she never went back to school. Throughout the rest of her life she lamented her lack of formal education. Still, it would be incorrect to call her uneducated. At the time of her death Ellen White had more than 1,000 volumes in her library. She was widely read and maintained an active correspondence, and her publications would fill a small bookcase.

Park Street Common and Ellen White's Injury

Ellen's education in Portland could not have continued for more than three or four years before her terrible accident. The details of the story—as told by Ellen White—began abruptly and tragically in 1836 or 1837, when she was about 9 years old.[12] This date is surmised, based on Ellen White's recollection of seeing a dramatic aurora borealis while recovering from her injury. She thought the celestial wonder was a harbinger of the coming of Jesus. It must have been remarkable, because during the centennial of the United States it was considered by one author to be one of the 100 greatest events between 1776 and 1876. The northern lights occurred on the night of November 14, 1837, and extended as far south as Georgia. The colors ranged from scarlet to white and covered much of the sky.[13]

Ellen was struck by a stone, angrily thrown by an older schoolmate, while crossing a public common heading toward home with her sister Elizabeth. Ellen vividly recalled what happened: "I turned my head to see how far she was behind me, and as I did so, she threw the stone and it hit me on the nose. A blinding, stunning sensation overpowered me, [and] I fell senseless."[14] When Ellen regained consciousness, she found herself in a nearby store covered with blood and her nose still bleeding freely onto her clothes and the floor. A sympathetic stranger offered her a ride home, but she refused out of concern for soiling his carriage with blood. She remembered, "After walking only a few

Spruce Street Harmon home
GPS: N 43°39.023' W 070°15.962'

rods,[15] I grew faint and dizzy. My twin sister and my schoolmate carried me home, about one-half mile."[16]

According to various nineteenth-century maps of Portland there was a park or "common" located about a third of a mile from their home toward the downtown area roughly east of their home.[17] It was located between Park Street and State Street and bounded north and south by Spring Street and Gray Street. It filled the middle portion of an entire city block. Ellen and her sister may have been returning from visiting the downtown area, where their father operated his hat shop, or maybe they were just playing in the park.[18] Today the park, or common, is a parking area for vehicles. Several historical homes from before the 1866 fire are located around its perimeter. These include a row house to the northeast that was built in the mid-1830s and various shops and historic homes. Perhaps it was to one of these shops or homes that Ellen Harmon was taken immediately after her accident.

Casco Street Christian Church

From March 11 to 23, 1840, William Miller visited Portland, Maine, where he gave a series of lectures on the second coming of Jesus. These lectures were held in the Christian or Freewill Baptist church located on the southeast corner of Casco and Cumberland streets.[19] A great crowd came to listen. As a young girl of 12, Ellen Harmon attended these meetings. She recalled:

> No wild excitement attended the meetings, but a deep solemnity pervaded the minds of those who heard. Not only was a great interest manifested in the city, but the country people flocked in day after day, bringing their lunch baskets, and remaining from morning until the close of the evening meeting.[20]

In connection with the series, special meetings were held during which sinners could prepare for the coming of Jesus. Conviction and revival spread through the entire city and beyond. It brought new energy to the various churches in Portland. Lorenzo Dow Fleming, pastor of the Casco Street Christian Church, reported that by July 6, 1840, a scant four months after the series, he had baptized 185 souls. He attributed most of these to the lectures of William Miller.[21] The Christian chapel

Site of Casco Street Christian Church
GPS: N 43°39.392' W 070°15.750'

Casco Street Christian Church after the discontinuance of its use as a church building

located on Temple Street was pastored by Samuel E. Brown. He reported that about 100 had joined his congregation as a result of Miller's meetings. As people were being baptized, Hiram Simonton wrote, "Some consider Mr. Miller crazy, others say he is a weak old man. But one thing diverts me a little: they all appear to be willing to receive members into their churches that date their conviction from hearing Mr. Miller preach."[22]

Caleb Bradley, a Congregationalist minister, described Miller's meetings in his personal diary. It traces his pilgrimage from doubt and suspicion to

amazement and qualified support.[23] The first diary entry that mentioned the meetings is dated March 12, 1840. "Heard Mr. Miller this p.m. explain the 2300 days mentioned in the 8th chapter of Daniel." The next day Bradley wrote: "Went into Miller's lecture—crowded house—subject—Vision of the latter days. Daniel 8:13, 14. The preacher seemed to make it appear very plain, people very attentive, many believed and some believed not." By March 15 Bradley is becoming more positive. "Attended Miller's lecture this evening, a very great crowd, judged to be 2,000 people. . . . He uses the Bible altogether and he thinks he is correct and I believe him sincere."

On Friday, March 20, Bradley noted that nearly everyone he spoke to in Portland had something to say about Miller's lectures. The topic that evening was the seven last plagues of Revelation 16, and the effect on the "crowded house" was dramatic. After noting that Miller focused on Jesus as the "Alpha and the Omega," Bradley wrote: "There appeared to be a very wonderful effect upon the congregation—all silent and still, all attention, all anxiety. Mr. Miller closed with a warm and feeling appreciation of the subject—pressed it home upon the hearts and *consciences* of his hearers. Those of you who wish to retire can now go if you choose, says Mr. Fleming, and those who are anxious are invited to remain and have prayer and ne'er a scene presented itself; better known to those who were present than can be described." Ellen Harmon was among the group that came forward for prayer. She wrote: "When sinners were invited forward to the anxious seat, hundreds responded to the call; and I, among the rest, pressed through the crowd and took my place with the seekers."[24]

Bradley's now enthusiastic comments continue day by day even after the conclusion of the meetings. On March 26 he wrote: "There is quite an excitement on the subject of religion, over the whole city; but especially in Casco Street Church, where Mr. Miller's lectures were held. Multitudes have come forward and acknowledged themselves *sinners* and are determined to take the *road* to *heaven*." At more than one point during the meetings Bradley mentioned that Miller was Bible-centered in his presentations. Now after the meetings "many had waked up and began to read their *Bibles*." Bradley concluded the entry for this day, "Thus ends another day and a few more days and time will be no longer."

Over the next few months the revival continued and increased in Portland and the surrounding area. On May 6, 1840, Bradley exclaimed: "The country is alive as it respects spiritual things—revivals in every part of the country—Portland is pervaded by the holy spirit—It is said that there is a general seriousness through the city—religion is the chief concern."

Miller described his Portland visit: "In no place that I ever visited have I found so little of self exaltation as in Portland. The people appear to be more on a level than any other city of my acquaintance. I saw none of the haughty, aristocratical pride which may be found in almost every other place of importance in the Union."[25]

Chestnut Street Methodist Church

The Chestnut Street Methodist Church in Portland was the home church for the Harmon family during the early 1840s. Robert and Eunice Harmon joined the church on February 26, 1840.[26] During the same year

Site of Casco Street Christian Church
GPS: N 43°39.392' W 070°15.750'

Ken Olin 2005

Site of Casco Street Christian Church

Sarah, Mary, and Robert, Jr., also joined, and Robert Harmon was made a class leader. In August, Robert Harmon helped found a branch congregation at the Brackett Street School near the Harmon home.

Until about the middle of 1842, Methodist pastors in Portland were sympathetic to the Millerite movement. Gershom F. Cox was the presiding elder in Portland between 1839 and 1842.[27] During this time he was very active in promoting the Millerite Advent message. At the July 20, 1842, Maine Methodist conference held in Gardiner, ministers who were supportive of Miller were moved to new locations. The *History of Methodism in Maine* reported: "Mr. Cox was removed from the district and appointed to Orrington, where he taught the doctrines of Miller, to the damage of the strong and flourishing society in that place." Charles Baker replaced Cox in the Portland district.[28] At the same time, William F. Farrington replaced John Hobart as pastor of the Chestnut Street church. A much more aggressive though reserved man, Farrington began to actively address matters of church discipline.

Miller came to Portland a second time in June of 1842 and received a less-than-warm welcome from the regular churches. The relationship between the Methodist church and Millerite believers became increasingly hostile. Many were expelled from their churches for believing in the soon coming of Jesus. The Harmon family was among those who were thus dealt with. During 1843 ministers began to be dismissed from their districts if they supported Miller's views.[29]

William F. Farrington (b. 1800)

Courtesy of the Center for Adventist Research

The class leaders' book for the Chestnut Street Church chronicles the process that led to the expulsion of the Harmon family from membership. Because of Robert Harmon's leadership position in the church and the esteem of other class leaders toward him, the discipline process was difficult and protracted. On February 6, 1843, Farrington formed the first of several committees to deal with the Harmons' "anti-Methodist conduct." It was a committee of two church leaders, L. Gooding and A. Bradbury. They failed to bring back a report. On March 27 Gideon Foster was made a committee of one to "visit [Brother] Harmon in reference to his irregularities." When he brought back a presumably positive report on April 23, it was "not accepted or laid on the table," and another committee of three was formed before whom Harmon was "cited to appear and answer for himself." This committee also did not bring a report, and on May 29 another three-person committee was formed "on Br. R. Harmon's irregularities." Finally on August 14, a "committee of trial" was formed "on the cases of Robert Harmon & those of his family who are members of the M. E. Church in this City all of whom having violated the rules of our Discipline in their long absence from our church and ordinances and supporting an Anti-Methodist doctrine and congregation Viz. Millerism, etc." One week later the committee's report was accepted, and Robert and Eunice Harmon together with their children Sarah, Robert, and Ellen were removed from membership for "breach of discipline." Mary was not excluded with her family, presumably because she had married Samuel Foss on July 5, 1842. Robert Harmon, Sr., appealed this decision to the quarterly meeting. On September 2, 1843, the quarterly meeting, with Charles Baker as presiding elder, upheld the action of the Chestnut Street church.[30] From reading the minutes and from Ellen White's recollection, it seems that the technicality used to remove them from membership was their nonattendance at class meetings. At the appeal Robert Harmon noted that other church members had also been absent from meetings and were not being removed from membership.[31]

The Harmon family were the first to be removed from membership for their Millerite views. The record of leaders' meetings during the succeeding months shows that several others were either voluntarily or involuntarily removed from membership.

Beethoven Hall

Musical culture in Portland began with Edward Howe in 1805. He became the founder of the Beethoven Musical Society. In 1824 the society estab-

Chestnut Street church (later structure)

Site of Beethoven Hall

Chestnut Street Methodist Church
GPS: N 43°39.568' W 070°15.472'

Site of Beethoven Hall
GPS: N 43°39.422' W 070°15.600'

lished its own music hall. For a time it had a "small, but remarkably sweet toned organ of its own." When the society disbanded in 1826, the organ was purchased by Howe and relocated to his home. In 1829 a new organization formed—the Handel and Haydn Society. Meetings were held in Beethoven Hall, which seated about 200 people.[32]

Adventists held meetings in Beethoven Hall following William Miller's 1840 meetings in the Casco Street Christian Church. This continued at least into 1845. Beethoven Hall was located on the third floor of a building on the east side of Congress Street near the head of Center Street near where Middle Street branches from Congress.[33]

Ellen White wrote of the meetings:

Notwithstanding the opposition of ministers and churches, Beethoven Hall, in the city of Portland, was nightly crowded; especially was there a large congregation on Sundays. All classes flocked to these meetings. Rich and poor, high and low, ministers and laymen, were all, from various causes, anxious to hear for themselves the doctrine of the second advent. Many came who, finding no room to stand, went away disappointed.

The order of the meetings was simple. A short and pointed discourse was usually given, then liberty was granted for general

exhortation. There was, as a rule, the most perfect stillness possible for so large a crowd. The Lord held the spirit of opposition in check while His servants explained the reasons of their faith. Sometimes the instrument was feeble, but the Spirit of God gave weight and power to His truth. The presence of the holy angels was felt in the assembly, and numbers were daily added to the little band of believers.[34]

Matthew F. Whittier, "the younger brother of the Quaker poet John Greenleaf Whittier and a resident of Portland, visited a Millerite meeting in Beethoven Hall during September 1844." He was not a "believer" and so is somewhat cynical in his choice of words. Nevertheless, he provides some interesting insights on the meetings and the Hall.

With considerable difficulty, on account of the crowd, we ascended the two flights of dark and dirty stairs, and with still greater difficulty elbowed our way into the hall. A motley crowd of all sizes, shapes, conditions and collors [sic] filled the hall and its galleries. . . . Clustered around a rude rostrum were the elect; most of them were in a kneeling posture. . . .

Around the hall hung pictures of strange uncouth animals, supposed to be the representation of those seen by Daniel and by St. John at Patmos.[35]

Levi S. Stockman (1814-1844)

Levi Stockman was a widely respected Methodist minister from East Poland, Maine, who became a Millerite preacher and played an important role in the conversion of Ellen Harmon. He was converted at the age of 15 and joined the Maine Methodist Conference at 22. From 1836 to 1843 he served as an itinerant preacher. He contracted pulmonary tuberculosis and moved to Portland, Maine. During the last year and a half of his life, he worked closely with the Millerites in Portland and other parts of Maine. His belief in the soon coming of Jesus led to his expulsion from the Maine Conference. This became a scandal for the Methodist Church. Many wondered how such a pious and honored minister could be treated in such a manner. Stockman was 30 when he passed away on June 25, 1844, leaving a wife and three children. His funeral was held in the Park Street Unitarian Church to accommodate the crowds that attended. He was buried in an unmarked grave in the Western Cemetery, Portland, Maine. After his death, even the Methodist paper described him as "one of the best and most acceptable preachers."[36] John Pearson, an Advent minister in Portland, wrote of Stockman on July 5, 1844: "We firmly believe that this year his sleeping dust will arise to the resurrection of life, and from the hand of Jesus receive that crown that fadeth not away."[37]

William Foy in Portland

During the first year of her prophetic ministry Ellen Harmon interacted with at least seven different prophetic claimants.[38] She considered the experiences of Hazen Foss and William Foy to be genuine. Foss lived in Poland, Maine, and is described further in other chapters. William Foy came to Portland, and lived there for a time after 1844. He was a tall Black man who actively shared his visions with Advent believers. Ellen wrote of Foy, "We went over to Cape Elizabeth to hear him lecture. Father always took me with him when we went, and he would be going in a sleigh, and he would invite me to get in, and I would ride with them. That was before I got any way acquainted with him." Foy apparently settled in Portland soon after the 1844 disappointment. When asked when she first saw him, Ellen responded, "It was there, at Beethoven Hall. They lived near the bridge where we went over to Cape Elizabeth, the family did." If one looks at a map of Portland from that time, the Foys must have lived only a few blocks from the Harmons. On January 3, 1845, with the help of Portland Adventists, John and Charles Pearson, Foy published a little tract describing his visions. It was

Longfellow boyhood home

Baptizing shore
GPS: N 43°39.717' W 070°14.859'

titled *The Christian Experience of William E. Foy Together With the Two Visions He Received in the Months of January and February 1842.* At one time Ellen Harmon had a copy and probably read it.[39] She also met and talked with Foy. At one meeting she sat with Foy's first wife, Ann.

His wife was so anxious. She sat looking at him, so that it disturbed him. "Now," said he, "you must not get where you can look at me when I am speaking." He had on an episcopalian robe. His wife sat by the side of me. She kept moving about and putting her head behind me. . . . She would be so anxious, repeating the words right after him with her lips. After the meeting was ended, and he came to look her up, she said to him, "I hid myself. You didn't see me." He was a very tall man, slightly colored. But it was remarkable [the] testimonies that he bore."[40]

Ellen Harmon always sat close to the stand or pulpit area in Beethoven Hall because it was easier for her to breathe. As mentioned previously, she had great difficulty with her lungs during the winter of 1844-1845. In the past William Foy has sometimes been confused with Hazen Foss. It should be noted that although William Foy never became a Seventh-day Adventist, he continued as a faithful Freewill Baptist minister and died many years later in East Sullivan, Maine.[41]

Ellen Harmon's Baptism in Casco Bay

Ellen White recalled that soon after returning from the Buxton, Maine, camp meeting, she was taken into the Methodist Church on probation.[42] The Chestnut Street Methodist Church records show that she was recommended for probation on September 20, 1841.

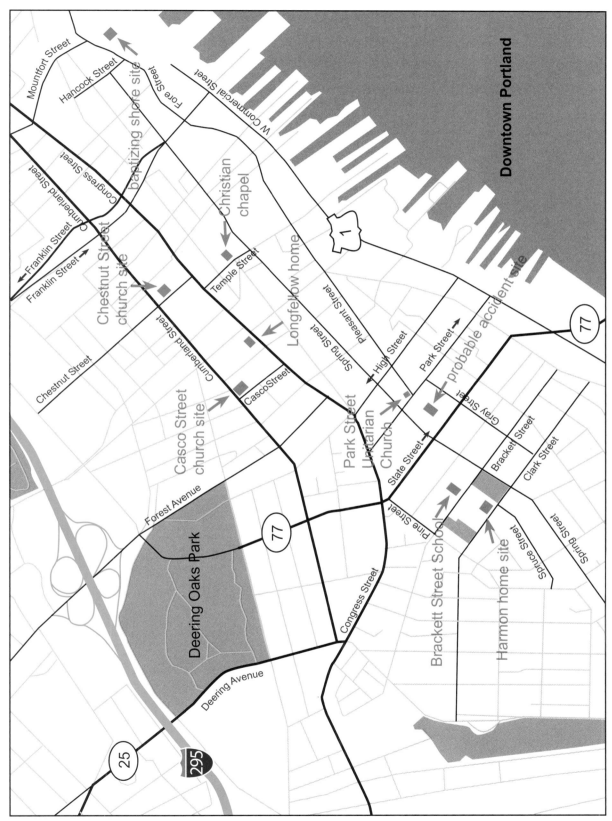

Adventist historic sites, Portland, Maine

The Methodist Church discipline required a minimum six-month probationary period before baptism. On May 23, 1842, the board recommended her for baptism. About a month later a group gathered on the shore of the baptizing place not far from Henry Wadsworth Longfellow's boyhood home to witness the baptism.[43] John Hobart baptized young Ellen and eleven others on June 26, 1842, in the cold water of the bay.[44] Today the approximate site of her baptism is on Fore Street a few blocks northeast of the Franklin Arterial (1A), which is now some distance inland.

Ellen graphically described the circumstances surrounding her baptism. "Finally the day was appointed for us to receive this solemn ordinance. Although usually enjoying, at this time, great peace, I frequently feared that I was not a true Christian, and was harassed by perplexing doubts as to my conversion. It was a windy day when we, twelve in number, were baptized, walking down into the sea. The waves ran high and dashed upon the shore, but in taking up this heavy cross, my peace was like a river. When I arose from the water, my strength was nearly gone, for the power of the Lord rested upon me."[45]

Notes

[1] *Portland* (Portland, Maine: Greater Portland Landmarks, Inc., 1999), pp. 28, 29.

[2] Ellen G. White to E. E. Franke, Sept. 1, 1903 (letter 193, 1903) (Silver Spring, Md.: Ellen G. White Estate).

[3] "Adventists' [sic] Meeting: Address by Elder Haskell on the Book of Daniel," Portland *Evening Express*, July 7, 1909, p. 14.

[4] D. E. Robinson, "At the Portland Camp-Meeting," *Review and Herald*, Dec. 9, 1909, p. 7.

[5] "Report of the Proceedings," *Signs of the Times*, Nov. 1, 1841, p. 113.

[6] J. N. Loughborough, "Some Individual Experience, A Companion to the Book *The Great Second Advent Movement*" (unpublished manuscript, Oct. 27, 1918), pp. 43, 44.

[7] Ellen G. White, *Spiritual Gifts*, vol. 2, pp. 69, 302.

[8] Ellen G. White, "Life Sketches Manuscript," pp. 8, 9.

[9] "Report of the School Committee," *Eastern Argus*, Mar. 31, 1829.

[10] "Sealed Proposals," *Eastern Argus*, May 3, 1836, p. 3.

[11] Maine Historical Society clippings. See Dec. 19, 1915, probably from the *Eastern Argus*.

[12] James White, "Mrs. Ellen G. White: Her Life, Christian Experience, and Labors," *Signs of the Times*, Jan. 6, 1876, p. 44.

[13] R. M. Devens, *Our First Century* (Springfield, Mass.: C. A. Nichols & Co., 1877), pp. 379-385.

[14] James White, "Mrs. Ellen G. White," p. 44.

[15] A rod is equal to five and a half yards.

[16] Ellen G. White, "Life Sketches Manuscript," p. 4.

[17] The common was between Park and State streets, with Spring Street to the north and Gray Street to the south.

[18] See Portland maps for 1836, 1851, 1866.

[19] An 1836 map of Portland has a sketch of the Casco Street Christian Church. It is captioned "Freewill Baptist."

[20] Ellen G. White, *Life Sketches* (1915), p. 20.

[21] L. D. Fleming, "Letter From L. D. Fleming," *Christian Palladium*, Aug. 1, 1840, pp. 105, 106.

[22] Hiram Simonton, "Letter to the Editor," *Christian Palladium*, June 15, 1840, p. 62.

[23] Caleb Bradley diary, Maine Historical Society, Portland, Maine.

[24] Ellen G. White, *Life Sketches* (1915), p. 21.

[25] William Miller, "Miller's Letters, No. 6," *Signs of the Times*, June 1, 1840, p. 37.

[26] Membership records of the Chestnut Street Methodist Church. Chestnut Street Methodist Episcopal Church, Portland, Maine.

[27] E. B. Randall, *A Statistical History of the Maine Conference of the M. E. Church From 1793 to 1891* (Portland, Maine: Lakeside Press, 1893), p. 163.

[28] Stephen Allen and W. H. Pilsbury, *History of Methodism in Maine: 1793-1886* (Augusta, Maine: Charles E. Nash, 1887), pp. 121-124.

[29] *Ibid.*, pp. 122, 123.

[30] "Records of the Leaders' Meetings," Sept. 2, 1836, to July 14, 1845. Chestnut Street Methodist Episcopal Church, Portland, Maine.

[31] Ellen G. White, *Life Sketches* (1915), p. 52.

[32] George Thornton Edwards, *Music and Musicians of Maine* (Portland, Maine: Southworth Press, 1928), pp. 42-62.

[33] "The Second Adventists," *Post Scrapbook* (Portland, Maine: Maine Historical Society), vol. 4, p. 106.

[34] Ellen G. White, *Life Sketches* (1915), p. 54.

[35] F. Whittier, Portland *Transcript*, Nov. 1, 1945 [sic], p. 228. Quoted from Frederick Hoyt, "We Lifted Up Our Voices Like a Trumpet: Millerites in Portland, Maine," *Spectrum*, August 1987, pp. 18, 20.

[36] B. F. Tefft, "Rev. L. S. Stockman," *Zion's Herald and Wesleyan Journal*, July 24, 1844, p. 120.

[37] John Pearson, "Letter From J. Pearson," *Advent Herald*, July 24, 1844, p. 194.

[38] Hazen Foss, William Foy, Dorinda Baker, Mary Hamlin, Phoebe Knapp, Miss Blaisdell, and Sarah Jordan.

[39] Most of the accounts in this section on Foy are from an interview between Ellen White and D. E. Robinson. See Ellen G. White, *Manuscript Releases*, vol. 17, p. 96.

[40] *Ibid.*

[41] Date taken from the tombstone.

[42] James White and Ellen G. White, *Life Sketches* (Battle Creek, Mich.: Seventh-day Adventist Pub. Assn., 1880), p. 145.

[43] "Old Baptising Shore," in *Post Scrapbook*, vol. 4, p. 101, from an 1890s newspaper article.

[44] The date of baptism and the pastor who baptized her are verified by Portland Chestnut Street Methodist Church records.

[45] James White and Ellen G. White, *Life Sketches* (1880), p. 145.

The Lighthouse

by Henry Wadsworth Longfellow

Katy Wolfer 2008

The rocky ledge runs far into the sea,
and on its outer point, some miles away,
the lighthouse lifts its massive masonry,
A pillar of fire by night, of cloud by day.

Even at this distance I can see the tides,
Upheaving, break unheard along its base,
A speechless wrath, that rises and subsides
in the white tip and tremor of the face.

And as the evening darkens, lo! how bright,
through the deep purple of the twilight air,
Beams forth the sudden radiance of its light,
with strange, unearthly splendor in the glare!

No one alone: from each projecting cape
And perilous reef along the ocean's verge,
Starts into life a dim, gigantic shape,
Holding its lantern o'er the restless surge.

Like the great giant Christopher it stands
Upon the brink of the tempestuous wave,
Wading far out among the rocks and sands,
The night o'er taken mariner to save.

And the great ships sail outward and return
Bending and bowing o'er the billowy swells,
And ever joyful, as they see it burn
They wave their silent welcome and farewells.

They come forth from the darkness, and their sails
Gleam for a moment only in the blaze,
And eager faces, as the light unveils
Gaze at the tower, and vanish while they gaze.

The mariner remembers when a child,
on his first voyage, he saw it fade and sink
And when returning from adventures wild,
He saw it rise again o'er ocean's brink.

Steadfast, serene, immovable, the same,
Year after year, through all the silent night
Burns on forevermore that quenchless flame,
Shines on that inextinguishable light!

It sees the ocean to its bosom clasp
The rocks and sea-sand with the kiss of peace:
It sees the wild winds lift it in their grasp,
And hold it up, and shake it like a fleece.

The startled waves leap over it; the storm
Smites it with all the scourges of the rain,
And steadily against its solid form
press the great shoulders of the hurricane.

The sea-bird wheeling round it, with the din
of wings and winds and solitary cries,
Blinded and maddened by the light within,
Dashes himself against the glare, and dies.

A new Prometheus, chained upon the rock,
Still grasping in his hand the fire of love,
it does not hear the cry, nor heed the shock,
but hails the mariner with words of love.

"Sail on!" it says: "sail on, ye stately ships!
And with your floating bridge the ocean span;
Be mine to guard this light from all eclipse.
Be yours to bring man neared unto man.

Katy Wolfer 2008

Topsham, Maine

"Fort Howland," the home of Stockbridge Howland in Topsham, Maine, is remembered as a center for early Sabbatarian Adventism. Topsham, which is about 25 miles north of Portland, is situated on the Androscoggin River just across from the larger town of Brunswick. Topsham received its name in 1717 while Maine was a part of the commonwealth of Massachusetts. During the 1840s Topsham's population was just under 2,000. One of its principal industries was mill factories along the Androscoggin River and its tributaries. Today one can still see restored mills and the remains of other mills from the bridge crossing from Brunswick to Topsham, and along the river.

During the formative years of 1845-1850 the homes of Stockbridge Howland and Robert Curtis were two of the most important places of meeting in the state of Maine for Sabbatarian Adventists. The Whites lived for a time with the Howlands. When the Whites traveled, they left little Henry, their firstborn son, in Topsham with the Howlands. Important conferences and Ellen White visions occurred in the Howland and Curtis homes. While the location of the Curtis home is still unknown, the location of the Howland residence is well established. Another even less known family was the Pattens. They were important in helping to counter the extreme sanctification fanaticism in Topsham described later in this chapter.

Robert and Mercy Curtis Home

In the spring of 1845, after returning to Portland from traveling in eastern Maine, Ellen Harmon made her way to Topsham.[1] There she attended meetings in homes of at least three different Adventist families—Curtis, Howland, and Patten. In 1845 many meetings were held at the Robert and Mercy Curtis home. On one occasion Ellen was taken off in vision and held the large Curtis family Bible. According to eyewitnesses she held the Bible at a 45-degree angle for several minutes. In this two-hour vision she walked about the room and even opened the Bible. As she turned the pages she quoted texts without looking at them.[2]

In November 1846 Ellen White was in the home of Robert and Mercy Curtis when she received her vision of the heavens with a view of various planets.[3] This vision convinced Joseph Bates that her visions were prophetic and not just "religious reveries."

The Patten Home

In the spring of 1845 James White and Ellen Harmon confronted "holy flesh" (extreme sanctification) fanatics in Topsham. Like the Millerite fanatic John Starkweather, the fanatical Adventists in Topsham

Stockbridge Howland home
GPS: N 43°55.567' W 069°57.770'

Stockbridge Howland home in Topsham, Maine, shown at its original location

believed that all of their impressions were holy. Some thought that unmarried men and women could lie together without impure thoughts. William H. Hyde, a 17-year-old Portland printer's son, became involved with this delusion. After he had contracted a serious case of "bloody dysentery" (perhaps cholera), he was visited and prayed for. Hyde agreed to leave the residence of the fanatics, and rode "four miles to the house of Brother Patten." After prayer Hyde was immediately healed and arose to eat a "farmer's dinner." This was before any understanding of health reform.[4] Not long after this Ellen Harmon was again in Portland, where she presumably had her third major vision, known as the new earth vision. It countered another group of fanatics known as spiritualizers. They spiritualized the Second Coming, the resurrection, the New Jerusalem, and even the person of Christ. In her vision Ellen White saw that the restoration of the earth and the New Jerusalem were literal. She described them vividly after coming out of vision. William Hyde was present and wrote a poem based on this vision that was published by J. V. Himes in the *Millennial Harp*. Today it can be sung from the current *Seventh-day Adventist Hymnal*. "We Have Heard" is the earliest song written for those who would become Sabbatarian Adventists. It is also the earliest song based on an Ellen White vision.

We do not have much information on the Patten family. Further research may bring more information to light.

Stockbridge Howland home

Stockbridge Howland Home (7 Elm Street, Topsham, Maine)

Stockbridge Howland was one of the closest friends and associates of James and Ellen White during the first years after their marriage.

Howland purchased his home on May 9, 1833, and continued to live there until he moved to Battle Creek in 1871.[5] During the 1830s Howland purchased and sold interests in mills located on a tributary of the Androscoggin River.

Howland sold his home in 1838 for $1,200 and then repurchased it on October 16, 1844, for the same price. It is curious that he repurchased his home in the week before the October 1844 date for the second coming of Jesus. It was after 1844 that the Topsham community became concerned that Howland's beliefs would cause him to sell his home again and then come to poverty. Consequently, on June 5, 1845, he was declared "an Insane & Lunatic person" and placed under guardianship.[6] This guardianship continued until 1859. A recollection described in the Nicola photo album suggests that Howland was asked to rebuild a bridge across the Kennebec River after it was washed away by a flood. He turned down the offer and told them he could not do the work since he was considered insane. It was obvious to everyone that this was not the case, and the matter went back to the probate court. The October 4, 1859, entry reads: "Howland was considered some years ago, by your predecessors in office, insane in some respects, and they had guardians appointed for him to prevent him from spending his property—now we consider him sane and capable of managing his own affairs."[7] His "rights of citizenship" were then fully restored.

The Howland home originally was located on the northeast corner of Main and Elm. At some point between 1875 and 1896 Woodbury B. Purinton moved the house across the street to its present location, which he also owned.[8]

On the southeast corner of the intersection of Main and Elm is the Baptist church built in 1835. The church was enlarged and improved in 1870. The Seventh-day Adventist church has at times rented this church for Sabbath services. Howland was Congregationalist, and not a member of the Baptist Church.[9]

Stockbridge Howland (1801-1883)

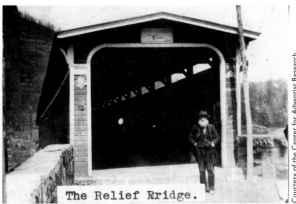

The Relief Bridge.

Bridge presumably built by Howland over the Kennebec River

James and Ellen White Family in Topsham

Many important things happened in Topsham. The key centers for James and Ellen White between 1846 and 1850 were Stockbridge Howland's home in Topsham; Otis Nichols' home in Dorchester, Massachusetts; Albert Belden's home in Rocky Hill, Connecticut; and Leonard Hastings' home in New Ipswich, New Hampshire. Of these four, probably Topsham was the most important.

In the spring of 1845 Ellen Harmon was in the Howland home. Frances Howland, their eldest daughter, was extremely ill with rheumatic fever. Her hands were swollen, and Ellen was deeply concerned for her "very dear friend." They all knelt in prayer, and soon Mercy Curtis felt convicted to go upstairs where Frances lay. She took her hand and said, "Sister Frances, in the name of the Lord arise, and be whole." Instantly Frances was healed. She dressed and came down to the parlor below. When the doctor came in, he was very surprised to see her fully restored.[10]

In April 1847 the Whites were at the Howland home, where Ellen had her Sabbath halo vision. It confirmed Joseph Bates' idea, based on Revelation 11:19, that the Sabbath had eschatological importance. Jesus had entered the Most Holy Place of the heavenly sanctuary, which contained the ark of the covenant. Within the ark were the Ten Commandments. Ellen White saw a brighter light surrounding the first four commandments but the fourth commandment had "a halo of glory . . . all around it."[11] The Sabbath was present truth because Jesus was before the ark in the second apartment of the heavenly sanctuary. Soon after this vision, across the river from Topsham in Brunswick, James White printed *A Word to the "Little Flock."*

United Baptist church, Topsham, Maine

Henry White (1847-1863)

In October 1847 the Howlands invited the Whites to live with them. They moved into the upstairs portion of the house and "commenced housekeeping with borrowed furniture." Rather than be dependent, James White worked "hauling stone for the railroad." James also worked cutting cordwood for 50 cents a day.

The Whites' eldest son, Henry, was perhaps most closely identified with "Fort Howland." It was to be his home for several of his younger years. He finally contracted pneumonia during a return visit at the age of 16, where he died. Ellen White remembered that she allowed herself and her child "one pint of milk each day" during the time they lived with the Howlands. On one occasion she had only "nine cents to buy milk for three mornings." She decided to skip buying milk for herself and instead bought "an apron to cover the bare arms" of her child.[12]

The Whites were still living in Topsham in April 1848 when a letter from E.L.H. Chamberlain in Middletown, Connecticut, urged them to attend the first of many Sabbatarian conferences. Later in 1848 an important conference was held at the Howland home. Over the weekend of October 20-22, 1848, they studied the meaning of the Sabbath as the seal of God. Less than a

month later in Dorchester, Massachusetts, Ellen White had a vision that James White should begin to publish the Sabbath and heavenly sanctuary message.

Following the October 1848 Topsham Sabbatarian conference, the Whites realized they could not take their son, Henry, everywhere with them. Henry spent most of the next several years living with the Howlands. It was not until the Whites relocated in Rochester, New York, that they could bring Henry back to live with them.[13] The 1850 census records show the name of Henry listed with the other Howland children as if he were one of their own.

During the fall of 1863 the Whites stayed in the Howland home while working in northern New England. While there Henry assisted with the completion of the 1863 prophetic chart by gluing them onto their cloth backing. In the process he chilled and contracted a cold that turned into pneumonia. His sudden death was a terrible shock for everyone. Funeral services were held in the Baptist church across the street from the Howland home and in Battle Creek, where he was buried. Henry's body was placed in a "metallic burial casket," and he was interred in the family plot in Oak Hill Cem-

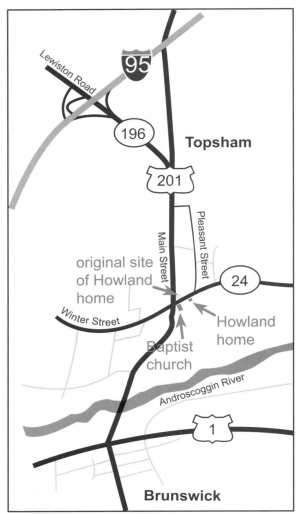

Howland sites, Topsham, Maine

[3] James White, *A Word to the "Little Flock"* (Gorham, Maine: James White), p. 22; Arthur L. White, *Ellen G. White: The Early Years*, pp. 113, 114.

[4] Ellen G. White, *Life Sketches* (Battle Creek, Mich.: Seventh-day Adventist Pub. Assn., 1888), pp. 200, 201.

[5] Uriah Smith, "Howland," *Review and Herald*, Apr. 17, 1883, p. 254.

[6] *Lincoln County Probate Records*, vol. 53, p. 122; vol. 59, p. 51. Superior Court, Bath, Maine.

[7] *Ibid.*, vol. 108, pp. 216, 217.

[8] *Lincoln County Records*, book 43, pp. 265, 266; *Estate of Woodbury B. Purinton Inventory*, vol. 5, p. 361.

[9] George Augustus Wheeler and Henry Warren Wheeler, *History of Brunswick, Topsham, and Harpswell, Maine* (Boston: Alfred Mudge & Son, 1878), pp. 654, 655.

[10] Ellen G. White, *Christian Experience and Teachings*, pp. 69, 71.

[11] *Ibid.*, p. 93.

[12] Ellen G. White, *Testimonies for the Church* (Mountain View, Calif.: Pacific Press, 1948), vol. 1, pp. 82, 83.

[13] James White, "Eastern Tour," *Review and Herald*, Nov. 1, 1853, p. 133.

[14] James White, "Eastern Tour," *Review and Herald*, Sept. 29, 1863, p. 140.

etery. A book, *An Appeal to the Youth,* was published to commemorate his death.

This chapter contains only highlights of events in the Howland home. James White summarized their feelings: "Here we had our first impressions of duty to preach and publish the message. . . . With this family we have ever found true friends and a hospitable home."[14]

Notes

[1] Ellen G. White, *Life Sketches* (1915), p. 74.

[2] J. N. Loughborough, *Rise and Progress of the Seventh-day Adventists*, pp. 106, 107. Loughborough quotes written memories of Frances Lunt (formerly the Frances Howland that was healed at that time) and Mrs. M. C. Truesdail, who was 15 at the time of the vision in 1845.

1863 Seventh-day Adventist prophetic chart

Courtesy of the White Estate

MASSACHUSETTS

Haverhill

South Lancaster

Boston

Old Sturbridge Village

Fairhaven

Catherine Parris 2008

Children fishing in Old Sturbridge Village, Massachusetts

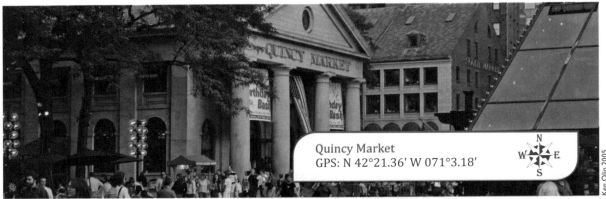

Quincy Market
GPS: N 42°21.36' W 071°3.18'

Ken Olin 2005

Quincy Market, Boston, Massachusetts

Boston, Massachusetts

Boston, Massachusetts, was the unofficial eastern headquarters of the Millerite movement during the 1840s. Joshua V. Himes, a Christian pastor in Boston, became the chief publicist, promoter, and organizer of the movement. At an Exeter, New Hampshire, meeting in 1839 Himes became acquainted with Miller and invited him to speak at the Chardon Street chapel in Boston. The results were dramatic and meetings were continued at the Marlboro chapel (connected to the Marlboro Hotel) to accommodate the crowds.[1] Other Advent meetings were on occasion held at the Marlboro chapel. In March 1840 Himes launched the *Signs of the Times*, the leading paper for the movement. It was renamed the *Advent Herald* in February 1844. Besides periodicals and broadsides, Himes published and widely circulated many tracts and books. The towns around Boston, which today are merged in the urban sprawl, contained many Millerite Adventists. Early Advent stories are sometimes connected to Boston and these outlying towns. Otis Nichols, a very early friend and supporter of James and Ellen White, lived southwest of Boston in Dorchester. Ellen White had her longest vision at the Thayer residence in Randolph just to the north of Dorchester. Correspondence in Millerite periodicals frequently came from the greater Boston region.

The 1844 map of downtown Boston in this chapter identifies several important Millerite sites. None of the original sites remain, and Boston has been reconfigured to a degree as a result of fires and development. This chapter does not contain pictures of the modern

Courtesy of Merlin D. Burt

Joshua V. Himes (1805-1895)

1843 Boston Almanac

First Christian church, Boston, Massachusetts

locations. The city of Boston is so changed and densely crowded that a modern visual is of less value. Through maps and pictures some conception can be gained of Advent sites in Boston. As indicated, J. V. Himes figured prominently in Boston. The location of his first church was at the corner of Summer and Sea streets—not far from the harbor docks at the southeast side of downtown Boston. The First Christian church predates the Millerite period but is of some interest because Himes was a pastor there from 1830 to 1837. The church was organized in 1804; the first pastors were Abner Jones, founder of the Freewill Baptist Church, and Elias Smith, founder of the Christian Connexion movement in northern New England.[2] Early Freewill Baptist Christians in New England were closely associated.

When Himes adopted Miller's views, he was pastor of the Chardon Street chapel. Himes organized the church on February 14, 1836, with 16 members and built the chapel in 1838. It comfortably seated about 500 people.[3] The First General Conference of Second Advent Believers was held in the Chardon Street chapel in October 1840.[4]

As the Millerite movement grew, it became necessary to provide a larger facility. A new "Second Advent tabernacle" on Howard Street that seated more than 3,000 was dedicated on May 4, 1843. It was located not far from the chapel.[5] The building was made of wood and put up hastily. When the building was constructed, it leaned into the street, and the "mayor, Martin Brimmer, compelled them to rebuild the wall." Those who attended remembered that the "interior was hung with pictures" representing the prophetic creatures of Daniel and Revelation.[6] Himes countered reports that the building was unstable. "Instead of its being a tottering building just ready to fall upon the heads of the audience," Himes wrote, the citizens of Boston "find that it is a large, pleasant, and well-supported place of worship."[7] After 1844 the building was converted to the Howard Athenaeum but burned in 1846. It was then rebuilt and continued to be used for theatrical performances.[8] (Not shown on map.)

After meeting for a time at the Central Hall on Milk Street, Himes returned in 1848 to the Chardon Street chapel. For the next few years it was named the Chardon Street Church of Second Adventists.[9] The current New Chardon Street is not at the same location as the Chardon Street of the 1840s.

Second Advent meetings were held at various locations in Boston during the exciting years between 1840

Chardon Street chapel

1843 Boston Almanac

and 1844. The Second General Advent Conference was held at the Melodeon on Washington Street during the week of May 24, 1842. Joseph Bates was the chairman of the conference.[10] This meeting prepared the way for the extensive camp meetings held during the summer and fall of 1842. It prepared the way for the East Kingston camp meeting and the purchase of the great tent that became such an important feature of large Millerite camp meetings.

The main office of the *Signs of the Times* was located at 14 Devonshire Street in an old exchange building. It was from this office that Himes and other Millerite leaders organized meetings, prepared publications, managed correspondence, and provided leadership to many aspects of the movement.

The Beacon Hill region of Boston was where William E. Foy, a Black Millerite minister, lived for a time and experienced visions. For more information on Foy and his visions, see chapters on East Sullivan and Portland, Maine. By 1860, according to Delbert Baker, almost two thirds of the city's Blacks lived on Beacon Hill.[11] Foy lived at 16 N. Grove Street at the base of the hill north of Cambridge Street toward the hospital.[12] Foy stated that he had visions during 1842 on Southack

Signs of the Times, Boston (last issue before 1844 disappointment)

Courtesy of the Center for Adventist Research

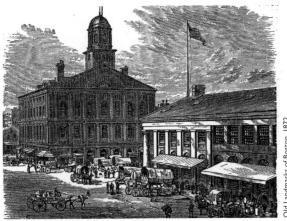

Old Landmarks of Boston, 1872

Faneuil Hall with Quincy Market, Boston, Massachusetts

Street and May Street.[13] Boston maps of the day do not indicate that there were churches on these streets, therefore the exact location is not known. Soon after his experience on May Street he was invited to share his testimony at the Broomfield Street church. This was most likely the Second Methodist chapel. No notice was given in the *Signs of the Times* of William Foy's experience. This is not surprising considering the opposition that Miller, Himes, and other key Advent leaders had to visions or ecstatic experiences.

Boston is, of course, an icon of the American Revolution. As one of America's oldest population centers, it was first incorporated in 1630. Today a favorite tourist destination is the Freedom Trail. This "trail" is really a three-mile directed tour through the central part of downtown Boston and across the Boston Inner Harbor. It takes the visitor by many historic buildings and sites from the Boston Common to Bunker Hill. Sites along the trail include the Park Street Church where, in 1829, William Lloyd Garrison gave his first public anti-slavery speech; the Old South Meeting House, where the Boston Tea Party began; the Old State House and Boston Massacre site; Faneuil Hall, a "Cradle of Liberty" where opposing views were freely aired; Quincy Market, a center of commerce built in 1825; the Old North Church, where Robert Newman signaled the approach of the British by using lanterns; the U.S.S *Constitution,* which is the oldest commissioned warship afloat; and the Bunker Hill monument, which marks the first major battle of the Revolutionary War.

Notes

[1] Josiah Litch, "The Rise and Progress of Adventism," *Advent Shield and Review*, May 1844, p. 57; Charles G. Finney, *Memoirs of Rev. Charles G. Finney* (New York: A. S. Barnes, 1876), p. 353.

[2] S. N. Dickinson, *The Boston Almanac for the Year 1843* (Boston: Thomas Groom & Co., 1843), p. 87.

[3] *Ibid.*, p. 118.

[4] Litch, p. 60.

[5] *Defence of Elder Joshua V. Himes* (Boston: Chardon Street church, 1851), p. 10; [J. V. Himes], "The Opening of the Tabernacle," *Signs of the Times*, May 10, 1843, p. 76.

[6] Samuel Adams Drake, *Old Landmarks and Historic Personages of Boston* (Boston: James R. Osgood and Co., 1875), pp. 367, 368.

[7] [J. V. Himes], "The Tabernacle," *Signs of the Times*, May 24, 1843, p. 96.

[8] Drake, p. 368.

[9] *Sketches of Boston, Past and Present and of Some Few Places in Its Vicinity* (Boston: Phillips, Sampson, and Co., 1851), p. 118.

[10] "General Conference in Boston," *Signs of the Times*, May 18, 1842, p. 56; "Boston Second Advent Conference," *Signs of the Times*, June 1, 1842, p. 68.

[11] Delbert W. Baker, *The Unknown Prophet*, p. 63.

[12] Dickinson, p. 57.

[13] William E. Foy, *The Christian Experience of William E. Foy Together With the Two Visions He Received in the Months of January and February 1842,* pp. 9, 15, 16.

THE

CHRISTIAN EXPERIENCE

OF

WILLIAM E. FOY

TOGETHER WITH THE

TWO VISIONS

HE RECEIVED IN THE MONTHS OF JAN. AND FEB. 1842

PORTLAND:
PUBLISHED BY J. AND C. H. PEARSON.
1845.

William Foy tract

1. Quincy Market. **2.** *Signs of the Times* office. **3.** Marlboro Hotel and chapel. **4.** Melodeon. **5.** Second Methodist chapel. **6.** Southack Street and May Street. **7.** North Grove Street. **8.** Chardon Street chapel. **9.** Second Advent tabernacle.

Joseph Bates (1792-1872)

Fairhaven Bridge
GPS: N 41°38.426' W 070°54.470'

N
W E
S

Courtesy of the New Bedford Whaling Museum

Fairhaven Bridge and Pope's Island panorama (1840s)

Fairhaven, Massachusetts

For Seventh-day Adventists, Fairhaven and New Bedford will ever be linked with Joseph Bates and his discovery of the Sabbath. It was here that Bates grew up and established his own family, and it was from here that he traveled the world, rising to captain and part owner of his own ship. It was in New Bedford and Fairhaven that he heard William Miller speak and became an ardent advocate of the soon coming of Jesus. It was here that he accepted the Sabbath and wrote tracts on topics that provided the theological foundation for the Seventh-day Adventist Church.

New Bedford was a whaling town during Joseph Bates' boyhood and young adult years. The great sea mammals furnished premium illuminating oil. New Bedford on the Acushnet River was also a seaport for other commerce. Not only whalers but also merchantmen sailed the seven seas in search of wealth. During the Revolutionary War New Bedford was a hideout for American privateers. The village of Fairhaven was originally a part of New Bedford, but became a distinct town in 1812. It was named for its beautiful setting that continues to this day. A long drawbridge through Pope Island connected the two towns. New Bedford was always the larger of the two cities. It has many interesting attractions that represent the rich history of the whaling industry and commerce during the nineteenth century. The Old Dartmouth Historical Society Whaling Mu-

seum is of particular interest to Adventists. In addition to whaling relics it contains original papers from Joseph Bates and his father.[1] To the south of New Bedford and Fairhaven is West Island, now accessible by bridge. It also has connections to the Adventist story.

Fairhaven has a number of very imposing Victorian municipal buildings, churches, and mansions. They include the Fairhaven High School, which is located in close proximity to the historic Fairhaven Academy, where Joseph Bates attended school as a boy; the Millicent Library, which is perhaps the most opulent library on the Eastern seaboard; and the Unitarian Memorial Church. These buildings were erected by the Henry H. Rogers family, who made a fortune in oil through their connection with John D. Rockefeller and the Standard Oil Company. At the time of Rogers' death in 1909 he was worth more than $100 million.

The Meadow Farm Boyhood Home of Joseph Bates

Joseph Bates was born on July 8, 1792, in Rochester, Massachusetts, about seven miles from New Bedford. He was the fifth of seven children born to Joseph Bates, Sr., and Deborah Nye. The Bates family moved into Meadow Farm in 1793 and lived there until 1835.[2] In 1835 Franklin Bates, Joseph Bates' younger brother,

Joseph Bates' boyhood home, Meadow Farm, 191 Main Street, Fairhaven, Massachusetts

sold the home to Anne Hathaway for $450. For the next 170 years and through six generations, the home belonged to the same family.[3] For many years the last couple to own the home, Hugh and Genevieve Darden, graciously received tour groups. In 2005, after Mrs. Darden's passing, the Seventh-day Adventist Church purchased the home and is in the process of restoring it. The current address is 191 Main Street.

William Wood built this historic home in 1742 on 150 acres that he purchased in 1735. Directly behind the house are the remains of an earlier house built by Thomas Tabor at some time between 1676 and 1680. The remaining wall is constructed with clamshell mortar. The Tabor house was destroyed by the "great gale" of 1869. [4] Its last resident was a Native American woman named Annis.[5] Joseph Bates lived in the Meadow Farm home until he went off to sea in 1807. From an upstairs window he could look out on the Acushnet River at the ships that came and went from their berthing. He became consumed with the desire to go to sea. "In my school-boy days," he wrote, "my most ardent desire was to become a sailor. I used to think how gratified I should be if I could only get on board a ship that was going on a voyage of discovery round the world."[6] Finally the day came in June 1807 when he was allowed to become a cabin boy on a ship called *Fanny,* bound for New York and London, England. Rather than following his father's hope that he turn to

Meadow Farm, Bates' boyhood home
GPS: N 41°38.777' W 070°54.504'

business enterprises, young Joseph would spend more than two decades as a seaman. His adventures are recorded in his autobiography, which even today provides fascinating and entertaining reading.

Painting of Tabor house next to the Bates home

Joseph Bates' boyhood home (circa 1890)

Fairhaven Academy

Joseph's father was one of the founders of New Bedford Academy, soon renamed Fairhaven Academy. When the school was built in 1798, Joseph Bates, Sr., was also elected treasurer. Joseph attended this school as a boy, and his picture is prominently displayed in one of the classrooms. Today Fairhaven Academy serves as the historical society building for the city. The building was moved to its present location in 1907.[7]

Fairhaven Academy

An Early Adventure at Sea

During Joseph Bates' return trip from his first sea voyage there was a large shark that continuously followed their ship. One Sunday as they were out at sea, young Joseph was sent aloft to the crow's nest on the

Fairhaven Academy
45 Center Street
Fairhaven, Massachusetts
GPS: N 41°38.606' W 070°54.409'

Fairhaven Academy (circa 1950)

New Bedford on the Acushnet River

main masthead to see if there were any ships in sight. On his way down he missed his step on the rope and fell some 60 feet into the ocean. He nearly hit the deck, but chanced to strike a rope that flipped him into the sea. The ship continued to travel, and Bates was nearly left behind. A rope was hurled to him, which he was able to grasp. He was then dragged back on deck. Some, who knew of his fear of the shark, asked if he had seen it while he was in the water. Bates began to tremble. Upon looking over the opposite side of the ship, he and the other seamen saw the shark serenely swimming there as if nothing had happened.[8]

A Most Remarkable Story: The Grave Robbers

Probably the most amazing story that Joseph Bates ever told from his eventful and full life was about a group of grave robbers. On Bates' first voyage he met a Mr. Lloyd, chief mate of a Philadelphia ship. While Lloyd was lodging in London, the police came to the house where he and a friend were staying. Fearing they would be considered disturbers of the peace, they fled into the street with nothing on but nightshirts. Lloyd hid in the marketplace while his friend went back for their clothes. In the middle of the night, while Mr. Lloyd was still waiting in the market, a gang of men came by intent on robbing the grave of a certain rich Jewish woman who had just been buried. They kidnapped Mr. Lloyd and brought him along to the cemetery, which was some two miles from the market. When he realized what the grave robbers were going to do, he begged to be released. They refused. The large flat stone that covered the grave was removed with a rope through an iron hook. This opened the vault of the Jewish family. The thieves were after the jewelry that was on the woman's person. The exciting question was "Who will go down and get the jewels?" Of course Mr. Lloyd was the man. He implored and entreated them not to make him do this dreadful deed, but they pushed him down

into the crypt and ordered him to strip off the jewels. After removing the necklaces and bracelets, he was ordered to take the rings from the corpse's fingers. He tried, but found that her fingers had swollen, which prevented the removal of the jewelry from them. The robbers passed down a knife and ordered Mr. Lloyd to cut off the fingers. He recalled to Bates, "I began to plead again, but they gave me to understand that there was no alternative; I must either do it or stay where I was. Almost dead with fear, I laid hold of her hands and cut her fingers off." When he had passed the jewels up, they dropped down the stone slab and ran away. Mr. Lloyd said, "I felt overwhelmed at my hopeless condition, doomed to die a most horrible death, and fearing every moment that the mangled corpse would lay hold of me. I listened to the rumbling sound of these robbers, until all was silent as death. The stone over me, I could not move. After a little I heard a distant rumbling of the ground, which continued to increase until I heard strange voices over the vault. I soon learned that this was another gang, most likely unknown to the first, and they were placing their rope to swing up the same stone slab. I at once decided what to do to save myself. As the slab came up, I leaped out of the vault in my white nightdress, or shirt. Horror-stricken, they all fled back toward the city, running with such speed that it was difficult for me to keep up behind them, and yet I feared that if they should stop, I should be discovered and taken. Before reaching the city, I had drawn up some nearer to the two hinder ones, when one of them cried out to his companion, *'Patrick! Patrick! The old woman is close to our heels!'* Onward they raced through the market and fled away from me, for I stopped here to hide myself. After a while my friend, having obtained my clothes, found me, and I returned home."[9]

Religious Experience: Follow the Light That You Have, and More Will Be Given.

Those are just two of many stories that this remarkable man related from his eventful life. Over the years Bates became a successful sea captain and even part owner of a ship and its cargo. He also found God and became a Christian. His wife, Prudence, had placed a pocket New Testament in his sea trunk, which contained a poem that caught his attention. He began to read the Bible and pray, and was converted in 1824. He tells of going into the jungles of South America to pray, and study his Bible. In 1827 he was baptized and became a member of the Christian church in Fairhaven.

Even before his conversion Bates was convicted that the lifestyle of a sailor was destructive. Alcohol and

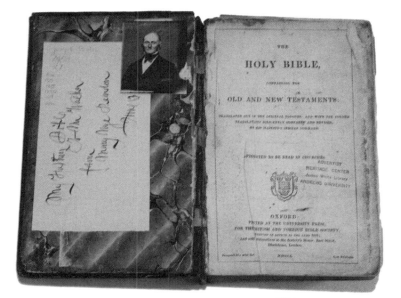

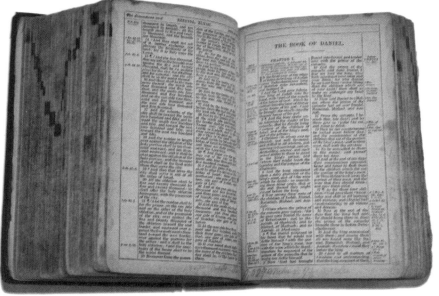

Joseph Bates' Bible used for Bible studies during the 1850s

cursing were the first to go. He became a teetotaling sea captain by the year 1824—a remarkable thing in those days. Then he was convinced he should abandon the use of tobacco. He therefore cast his pipe into the sea and made an end of that vice. In time he even discarded tea and coffee.

Not content merely to transform his own life, Bates required that his ship be an alcohol-free zone. He also prohibited swearing. With such rules, many thought that he would be unable to get sailors to serve on his ship. Some questioned whether he could keep order

without the promise of liquor. But the opposite soon proved to be the case. His became an orderly ship at sea and at port. It was true that some of his men felt it was a sailor's right to drink and swear. But on reflection some seemed grateful.

After finishing his career as a sea captain in June 1828, Bates retired with a modest fortune of more than $10,000.[10] A firm Christian believer and activist, he participated in the temperance and abolitionist movements. He also was very active in the Christian church. In 1831/1832 Bates wrote: "I then began to feel the

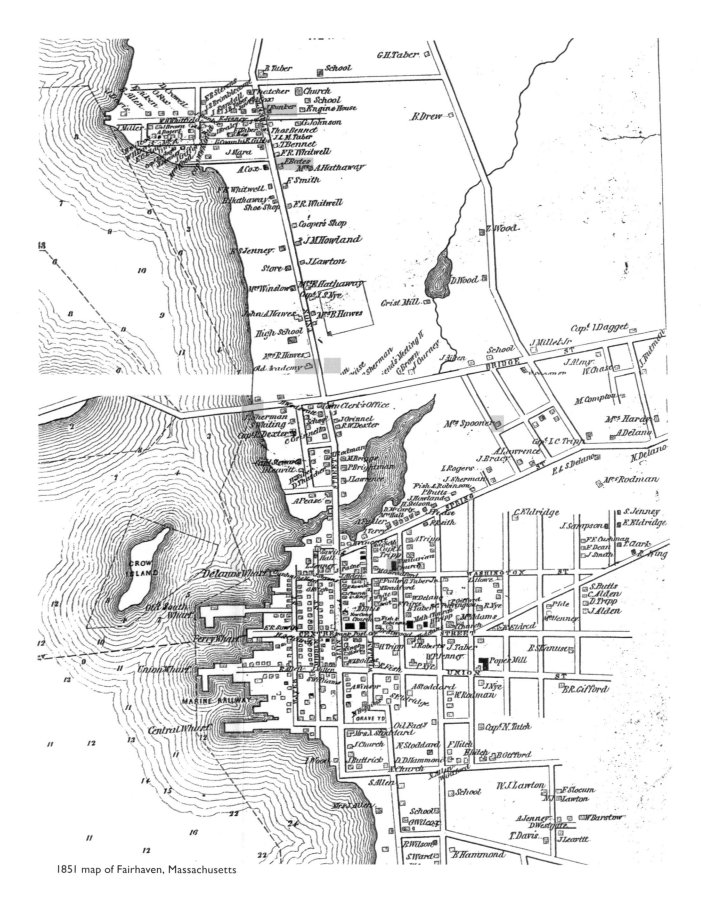

1851 map of Fairhaven, Massachusetts

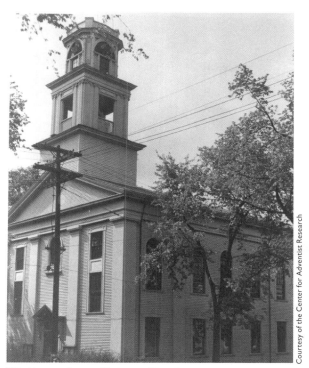

Washington Street Christian Church

Northeast Maritime Institute

importance of taking a decided stand on the side of the oppressed. My labor in the cause of temperance had caused a pretty thorough sifting of my friends, and I felt that I had no more that I wished to part with; but duty was clear that I could not be a consistent Christian if I stood on the side of the oppressor, for God was not there. Neither could I claim his promises if I stood on neutral ground. Hence, my only alternative was to plead for the slave, and thus I decided."[11]

Such convictions and courageous determination, speak volumes about Bates' character. He was determined to be true to God no matter the cost. He followed the light he received, and more was given. This characteristic would enable him to take his stand for the Advent message and take a prominent place in its proclamation, and in sharing the Sabbath.

The Washington Street Christian Church

Two of the principal founders of the Seventh-day Adventist Church were Christian Connexion ministers—James White and Joseph Bates. Ellen White was from a Methodist background. Bates rose to some prominence in the New England branch of the Christian Church.

Joseph Bates became more active in the Christian Church after retiring from traveling the world. He and a

Washington Street Christian Church
32 Washington Street
Fairhaven, Massachusetts
GPS: N 41°38.243' W 070°54.212'

few other prominent leaders of the Christian Church in Fairhaven built the Washington Street Christian Church in 1832. He wrote of the church with these words: "Up to 1832, the Christian Church in Fairhaven, with which I had united, had occupied a rented hall; and they now began to feel the need of having a house of worship of their own in a more convenient place. Four of the brethren [including Bates] united and built one, which was called the Washington-Street Christian meeting-house. Soon after it was finished and dedicated, we commenced a series of religious meetings, in which the Lord graciously answered our prayers and poured out his Spirit upon us, and many souls were converted."[12] Previously the Christian church had met in the Academy Hall. Presumably this is a reference to the Fairhaven Academy, which is now the historical society for the town. Located on 32 Washington Street, the Christian church was the site of a weeklong series of lectures presented by William Miller during March 13-19, 1841. The *Signs of the Times* noted that "the effect has been powerful."[13] "As a result of his preaching, thirty-three persons left the church, most of whom

Bates home on Mulberry Street
GPS: N 41°38.470' W 070°54.063'

19 Mulberry Street
Fairhaven, Massachusetts

The Bates home on Mulberry Street

Prudence Bates (1793-1870)

Building a Home for Prudence Bates on Mulberry Street

After retiring from a life at sea, Bates sought to provide a pleasant situation for his wife, Prudence, who had spent so many years waiting for him to come back from long voyages. He sold his previous residence and in 1832 began to build the Mulberry Street farm. He built a home and barn and planted three orchards of mulberry trees to raise silkworms.[16] The current address of the home is 19 Mulberry Street, in Fairhaven. The records of his purchases and construction costs for this home are found at the research library of the New Bedford Whaling Museum and at the courthouse. He spent a lot of money on the development of this property. Bates wrote of his endeavors: "I sold my place of residence in the year 1831, and was occupied much of my time in 1832 in locating my dwelling-house and outbuildings on my little farm. . . . After finishing my buildings on my farm, before referred to, I commenced the work of raising mulberry trees, to obtain their foliage to feed the silkworm, designing to enter into the culture of silk. I had erected a school-house on my place, in which I designed to have a manual-labor school for youth."[17]

The Bates family lived on Mulberry Street from 1832 until Bates sold the farm on February 16, 1844, to Noah Spooner for $4,550.[18] Over the next few months or years he spent this money on the proclamation of the Advent movement. After 1844, it is less clear where the

united with a number from the Methodist Episcopal Church and formed the nucleus of the Second Advent Society."[14] This group met in private homes and in Fountain Hall.[15] In 1902 the former Christian church became a school and then in 1942 the Fairhaven Boys Club. In 1965 the club had outgrown the church, and a brick addition was added. Currently the facility belongs to the Northeast Maritime Institute. It has been nicely restored but with some modifications.

Bunker home on Main Street

Bates family lived in Fairhaven. Bates did not own a home, and rentals were not as carefully recorded in directories and other town publications. Fortunately there is extant correspondence from the John Bunker family to document where the Bateses were living after the fall 1844 disappointment.

Living at 209 Main Street in Fairhaven

At least by the summer of 1845 Joseph Bates and his family were living in the John Bunker home at 209 Main Street, located about a block north of Bates' boyhood home. Bunker correspondence contains two references, one in July 1845 and the other in December 1847, that indicate that Bates and his family lived in the home.[19] The 1850 U.S. Federal Census record for Fairhaven shows Joseph Bates and his entire family living adjacent to John and Elizabeth Bunker.[20] Perhaps there was an additional dwelling house connected to the Bunker home and carriage house. The 1855 state census also lists the Bateses as still living in connection with the Bunker family. The Bunker home can be located on the 1851 map of Fairhaven; today it is one of the town's designated historic properties.[21] Chet Jordan, who served as caretaker at the Bates boyhood home during 2007 and 2008, received from a neighbor a copy of a newspaper clipping from 1948. This article is about Annie Blackwell, who is thought to have lived in the Bunker house. She stated that Joseph Bates lived

Katy Wolfer 2008

Bunker home
GPS: N 41°38.867' W 070°54.536'

in the house and that "the Fairhaven kitchen in which he did much of his writing" was used by Blackwell as a bedroom. It is gratifying to know the location of the York shilling story and where Bates published his most important tracts that initiated key theological concepts for the Seventh-day Adventist Church.

The Advent Message

It was through a minister of the Christian Connexion that Bates came to accept the Advent message in the fall of 1839.[22] In the spring of 1840 William Miller delivered a series of lectures in the New Bedford North Christian Church.[23] Bates was invited to attend and was much impressed. He exclaimed, "That is the truth!" Bates was always one to put his whole being into whatever he believed. After purchasing and reading William Miller's lectures, he was convinced that Jesus was coming "about 1843."[24] Bates is listed as one of the organizers of the first General Conference of the Second Coming held in Boston in October 1840.[25] Bates also may have arranged for Miller to speak at the Washington Street Christian Church in March 1841. Over the next few years Bates spent his personal wealth in promoting the proclamation of the coming of Jesus.

He preached and ministered throughout the East and even into Maryland.

Evangelism in a Slave State

One story from Bates' travels is the trip to Maryland with Heman S. Gurney, an Adventist blacksmith who was also an excellent singer. They embarked on their daring venture during February and early March 1844, soon after Bates sold his farm on Mulberry Street. In general, Millerite preachers were not welcome in slave states. Slave owners were suspicious that the theology of the Second Coming was merely a guise to free their slaves. Even with the risk of physical injury, Bates and Gurney departed. As they traveled from Kent Island down the east side of Chesapeake Bay, they came to Centreville. There they met a judge named Mr. Hopper, who showed some interest in the Advent message. This man asked, "Mr. Bates, I understand that you are an abolitionist, and have come here to get away our slaves." Bates responded: "Yes, Judge, I am an abolitionist, and have come to get your slaves, and *you too*! . . . We teach that Christ is coming, and we want you all saved."[26] After a few days of meetings, the judge was favorably

impressed with Bates and Gurney. He brought them an article from the Baltimore *Patriot* that noticed "two men" [Bates and Gurney] who were threatened with "riding on a rail." The paper also noticed their response, which Bates loosely quotes in his book. "They were all ready, and if they would put a saddle on the rail, it would be better to ride than to walk!"[27] This shows the natural spunk and Yankee grit of Captain Bates (who was now Elder Bates).

Perhaps the most emotionally touching part of this story is the response of the slaves to Second Advent preaching. Bates noted that "the people came out to hear, and listened attentively, particularly the slaves, who had to stand on the back side of the white congregation. . . . They heard Bro. Gurney sing the hymn, 'I'm a pilgrim and I'm a stranger.' One of the colored men came to our lodgings to beg one of the printed copies. Bro. [Gurney] had but one. Said he, 'I'll give you a quarter of a dollar for it;' probably it was all the money the poor fellow had. He lingered as though he could not be denied. Bro. [Gurney] then copied it for him, which pleased him very much."[28]

The hymn "I'm a Pilgrim" is included in Joshua V. Himes' 1843 *Millennial Harp*. James White also included it in the first Sabbatarian Adventist hymnbook, *Hymns for God's Peculiar People That Keep the Commandments of God and the Faith of Jesus*. It has continued to be retained in Seventh-day Adventist hymnals to the present.

TRACT,

SHOWING THAT THE SEVENTH DAY

SHOULD BE OBSERVED AS THE SABBATH,

INSTEAD OF THE FIRST DAY;

"ACCORDING TO THE COMMANDMENT."

BY T. M. PREBLE.

NASHUA:
PRINTED BY MURRAY & KIMBALL.
1845.

1845 tract on the Sabbath by T. M. Preble

Thomas M. Preble

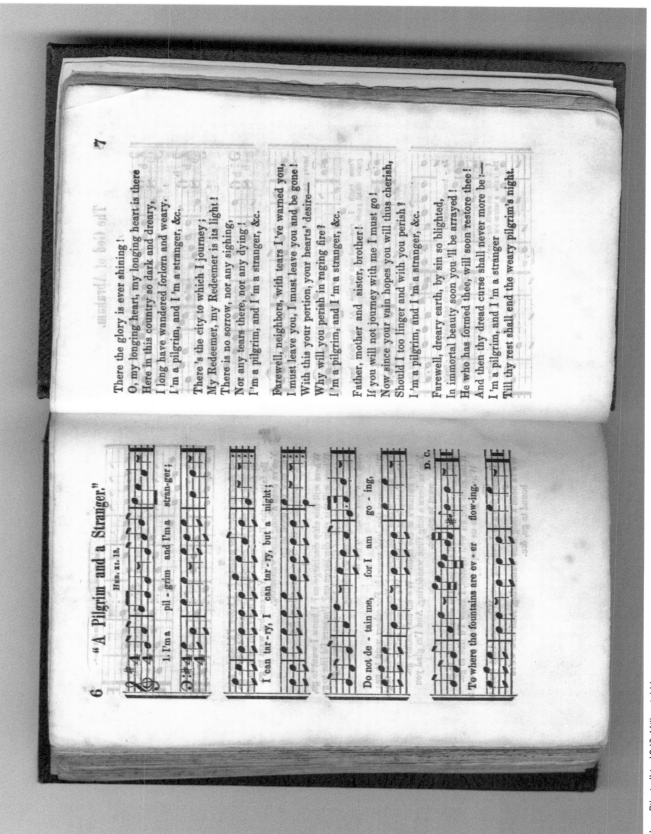

"I'm a Pilgrim" in 1843 *Millennial Harp*

Accepting the Sabbath

The seventh-day Sabbath was first introduced to Millerites by Seventh Day Baptists. In the summer of 1844 a Millerite preacher in New Hampshire named T. M. Preble accepted the Sabbath. In February 1845 he wrote an article on the Sabbath in the Maine Millerite paper entitled *Hope of Israel*. Bates read this article and undoubtedly Preble's subsequent tract and became convicted that the Sabbath was Bible truth.[29] For a time between February/March 1845 and the summer of 1846 his faith wavered because of fanatical spiritualizers who promoted the Sabbath in a confusing and unbiblical manner.[30]

Story of Bates and his trip to Washington, New Hampshire

To deepen his knowledge about the Sabbath, Joseph Bates traveled to New Hampshire to visit with Frederick Wheeler and Cyrus Farnsworth. It is not clear whether this happened in 1845 or 1846. Perhaps Bates did not have money to ride, and decided to walk the many miles from Fairhaven, Massachusetts, to Washington, New Hampshire. As the story goes, he arrived late in the evening where Frederick Wheeler was staying in Hillsborough and woke the family up. Wheeler's 11-year-old son George remembered Bates' late arrival. So urgent was Bates to study that he and Wheeler stayed up through the night.[31] The next day Wheeler and Bates went to Cyrus Farnsworth's home by Millen Pond not far from the Adventist church. There under the maple trees, Wheeler and Bates together with Farnsworth studied the Bible regarding the Sabbath. Returning to Fairhaven, Bates was crossing the bridge that spanned the Acushnet River from New Bedford. He met a friend from Fairhaven and West Island whose full name was James Madison Monroe Hall. Hall asked Bates what the news was. Bates shot right back: "The news is that the seventh day is the Sabbath." After a short time Hall became a convert to the Sabbath doctrine.

Heman S. Gurney and Fairhaven

Heman S. Gurney was an unmarried blacksmith in Fairhaven. He first discovered William Miller's writings in 1838, but it was in 1840 that Joseph Bates came into Gurney's shop with the first issue of the *Signs of the Times*. He embraced the Advent message and remained a part of the "front guard" of the movement. In the spring of 1845 Bates brought T. M. Preble's tract on the Sab-

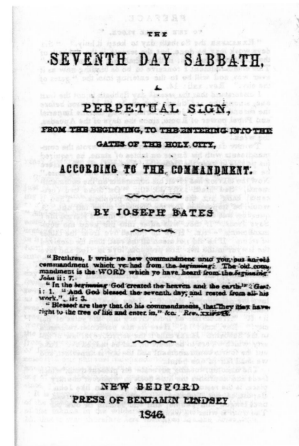

First tract on the Sabbath by Joseph Bates

bath to an Advent meeting in Fairhaven. Gurney and a few others decided to join Bates in keeping the Sabbath.

Gurney was also instrumental in the publication of Ellen White's first broadside. He heard Ellen Harmon (White) describe her first vision at the "Advent hall" in New Bedford presumably early in 1846. He "was slow to advocate her course," though he "could see no reason to find fault with her." "She appeared like a humble, conscientious Christian." He learned her name and address and decided to check out her story. So he traveled up to Portland, Maine, and met her father, Robert Harmon, in his "humble cottage." He also contacted several other people in Portland who knew her. After spending "a number of weeks" in the area, he was "convinced that the fountain was good, and that God had called sister Harmon to an important work." He together with James White arranged for the printing of *To the Little Remnant Scattered Abroad* in April 1846 as a simple broadside.[32] A total of 250 copies were published, with Gurney providing half the cost. Thus we have Gurney to thank for the first publication by Ellen White. Gurney

Heman S. Gurney (1817-1896)

Courtesy of the Center for Adventist Research

often saw Ellen Harmon in vision. He was with her when she had a vision on a boat just before a raging storm as they traveled to West Island to visit the Hall family. This helped confirm, for some, that her visions were not a result of mesmerism (or hypnotism). The circumstances were not conducive to hypnotic influence.

In 1853 Gurney married the widow Anne E. Randall, daughter of William Gifford, who also was among the first Sabbathkeepers in Fairhaven.[33] They had three children and moved to Jackson, Michigan, in 1856 and then to Memphis, Michigan, about 1865. Gurney remained active as a blacksmith and evangelist the rest of his life. It is not known where he lived in Fairhaven or the exact location of his blacksmith shop.

Spreading the Sabbath Message

Bates is remembered for his zeal for the Sabbath and evangelism. He would often say, "**O how I do love this Sabbath.**" He became an apostle for the Sabbath and is largely responsible for the theological foundation of Sabbatarian Adventism and the Seventh-day Adventist Church. In August 1846 he published his tract *The Seventh Day Sabbath: A Perpetual Sign.* James and Ellen White, newly married, read the tract and accepted the Sabbath. Bates continued to travel during 1846 promoting his tract, resulting in various ones, including Hiram Edson, O.R.L. Crosier, and Franklin Hahn, accepting the Sabbath. For more on the Sabbath story, see the Washington, New Hampshire, chapter.

During the 1850s Bates was probably the movement's most effective evangelist. He gave Bible studies throughout New England and beyond. Many of his converts went on to become leaders and ministers in the Seventh-day Adventist Church during the 1860s and 1870s.

Bates' Third Tract on the Sabbath and a Single York Shilling

The story of Joseph Bates' third tract[34] on the Sabbath should be told in Fairhaven. James White wrote of this tract with these words: "In the autumn of 1847, Bro. Bates sat down to write a work of more than one hundred pages, with only a York shilling at his command."[35] A York shilling was worth 12 and a half cents. A shortage of funds was certainly not enough to stop Joseph Bates from sharing the good news of the Sabbath. He had gone from having thousands of dollars in 1844 to a state of poverty.

It seems that Bates kept information on their bleak financial condition from his wife. While his pen was busy at work writing, Prudence told him she needed some flour and a few other sundries to finish a baking project. Bates asked, "How much flour do you lack?"

"About four pounds" was her reply. Bates then went to the store and purchased the four pounds of flour and the other articles with his last shilling. When he returned, his wife exclaimed in surprise, "Have you, Captain Bates, a man who has sailed vessels out of New Bedford to all parts of the world, been out and bought *four* pounds of flour?"

Bates responded, "Wife, I spent for those articles the last money I have on earth."

Bitterly Prudence sobbed and exclaimed, "What are we going to do?"

Bates stood to his feet and with all the dignity of a captain directing his vessel said, "I am going to write a book; I am going to circulate it, and spread this Sabbath truth before the world."

Five cent postage-paid stampless letter, York shilling (front and back)

Benjamin Lindsey

"Well," said Prudence, "what are we going to live on?"

Bates replied with a smile, "The Lord is going to open the way."

Prudence, who was not yet convicted on the importance of the Sabbath, replied, "That's what you always say," burst into tears, and left the room.

About a half hour later as Bates was writing on his book, he felt impressed to go to the post office. Once there he found a letter waiting for him with postage due. In those days prepayment was optional. Elder Bates was probably embarrassed to tell the postmaster, Mr. Drew—a man he knew well—that he didn't have the five cents necessary to pay the postage. Drew told him to take the letter along and pay later. Ever a careful man, Bates refused and asked the postmaster to open the letter. Out came a $10 bill. After paying the required postage, Bates went to buy provisions. He purchased "a barrel of flour for $4, besides potatoes, sugar, and other necessary articles. When giving orders where they were to be delivered, he said, 'Probably the woman will say they don't belong there, but don't you pay any attention to what she says; unload the goods on the front porch.'" Joseph Bates must have had a sense of humor. While the delivery was in process, he went across the bridge to New Bedford and arranged with a printer named Benjamin Lindsey—whom he had used previously—to publish 1,000 copies of this new tract. The agreement was that Bates would bring the copy pages to the printer as they were written. The pages would then be quickly typeset with proofs prepared. The finished publication was to be kept in the printer's office until the bill was paid in full. After these arrangements, Bates purchased paper and pens to continue his work and returned home. Slipping into his chair, he continued writing—probably with a twinkle in his eyes and maybe a suppressed smile on his face.

Soon Prudence came and excitedly said, "Joseph, just look out on the front porch! Where did that stuff come from? A drayman came here and would unload it."

"Well," said Bates, "I guess it's all right."

"But," said Mrs. Bates, "where did it come from?"

"Well," said Bates, "the Lord sent it."

"Yes," said Mrs. Bates, "the Lord sent it; that's what you always say."

Joseph Bates then passed the letter he had received to his wife, saying, "Read this, and you will know where it came from." J. N. Loughborough reported the story as he heard it from Bates: "She read it, and again retired for another cry, but it was of a different character from the first; and on returning she humbly asked his pardon for her lack of faith."[36]

As he finished *A Vindication of the Seventh-day Sabbath*, Bates wrote these words in the preface: "I am unable to pay the printer, your means—as God has given you ability—will be needed. I trust that God's true children are ready."[37] Unknown to him, Heman Gurney had collected on an unexpected debt and used part of the money to retire the balance. Years later Gurney said, "Brother Bates never knew to the day of his death *who* paid the balance of the book bill."[38] Some question remains as to whether Gurney retired the debt for the tract *A Vindication* or Bates' first Sabbath tract, *The Seventh Day Sabbath: A Perpetual Sign*.

Notes

[1] 18 Johnny Cake Hill, New Bedford, Massachusetts 02740.

[2] Godfrey T. Anderson, *Outrider of the Apocalypse: Life and Times of Joseph Bates* (Mountain View, Calif.: Pacific Press, 1972), pp. 13, 14, 16.

[3] Genevieve M. Darden to "Dear Carolyn," Aug. 20, 1987.

[4] D. Hamilton Hurd, comp., *History of Bristol County, Massachusetts* (Philadelphia: J. W. Lewis & Co., 1883), p. 268.

[5] Genevieve M. Darden to "Dear Rita," Aug. 14, 1984.

[6] James White, ed., *The Early Life and Later Experience and Labors of Elder Joseph Bates* (Battle Creek, Mich.: Seventh-day Adventist Pub. Assn., 1877), p. 18.

[7] Charles A. Harris, *Old-time Fairhaven* (New Bedford, Mass.: Reynolds Printing, 1954), vol. 3, pp. 118-215.

[8] James White, ed., *The Early Life and Later Experience*, pp. 24-26.

[9] *Ibid.*, pp. 21-23.

[10] *Ibid.*, p. 309.

[11] *Ibid.*, pp. 243, 244.

[12] *Ibid.*, p. 240.

[13] [J. V. Himes,] "Lectures at the Marlboro Chapel," *Signs of the Times*, Apr. 1, 1841, p. 5.

[14] James L. Gillingham et al., *A Brief History of the Town of Fairhaven, Massachusetts* (n.p.: n.p., 1903), pp. 45, 46.

[15] Leonard Bolles Ellis, *History of New Bedford and Its Vicinity: 1602-1892* (Syracuse, N.Y.: D. Mason & Co., 1890), p. 395.

[16] Joseph Bates, *The Autobiography of Elder Joseph Bates* (Battle Creek, Mich.: Seventh-day Adventist Pub. Assn., 1868), pp. 242, 243.

[17] *Ibid.*, pp. 235-242.

[18] Based on deed records in Bristol County, Massachusetts.

[19] John Bunker to "Dear Child," July 16, 1845; John Bunker to "Dear Daughter," Dec. 23, 1847; John Bunker to "Dear Son," Jan. 17, 1849.

[20] In the census: John Bunker (66), Elizabeth Bunker (64), Clarisa Foster (15), Joseph Bates (58), Prudence M. Bates (58), Mary Nye (85), Eliza Bates (29), Mary N. Bates (17), Joseph Bates, Jr. (20), William Stott (41), and Anna Stott (8). As mariners: John Bunker, Joseph Bates, Jr., and William Stott. Bunker's estate is valued at $2,500.

[21] H. F. Walling, Surveyor, *Map of the City of New Bedford and the Village of Fair Haven* (New Bedford, Mass.: C. & A. Taber, 1851).

[22] Bates, *Autobiography*, p. 243.

[23] *History of the Churches of New Bedford* (New Bedford, Mass.: E. Antony & Sons, 1869), p. 116.

[24] Bates, *Autobiography*, pp. 243, 244.

[25] *Ibid.*, pp. 248-250; "A General Conference of the Second Coming of the Lord Jesus Christ," *Signs of the Times*, Sept. 15, 1840, p. 92.

[26] Bates, *Autobiography*, pp. 280, 281.

[27] *Ibid.*, p. 282.

[28] *Ibid.*, pp. 283, 284.

[29] Joseph Bates, *The Seventh Day Sabbath: A Perpetual Sign* (New Bedford, Mass.: Benjamin Lindsey, 1846), p. 40.

[30] *Ibid.*; T. M. Preble, "Eld. Preble on the Sabbath," *Review and Herald*, Aug. 23, 1870, p. 73 (reprinted from *Hope of Israel*, Feb. 28, 1845); T. M. Preble, *Tract, Showing That the Seventh Day Should Be Observed as the Sabbath* (Nashua, N.H.: Murray and Kimball, 1845).

[31] W. A. Spicer, *Pioneer Days of the Advent Movement* (Washington, D.C.: Review and Herald, 1941), p. 50.

[32] H. S. Gurney, "Recollections of Early Advent Experience," *Review and Herald*, Jan. 3, 1888, p. 2; H. S. Gurney, "Gurney Statement Re 'To the Remnant,'" May 15, 1891.

[33] H. S. Gurney, "Another Nonagenarian Adventist," *Review and Herald*, June 12, 1894, p. 372.

[34] Joseph Bates, *A Vindication of the Seventh-day Sabbath* (New Bedford, Mass.: Benjamin Lindsey, 1848).

[35] James White, *Life Incidents,* p. 269.

[36] J. N. Loughborough, *The Great Second Advent Movement,* pp. 251-255.

[37] Bates, *A Vindication of the Seventh-day Sabbath*, p. 1.

[38] Loughborough, *The Great Second Advent Movement*, p. 254.

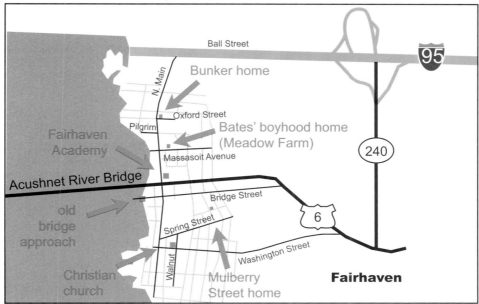

Bates sites, Fairhaven, Massachusetts

Hazen Foss grave
GPS: N 42°45.914' W 071°04.178'

Merlin D. Burt 2010

Foss grave in Elmwood Cemetery, Haverhill, Massachusetts

Haverhill, Massachusetts

Elmwood Cemetery in Haverhill, Massachusetts, is where Hazen Foss (1819-1893) is buried. There are three entrances to the cemetery. To reach his grave, enter the main gate near a white building. Next, take the third road to the right. Proceed past a road to the left and turn left at the cross street. Turn right at the first dirt lane. The grave of G. H. Hill is on the corner. Hazen Foss is buried near the far end of the lane on the left with other family members.

Foss, who received visions before the 1844 disappointment, was a "shirttail" relative of Ellen White's. Ellen's older sister Mary married Samuel Foss, who was Hazen's brother. After the fall 1844 date passed, Hazen Foss felt he had been deceived. In a second vision he was warned that if he refused to share what he had been shown, the work would be taken from him and given to another. Fearing rejection by other Adventists, Hazen did nothing. He finally heard a voice that said, in effect, "You have grieved the Spirit of the Lord." In horror at his own stubbornness, he called a meeting but was unable to recall the vision. After several attempts he concluded that the Spirit of God had left him. Those present described the meeting as the most terrible they had ever attended. When Ellen Harmon visited Poland, Maine, for the first time following her December 1844 vision, Hazen heard her describe her vision (see the chapter on Poland, Maine). He came to see Ellen at his

brother-in-law's home where she was staying and told her that what she had shared was similar to what he had been shown. He warned her to obey God and remain faithful. Hazen told her that he was a lost man. In later years family members and friends remembered that he showed no further interest in religion.

Sometimes people confuse Hazen Foss with William E. Foy (1819-1893). Foy was a Black man who also received visions previous to the 1844 disappointment. He also met Ellen Harmon on a few occasions when speaking in Portland, Maine. Unlike Foss, Foy remained faithful to his commission. Though he never kept the seventh-day Sabbath, Foy continued the rest of his life as a Freewill Baptist preacher. He is buried in East Sullivan, Maine, in Birch Tree Cemetery (see the chapter on East Sullivan, Maine).

Merlin D. Burt 2010

Hazen Foss grave, Haverhill, Massachusetts

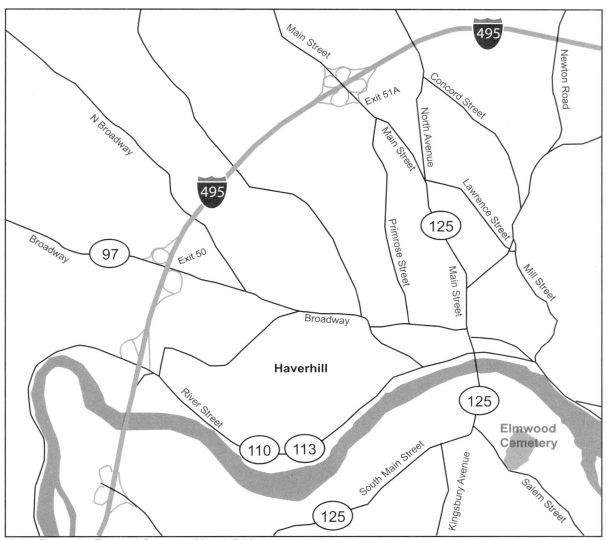

Hazen Foss grave, Elmwood Cemetery, Haverhill, Massachusetts

Hazen Foss (1819-1893)

Photo courtesy of the Ellen G. White Estate

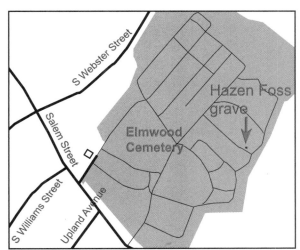

Expanded view of Elmwood Cemetery

Katy Wolfer 2008

Old Sturbridge Village

To visit Old Sturbridge Village is to enter the world of rural New England during America's early years (1790-1840) before the Industrial Revolution. It is the world of the Millerite movement and early Adventism. Old Sturbridge is a reconstruction of the actual town, with many buildings added, modified, or idealized. It has much of the early and mid-nineteenth-century character. The village is operated in context, so visitors see events and activities that would have occurred during the particular time of year they visit. If people visit in the spring, they will see planting activities, and in the

fall they will see harvest activities. In early nineteenth-century New England each season had its own requirements and experiences.

The visitor should see the printshop and how broadsides and other publications were made. It gives a better understanding of how James White printed the *Review and Herald* in Rochester, New York. James White's father was a cobbler, so the cobbler's shop is interesting. The schoolhouse gives one an idea of how Adventist pioneers were educated. The mills are also important to

Katy Wolfer 2008

Katy Wolfer 2008

see. Of particular interest are the sawmill and carding mill. Water power was critically important, and towns were usually established based on the elevation gradients and flow patterns of rivers. Sturbridge is ideally situated on the Quinebaug River. The formation of a mill pond was essential to most early American towns. A stop at the blacksmith shop is fascinating. Some Adventist pioneers were blacksmiths, and seeing how they worked is enlightening. The gift shop and the bookstore in particular are worth seeing. There are many reproduction items from nineteenth-century America, and the book collection is extensive.

There were Millerite Adventists who lived and worked in the original Sturbridge. F. G. Brown wrote from Sturbridge on November 18, 1844, soon after the disappointment. "I had no idea I loved Jesus so passionately, until after the tenth [the "tenth day of the seventh month" was the biblical date for the Day of Atonement, which turned into the disappointment of October 22, 1844]. It was the first disappointment I had ever experienced of the kind. You know I always thought that '43

must pass in order to fulfill various prophecies relative to the prolonging of the days, and failing of every vision, the tarrying of the vision, peace and safety, etc. But *my* time has now come for the Lord to make His appearing, and I was sadly, sadly disappointed in not seeing Him."*

Notes

* F. G. Brown, "Letter From Brother F. G. Brown," *Advent Herald*, Dec. 11, 1844, pp. 138, 139.

Old Sturbridge Village
1 Old Sturbridge Village Road
Sturbridge, Massachusetts

GPS coordinates:
N 42°06.467'
W 072°05.933'

Young docents in Sturbridge Village

Founder's Hall
GPS: N 42°26.737' W 071°41.114'

Katy Wolfer 2008

Founder's Hall, Atlantic Union College, 338 Main Street, South Lancaster, Massachusetts

South Lancaster, Massachusetts

South Lancaster, Massachusetts, is the location of South Lancaster Academy and Atlantic Union College. This academy and Healdsburg College both began in 1882. Healdsburg College moved to Angwin, California, and became Pacific Union College. Battle Creek College moved to Berrien Springs, Michigan, and became Emmanuel Missionary College, then Andrews University. South Lancaster Academy, founded by S. N. Haskell, became a junior college in 1918 and Atlantic Union College in 1922. It is the oldest Seventh-day Adventist academic center at its original location. The

old academy building, now restored as Founder's Hall, was built in 1884. It contains a small but very interesting museum that includes many original artifacts. Displayed in the Miller chapel on the upper floor are an original 1843 prophetic chart, a pulpit from which William Miller spoke, and two paintings by Horace Bundy. The 1857 Bundy paintings are full-length matching representations of William and Lucy Miller. The venerable Founder's Hall is the oldest Seventh-day Adventist educational building still standing.

William Miller (1782-1849)

Photo courtesy of Atlantic Union College

Lucy P. Miller (1782-1854)

Photo courtesy of Atlantic Union College

Village church, South Lancaster, Massachusettes

Bulfinch Church, Lancaster, Massachusettes

Stephen Nelson Haskell (1833-1922)

One other significant Seventh-day Adventist historical building in South Lancaster is the Village Seventh-day Adventist Church. It was built at its present location in 1877 and enlarged in 1897. In February-March 1899 the thirty-third session of the General Conference was held in this church.

Also in Lancaster is the former Congregationalist Bulfinch Church on 725 Main Street, which was dedicated in 1816. Created by Charles Bulfinch (1763-1844), it is one of the finest examples of Federal-style architecture in existence. The church bell was cast by Paul Revere or his sons in 1816. It cracked and was recast in 1822. It has been in use since that time. Other buildings designed by Bulfinch include the central portion of the United States Capitol in Washington, D.C., and the enlarged Faneuil Hall near Quincy Market in Boston.

North Lancaster and the J. N. Andrews Home

J. N. Andrews moved to Lancaster, Massachusetts, with his two children, Charles and Mary, after his wife died of a stroke in 1872. Their home is located at 1444 Main Street on Route 117 in North Lancaster. Andrews lived here until 1874, when he went to Europe as the first official Seventh-day Adventist overseas missionary. In this house he completed the second edition of his *History of the Sabbath*. North Lancaster was an advantageous location for Andrews, since he was able to make frequent research trips into Boston. This home was a place of spiritual and emotional trial for Andrews. His son remembered him being harassed by the devil while living here.

J. N. Andrews home
GPS: N 42°28.323' W 071°40.860'

John Nevins Andrews home
1444 Main Street, North Lancaster, Massachusetts

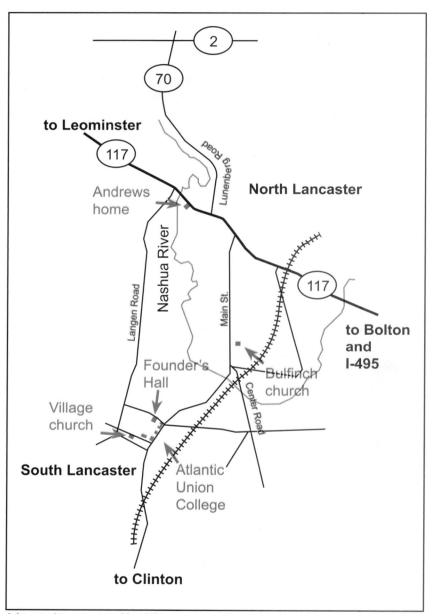

Adventist historic sites, North Lancaster, and South Lancaster, Massachusetts

ADVENTIST PIONEER PLACES

NEW HAMPSHIRE

Washington, New Hampshire, Seventh-day Adventist Church

Katy Wolfer 2008

Funds were raised for the "great tent" at East Kingston, New Hampshire, camp meeting

East Kingston, New Hampshire

The short distance of coastal New Hampshire between Massachusetts and Maine contains two important Millerite sites, Exeter and East Kingston. The Exeter, New Hampshire, camp meeting is discussed in the next chapter.

Not far to the east of the current Interstate 95 toll road is East Kingston, the site of the first Millerite camp meeting in the United States. The camp meeting was held from June 28 to July 5, 1842, in a beautiful hemlock grove, north of the town next to the railroad line connecting north to Maine and south to Massachusetts. The railroad established a temporary station at the site of the camp meeting and allowed a discounted fare.

Camp meetings were not invented by Millerites. In America, camp meetings began at the turn of the nineteenth century, first in Kentucky and then throughout the nation. Methodists in particular adopted this style of revivalism. The Second Great Awakening in America had three foci of activity: university revivals, camp meetings, and protracted town meetings. The Millerite movement, as a part of this great awakening, followed the revival style of the day. The East Kingston meeting was comparable to other camp meetings held between 1800 and 1845 during the Second Great Awakening.

The principal speaker at the East Kingston meeting was William Miller, who presented his course of lectures on Bible prophecy. The success of the meetings inspired those in attendance to raise $1,000 for a "great tent" to protect attendees from sun and rain. The tent was quickly purchased and first pitched in Concord, New Hampshire, some 36 miles northwest from East Kingston.

The number present was estimated between from 7,000 to 10,000 and as high as 10,000 to 15,000 people. 26 towns were represented with separate larger meeting tents, with people pitching personal tents near their meeting tent. An open stand was set up for the general meetings, and Miller spoke with great effect to the vast crowd. Apollos Hale reflected that this meeting marked the "commencement of a new era in the Second Advent cause." According to Hale, "all parts of New England

Nineteenth-century camp meeting view

. . . Old England, and Canada were represented at the meeting." He also observed that people from nearly every religious orientation attended, including "Universalists, Deists and Infidels."

John Greenleaf Whittier attended this camp meeting as it began and found the meetings very interesting. He wrote the following description:

Three or four years ago, on my way eastward, I spent an hour or two at a campground of the Second Advent in East Kingston. The spot was well chosen. A tall growth of pine and hemlock threw its melancholy shadow over the multitude, who were arranged upon rough seats of boards and logs. Several hundred—perhaps a thousand people—were present, and more were rapidly coming. Drawn about in a circle, forming a background of snowy whiteness to the dark masses of men and foliage, were the white tents, and back of them the provision-stalls and cook-shops. When I reached the ground, a hymn, the words of which I could not distinguish, was pealing through the dim aisles of the forest. I could readily perceive that it had its effect upon the multitude before me, kindling to higher intensity their already excited enthusiasm. The preachers were placed in a rude pulpit of rough boards, carpeted only by the dead forest-leaves and flowers, and tasseled, not with silk and velvet, but with the green boughs of the somber hemlocks around it. One of them followed the music in an earnest exhortation on the duty of preparing for the great event. Occasionally he was really eloquent, and his description of the last day had the ghastly distinctness of Anelli's painting of the End of the World.

Suspended from the front of the rude pulpit were two broad sheets of canvas, upon one of which was the figure of a man, the head of gold, the breast and arms of silver, the belly of brass, the legs of iron, and feet of clay—the dream of Nebuchadnezzar. On the other were depicted the wonders of the Apocalyptic vision—the beasts, the dragons, the scarlet woman seen by the seer of Patmos, Oriental types, figures, and mystic symbols, translated into staring Yankee realities, and exhibited like the beasts of a traveling menagerie. One horrible image, with its hideous heads and scaly caudal extremity, reminded me of the tremendous line of Milton, who, in speaking of the same evil dragon, describes him as "swinging the scaly horrors of his folded tail."

To an imaginative mind the scene was full of novel interest. The white circle of tents; the dim wood arches; the upturned, earnest faces; the loud voices of the speakers, burdened with the awful symbolic language of the Bible; the smoke from the fires, rising like incense—carried me back to those days of primitive worship which tradition faintly whispers of, when on the hill-tops and in the shade of old woods Religion had her first altars, with every man for her priest and the whole universe for her temple.[*]

The location of the East Kingston camp meeting has not been fully verified. The map and directions are for the traditional site. The traditional location now has homes where once stood the grove and assembly of tents.

Notes

[*] John Greenleaf Whittier, *The Writings of John Greenleaf Whittier* (Boston: Houghton Mifflin and Co., 1892), vol. 5, pp. 424-426.

Site of East Kingston camp meeting
GPS: N 42°56.167' W 071°00.025'

Merlin D. Burt 2010

45 Sandborn Road, East Kingston Township, New Hampshire, traditional site of a Millerite camp meeting

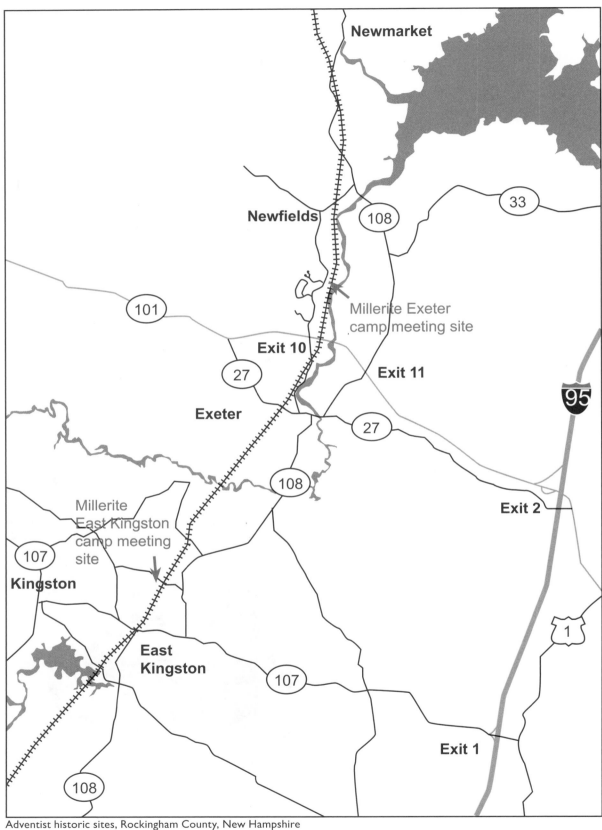

Newmarket

Newfields

108

33

101

Millerite Exeter
camp meeting site

Exit 10

27

Exit 11

Exeter

27

95

108

Millerite
East Kingston
camp meeting
site

Exit 2

107

Kingston

East
Kingston

107

1

Exit 1

108

Adventist historic sites, Rockingham County, New Hampshire

Site of Exeter camp meeting
GPS: N 43°01.037' W 070°56.471'

Merlin D. Burt 2010

Site of Millerite camp meeting, 80 Newfields Road, Exeter, New Hampshire

Exeter, New Hampshire

Exeter, New Hampshire, is located west of Interstate 95 off Route 101 northeast of East Kingston, in the county of Rockingham. Both towns were important camp meeting sites because of their convenient proximity to the railroad. The August 12-17, 1844, Exeter camp meeting ignited the most powerful proclamation of the second coming of Jesus that swept across the northern United States. Called the "true Midnight Cry," it focused the nation's attention on Yom Kippur or the Day of Atonement of the Jewish year 1844, which corresponded to October 22, 1844. On August 22, 1844, Samuel Snow published a paper called *The True Midnight Cry*, with the message he shared at Exeter. His concluding words were of breathtaking import: "Our blessed Lord will therefore come, to the astonishment of all them that dwell upon the earth, and to the salvation of those who truly look for him, on the *tenth day* of the *seventh month* of the *year of jubilee*: *and* that is the *present* year, 1844."[1]

During 1844 Millerite Adventists first looked for Jesus to come in the spring. There was a disappointment by mid-April after Jesus did not come. William Miller had published his belief that Jesus would come sometime between March 21, 1843, and March 21, 1844. But before the March date arrived, many believed that the date should be revised to mid-April based on the Jewish Karaite calendar. Though disappointed, few Millerites abandoned the movement. During the summer of 1844 Miller and other Adventist preachers continued to travel and give lectures, confident that the

Lord would come soon and that the delay was on account of some miscalculation of the time.

The 1844 Exeter camp meeting, though not as large as the 1842 East Kingston camp meeting, was sizable. Twenty different towns were represented, with large tents surrounded by smaller tents for personal accommodation.[2] James White, who was present, described

Courtesy of the Center for Adventist Research

Samuel S. Snow (1806-1870)

the arrangement: "There were many tents upon the ground, some of them resembling houses of worship, in size and shape, more than the small tents usually seen upon Methodist camp grounds. These furnished ample accommodations for the thousands of believers present."[3] White remembered that fanaticism appeared in the form of "holy flesh" perfectionism. The tent from Watertown, Massachusetts, was next to the Portland, Maine, tent, where James White and others were meeting. The Watertown group became increasingly disruptive, with loud shouting and hand clapping. To get away from their influence, the Portland believers moved their tent to a different part of the campground.

White recalled that as the meetings continued a "general gloom" spread over the campground. People were warned away from the Watertown tent. But this caused crowds of curious people to attend. The fanaticism spread and the general meetings failed to move the people. It was during one of these that Joseph Bates was reciting anew the evidences for the soon coming of Jesus. A woman stood and said "with a clear, strong, yet pleasant voice, . . . 'It is too late, Bro.———. It is too late.'"[4] Bates sat down, and Samuel Snow rose to speak. He continued his presentation the next day and connected the Day of Atonement cleansing of the sanctuary on the tenth day of the seventh month to the 2300 days of Daniel 8:14. He thus concluded that Jesus would come in the fall of 1844. James White wrote:

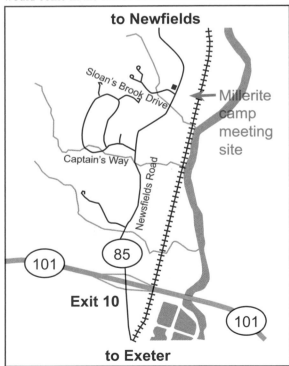

Millerite camp meeting site, Exeter, New Hampshire

"The deepest solemnity pervaded the entire encampment. . . . But what of the Watertown fanatics? In the intense interest upon the subject of time, taken by the entire crowd, these were forgotten. No one seemed to be affected by them, or troubled about them. In fact, they were quiet till they left the ground."[5]

Either at the Exeter camp meeting or soon after, Snow concluded that based on the Karaite calendar, Jesus would come in October 1844. The power of the proclamation during the weeks between August and October is hard to portray adequately. Tens of thousands were converted, sins were confessed, lives transformed, and nearly all those converts looked with anticipation to meet Jesus. This short but powerful proclamation has continued to be referred to by Seventh-day Adventists as the Midnight Cry. William Miller and other key leaders were among the last to accept the fall date. The movement seemed to progress with its own compelling power. Few wrote specifically of the actual October 22, 1844, date. Most (including Snow) more cryptically referred to the tenth day of the seventh month. This day was the only date Adventists generally set for the Second Coming. There were a sizable number who also looked to October 23, 1844, particularly in western New York and Ohio.

The 1844 camp meeting was the second Millerite gathering in Exeter. From September 26 to October 3, 1843, a camp meeting had been held at the same location as the 1844 meeting. A great deal of excitement was generated in the Exeter area because it was announced that William Miller would be present. Several articles appeared in the local paper regarding the 1843 meetings. One correspondent came early to the meeting with the hope of seeing Miller. Not seeing him, he wrote cynically: "I have been to the Camp Ground this afternoon—and was impelled to go from the desire I had to see the Rev. Mr. Miller. . . . But I was disappointed. His *advent* did not take place."[6] Miller did arrive and was on the ground for two days and spoke to the assembled thousands. The description of another correspondent to the local paper adds some color to the meetings: "At half past 6 o'clock the people were again called together by the Preacher's bell for the evening service." After the meetings the "Railroad bell" sounded its "shrill whistle of the Engine" and "summoned those of us who had no bed in the camp to seek one elsewhere." "We left the ground, not converts, by any means, to the peculiar doctrines advocated there; but with a very favorable opinion of the devotedness and piety of many humble christians who had honestly embraced those doctrines."[7]

The site of the Exeter camp meeting is still partially an open field. From the road the visitor can look down the gradual hill to the railroad tracks. Trees obscure the river that is just beyond the railroad tracks. An early resident of Exeter remembered the 1844 camp meeting. "My earliest recollection of the Advent meetings was one held in a grove nearly opposite the Arthur Haley house." The announcement in the Exeter newspaper also announced that the camp meeting commenced "in Haley's grove," where the Methodists had met the previous week.[8] Arthur Haley, the owner of the grove where the 1843 and 1844 camp meetings were held, became a leader in the Exeter Advent Christian Church, along with several others with a last name of Haley.[9]

Phillips Exeter Academy
GPS: N 42°58.772' W 070°57.013'

53 Front Street, Exeter, New Hampshire

Phillips Exeter Academy

The town of Exeter is the third-oldest town in New Hampshire and was the seat of the legislature during the Revolutionary War. The town is located on the Exeter River, a branch of the Piscataqua River. The approximately 3,000 residents were provided power for mills and other machinery from an excellent falls at Exeter.

John Phillips, an Exeter merchant, with his second wife, Elizabeth, founded Phillips Exeter Academy in 1781. The distinguished educational institution was established as a "public free school." The deed of gift stipulated that the academy "shall ever be equally open to youth of requisite qualifications from every quarter."[10] Started in one building, the school has grown to cover several blocks, with many imposing and architecturally beautiful buildings. It is reported that today

the academy has one of the largest preparatory school libraries in the world.

From 1848 to 1851 Uriah Smith was a student at Phillips Exeter Academy. He began his course of study at the age of 16. At the time of his enrollment the academy was a small school for boys and young men meeting in a single enlarged school building. There were three instructors at the school. The principal, Gideon L. Soule, gave leadership to the academy for 35 years.[11] Smith attended the entire three-year course of study at the academy. His grade report shows that he was a good student. By the end of his course he was receiving the highest grades. The academy provided Smith with a classical education in English grammar, Latin, Greek, mathematics, and classical history. The school sought to prepare students for leadership and civic responsibil-

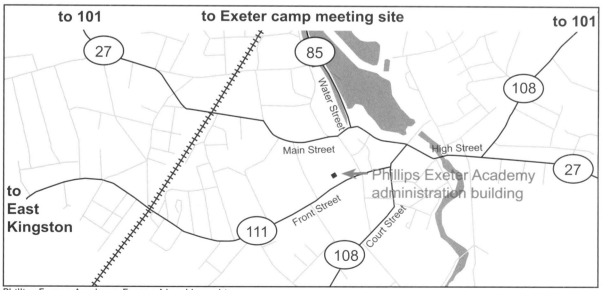

Phillips Exeter Academy, Exeter, New Hampshire

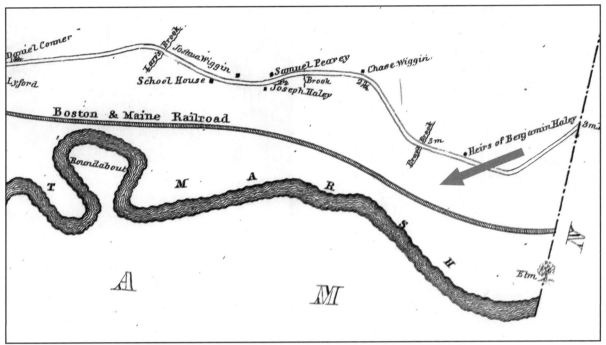

Map showing site of Exeter camp meeting; Joseph Dow, *Plan of the Town of Exeter*, 1845

ity in a society that was still dominated by small towns with an agrarian orientation. During the years that Smith was at the academy the enrollment ranged from 69 to 80.[12] Though small by modern standards, this school stood out as one of the more prestigious institutions in New Hampshire, with high academic requirements. To this day it remains a respected preparatory school for future leaders in America.

The original building where Smith attended classes is no longer standing. There have been four successive buildings where the current central administration building stands. The first school building was moved several times before being moved to its current location in 1999. It is called the Wells Kerr House. The second administration building (when Smith would have attended) is represented only in a picture. Phillips Exeter Academy is proud that Abraham Lincoln's son Todd was a student during the 1860s, while the second administration building was still in use.

Smith's years at Exeter included the advanced class. In an 1899 reflection, Smith wrote regarding his personal history: "Graduated at Phillips Exeter Academy in 1851 prepared to enter the sophomore class at Harvard. Sickness and death of my father in 1852 arrested further schooling."[13] Instead of continuing his schooling, Smith took a position as a public school teacher until 1853, when he connected with the publication of the *Review*

and Herald in Rochester, New York. He maintained a nearly continuous connection with the Review and Herald office for the next 50 years, until his death in 1903. For many of those years he was the editor of the *Review and Herald*. He was also widely respected for his work as an author, wood engraver, and inventor.[14] (For further information on Uriah Smith, see the chapter on West Wilton, New Hampshire.)

Notes

1 Samuel S. Snow and E. Hall, Jr., *The True Midnight Cry*, Aug. 22, 1844, pp. 1-4.

2 "The Exeter Campmeeting," *Advent Herald*, Aug. 21, 1844, p. 20.

3 James White, *Life Incidents,* p. 154. See also Joseph Bates, *Second Advent Waymarks and High Heaps, or a Connected View of the Fulfillment of Prophecy by God's Peculiar People From the Year 1840 to 1847* (New Bedford, Mass.: Benjamin Lindsey, 1847), pp. 30, 31.

4 James White, *Life Incidents*, p. 159.

5 *Ibid.*, p. 163.

6 "Second Advent Camp Meeting," *Exeter News-Letter*, Oct. 2, 1843, p. 2.

7 "More of the Camp Meeting," *Exeter News-Letter*, Oct. 2, 1843, p. 3.

8 B. F. Swasey, "The Advent Camp Meetings in 1843-4, *Exeter News-Letter*, Mar. 6, 1908, p. 42; "The Camp Meeting," *Exeter News-Letter*, Sept. 25, 1843, p. 2; S. Swett, "Second Advent Camp Meeting," *Signs of the Times*, Sept. 20, 1843, p. 40.

9 "A History and Data Concerning Advent Christian Church, Inc., Exeter, New Hampshire," from Advent Christian church records in Exeter, 1869-1877, Exeter Historical Society, Exeter, New Hampshire.

10 Julia Heskel and Davis Dyer, *After the Harkeness Gift: A History of Phillips Exeter Academy Since 1930* (Lebanon, N.H.: University Press of New England, 2008), pp. 12, 13.

11 Myron R. Williams, *The Story of Phillips Exeter* (Exeter, N.H.: Phillips Exeter Academy, 1957), pp. 40-51.

12 *Catalogue of the Officers and Students of Phillips Exeter Academy for the Academical Year 1848-9* (Exeter, N.H.: Wood and Furber, 1849), pp. 2-5.

13 Written by Uriah Smith in 1899 at the request of the New Hampshire state librarian; from Barbara Hoare (granddaughter of Uriah Smith), "Notes on the Life of Uriah Smith" (n.p., n.d.).

14 A. G. Daniells, "Uriah Smith" (a sketch read at Smith's funeral), Mar. 8, 1903; *American Biographical History of Eminent and Self-made Men*, Michigan Volume (Cincinnati: Western Biographical Publishing, 1878), pp. 91, 92.

Second school building, Phillips Exeter Academy, where Uriah Smith attended, 1848-1851

Gradebook for April 25, 1849, to July 31, 1849, Phillips Exeter Academy, with Uriah Smith's grade record

ch:	George Boynton	"	"	17	Peterboro
ch:	David L. Hobbs	"	"	16	North Hampton
	Amasa Fogg	"	"	20	Parsonsfield, Me.
	Edwd. I. Purdy	"	27	13	Exeter
	Chas. B. Crockett	May 8		14	Boston Mass
	Robert Russell	"	14	14	Biddeford Me
	Stephen H. Brooks	"	22	14	Exeter
	Richard A. Barrett	"	15	15	St. Louis Mo
	George W. Sawyer	Aug: 29		18	Wakefield.
ch:	Uriah Smith	"	30	16	Wilton
	Walter S. Gove	"	"	16	New Orleans La.

Phillips Exeter Academy admission record showing Uriah Smith admitted August 30, 1848, to the classical course. He was age 16.

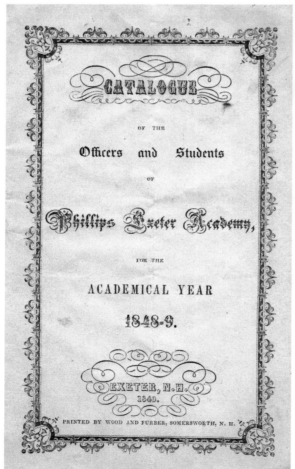

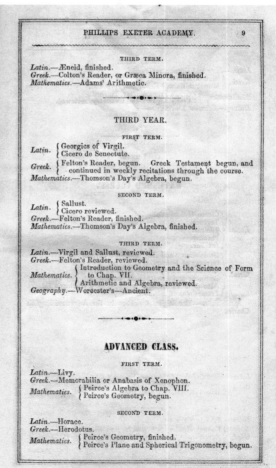

School catalog for 1848-1849 showing three-year course with advanced class. Uriah Smith completed this course of study.

Leonard Hastings' potato field
GPS: N 42°46.720' W 071°52.272'

Merlin D. Burt 2010

Site of Leonard Hastings' potato field, New Ipswich, New Hampshire

New Ipswich, New Hampshire

Leonard Hastings

About 12 miles south of West Wilton is the town of New Ipswich, New Hampshire, with the home and graves of Leonard and Elvira Hastings. Leonard Hastings was a frequent correspondent and early financial supporter of Sabbatarian Adventist founders Joseph Bates and James and Ellen White. The support, friendship, and influence is reflected in the frequent letters and published references in Adventist papers. During the late 1840s and early 1850s, before the establishment of the publishing office in Rochester, New York, the Hastings home was a place to visit for the Whites, Bateses, and others. Leonard Hastings remains important because early correspondence to him that provides vital information on the earliest days of Sabbatarian Adventism has survived.

In March 1849 the Whites visited the Hastingses in New Ipswich. When they arrived Friday evening (March 9), they were met by a tearful Elvira. Her infant son, John, was suffering from severe colic. This had affected Elvira's own health. The Whites prayed for and anointed the child. He stopped crying, and Elvira was much relieved. Ellen White received a vision and saw an angel hovering over Elvira to strengthen her. She wrote: "Our interview with that dear family was precious. Our hearts were knit together, especially was the heart of sister Hastings knit with mine, as were David's and Jonathan's. Our union was not marred while she lived."[1]

Courtesy of the Ellen G. White Estate

Leonard Hastings (1803-1883)

Elvira passed away suddenly on February 28, 1850. An unfinished letter written a few days before her death was published in the *Advent Review*. Elvira's death was a great sorrow to Ellen White. The most important development following this loss was the turning of the hearts of the Hastings children toward God. On Sabbath, June 22, 1850, James White baptized the four oldest Hastings children—Harriet, George, Sarah, and Emma.[2] This dramatic conversion of Adventist children who had come of age since the 1844 disappointment helped Sabbatarian Adventists to realize that God was still working to bring souls to conversion.

For Adventists today, Hastings is perhaps best known for his "potato patch." Before the fall 1844 time expectation, he neglected to dig his potatoes, much to the concern of his neighbors. When Jesus did not come, he dug his potatoes in the spring of 1845 and provided seed stock at a very favorable price. This advantage was because of a potato blight (*phytophthora infestans*) that affected the region. Originating in central Mexico, it first appeared in Philadelphia and New York City in early 1843. By 1845 the blight had spread as far as Illinois and Nova Scotia. The same infestation crossed the Atlantic to the British Isles and continental Europe in 1845 and was responsible for the great famine in Ireland during the later half of the 1840s.[3]

Leonard and Elvira Hastings Farm Site and the Central Cemetery

New Ipswich is located on Highway 124 between Highways 202 and 31 in southern New Hampshire, a few miles north of Fitchburg, Massachusetts. To find the "potato patch" and home site, proceed west from the center of New Ipswich on Highway 123/124 for .3 miles to Appleton Road. Turn right and go a little more than one mile to Boynton Hill Road. Turn right onto the dirt road and proceed another half mile to near the top of the hill, but do not cross under the high-tension power lines. On the left is a farm entrance into an open field. This was the location of Leonard Hastings' potato field. To the right opposite, a bit further down the hill, is the site of Leonard Hastings' home.

To visit the graves of Leonard and Elvira Hastings, turn off Highway 124 on 123A south from New Ipswich town center. Proceed .6 mile to Central Cemetery. Turn right through the gate and proceed west to the pond on your left. Just beyond the pond is a narrow road and a wider entrance where you can park. It is probably best to proceed on foot from this point. Continue past the pond (on your left) on the narrow road to the far end of the cemetery. The Hastings' monument is up the hill, the fourth row on your right.

Notes

[1] Ellen G. White, *Spiritual Gifts*, vol. 2, p. 111.

[2] James White, "Our Tour East," *Advent Review*, August 1850, pp. 14, 15; 1850 U.S. Federal Census records.

[3] John Reader, "The Fungus That Conquered Europe," New York *Times*, Mar. 17, 2008; Cecil Woodham-Smith, *The Great Hunger: Ireland 1845-1849* (New York: Harper & Row, 1962); Christine Kinealy, *This Great Calamity: The Irish Famine 1845-52* (Dublin: Gill & Macmillan, 1994).

Parking area near Hastings grave
GPS: N 42°44.999' W 071°51.318'

Merlin D. Burt 2010

Central Cemetery, New Ipswich, New Hampshire

Merlin D. Burt 2010

Leonard and Elvira Hastings graves

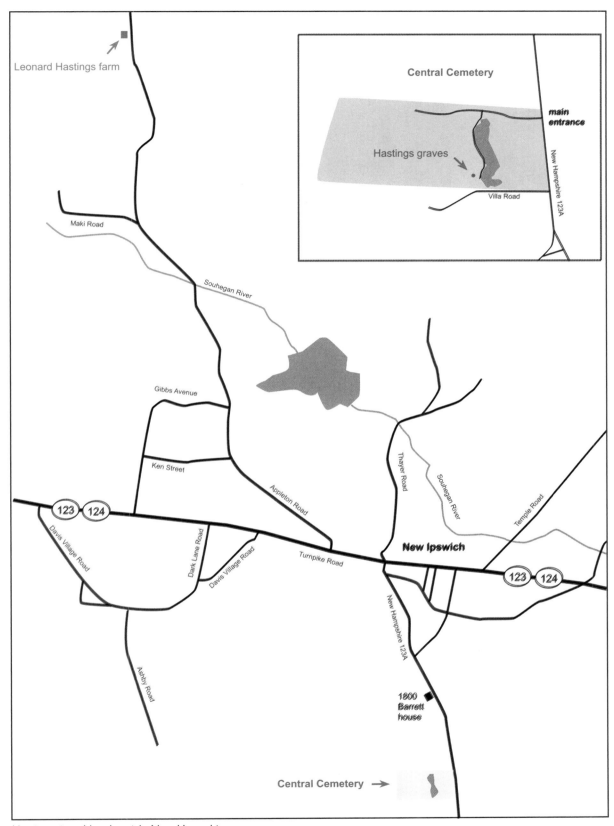

Hastings sites, New Ipswich, New Hampshire

Leonard Hastings farm

Central Cemetery

main
entrance

Hastings graves

Villa Road

New Hampshire 123A

Maki Road

Souhegan River

Gibbs Avenue

Ken Street

Appleton Road

Thayer Road

Souhegan River

Temple Road

123 124

Davis Village Road

Dark Lane Road

Davis Village Road

Turnpike Road

New Ipswich

123 124

New Hampshire 123A

Ashby Road

1800
Barrett
house

Central Cemetery →

Washington, New Hampshire, church
GPS: N 43°09.206' W 072°07.587'

Washington, New Hampshire, Seventh-day Adventist Church

Katy Wolfer

Washington, New Hampshire

Washington, New Hampshire, is often described as the birthplace of the Seventh-day Adventist Church. Though this is not entirely accurate, it certainly is the location of the earliest Sabbathkeeping Millerite church that continues to this day as a Seventh-day Adventist church. Picturesque Washington, New Hampshire,

Town square, Washington, New Hampshire

Ken Olin 2005

with its changes in elevation and distinct New England appearance, was incorporated on December 13, 1776. The residents have long been proud that their town was the first to be incorporated after George Washington. It never fails to inspire the new visitor to see the white cupolas of the town hall, Congregationalist church, and schoolhouse/police station come into view as one drives into town. The town hall has been in use for more than 200 years, while the schoolhouse dates to the 1880s. The previous school was a small brick structure known as the Center School. The white public buildings are located close together on the town common. Washington has always been a rural agrarian community. In 1830 the population peaked at 1,135. To recapture a mid-nineteenth-century perspective, one must visualize the rolling hills as mostly cleared of trees, revealing agriculture and picturesque farms together with river mills and logging operations. With the coming of the railroad, tourism brought people seeking fresh air and healthy water. Today Millen Pond and about 25 other small lakes in the region help make this town a vacation and retreat destination. Around Millen Pond many cottages and the occasional private pontoon airplane reveal that some have discovered one of New Hampshire's hidden beauty spots.

Washington is situated some nine miles north of West Hillsborough. Hillsborough remains associated with Washington in Adventist thinking because Frederick Wheeler lived there. A few years ago the presumed location of the schoolhouse where Wheeler first preached the Sabbath was discovered. West Hillsborough was also the location of a Millerite camp meeting and the home of Washington Barnes.

In the spring of 1842 a classic white meetinghouse was built about three miles from the Washington town center, and a "Christian Society" was formed. The building was funded in a typical New England manner—through the sale of pews. In December of 1842 Joshua Goodwin brought the Millerite Advent message to the towns of Lempster and Marlow near Washington. He reported from Washington on January 11, 1843: "The Lord is reviving His work graciously in this section of country. Never did I witness a more powerful work of God than I have witnessed in this section for some six or eight weeks past."[1] During 1843 the majority of the Christian congregation had adopted the Advent message. By the end of 1844, through the influence of Rachel Oaks and Frederick Wheeler, more than a dozen of the congregation had become Sabbathkeepers. An official Seventh-day Adventist congregation was finally organized in 1862.

The classic lines of the church with its white clapboard exterior, plain gable roof, and dual doors draw the mind of the visitor to an earlier and simpler time. The old cemetery and the more recently constructed Sabbath Trail enhance the peaceful setting of the church. The church seats about 120 people with a small still-active congregation that meets there from about April to October each year. The road to the church is not plowed during the winter.

The milelong Sabbath Trail winds through the woods behind the church and traces the history of the Sabbath from Creation to the present on 31 granite stones. There are benches at each site where one can sit and reflect on the inscription. The design was conceived by Pastor Merlin Knowles in 1995 and completed in 1998.

To get to the church, proceed, from the gazebo in the center of Washington, 2.1 miles on Faxon Hill Road (the road to Millen Pond). Turn left onto King Street, a dirt road, and go 0.3 miles to the parking lot and church, which are on the left.

Frederick Wheeler and Hillsborough, New Hampshire

Frederick Wheeler lived in the town of West Hillsborough, New Hampshire, also known as the upper village. An itinerate Methodist minister, he accepted the Millerite Advent faith toward the end of 1842. Describ-

Frederick Wheeler (1811-1910)

ing his experience, he wrote: "My conversion was not a conversion to a mere theory, but it was the power of God sending home the truth and filling my entire being with His presence."[2] George, son of Frederick and Lydia Wheeler, remembered the commitment and dedication of his parents. In anticipation of the Second Coming they sold their home and moved in with Washington Barnes. The wives of Washington and Frederick were sisters. George remembered that there were other families living with the Barneses. The children slept in the attic, and families were separated by blankets nailed to the rafters. The Wheelers had virtually nothing after the 1844 disappointment, though Frederick Wheeler did have a horse and wagon that he used to preach in different places. To survive, Wheeler hired himself out to work on a farm three days a week and preached the rest of the time in New Hampshire and Vermont. When George was asked about his father's first seventh-day Sabbath sermon, he said, "Father preached it first in the Washington Barnes red schoolhouse in the town of Hillsborough, and continued to hold meetings there for some time until the tax payers complained about it. Then Ev. [sic] Barnes cleared out his wheelwright and plow shop, and meetings were held there."[3]

Wheeler was probably the first Sabbathkeeping Adventist minister in North America. It was some time between March and May of 1844 that he accepted the Sabbath through the efforts of a Seventh Day Baptist widow named Rachel Oaks.[4] W. A. Spicer published the following information from F. W. Bartle, a neighbor of Frederick Wheeler's when they lived in New York. Bartle wrote:

He [F. Wheeler] told me that they had held a quarterly meeting in the church, celebrating the Lord's supper. In his sermon about the service he made the remark that all persons confessing communion with Christ in such a service should be ready to follow Him, and obey God and keep His commandments in all things. Later, he said, he met Mrs. Preston [Rachel Oaks Preston], who reminded him of his remarks about the meaning of communion with Christ. "I came near getting up in the meeting at that point," she told him, "and saying something." "What was it you had in mind to say?" he asked her. "I wanted to tell you that you would better set that communion table back and put the cloth over it, until you begin to keep the commandments of God." Elder Wheeler told me that these words cut him deeper than anything that he had ever had spoken to him. He thought it over, and soon he began to keep the Sabbath.[5]

While convincing Wheeler of the Sabbath must have encouraged Rachel Oaks, she found it more difficult to influence the rest of the Adventists at the Christian church in Washington. They were so focused on the second coming of Jesus that they didn't see the importance of the Sabbath. In her obituary, S. N. Haskell wrote, "In 1844, after the passing of the time, she introduced the Sabbath among the Adventists."[6]

Most of the Farnsworth family and those associated with the Washington church understood that the Farnsworth family and most of the other members did not accept the Sabbath until after the October 1844 disappointment. There is conflicting information on some of the details. This overview attempts to provide the best synthesis from the extant records.

Soon after Wheeler accepted the Sabbath, a Millerite camp meeting was held in Hillsborough, near the Washington Barnes farm. George Wheeler, eldest son of Frederick, was 10 years old at the time and recollected how the primitive camp was set up in a grove of trees,

with between 300 and 400 present. The seats were made by stringing long tree trunks on the ground and attaching rough hemlock boards for seating. The only musical accompaniment, if it could be called musical, was provided by about a dozen "song leaders" who beat the time using poles. The tents were made of staked coarse sheeting over forked poles. The Barnes family sold or gave biscuits and other necessities to the campers, and a farmer provided milk. Little is known of the details of this camp meeting, but it may have been the first during which the Sabbath was presented to Millerite Adventists by Frederick Wheeler. During the summer of 1844 another Adventist minister in New Hampshire named T. M. Preble accepted the Sabbath, perhaps under the influence of Frederick Wheeler. Preble in turn wrote an article and tract on the Sabbath in February and March 1845 that convinced Joseph Bates. Bates then wrote tracts, which convinced others, such as James and Ellen White and Hiram Edson, to keep the Sabbath. Thus the Sabbatarian Adventist movement was formed that later became the Seventh-day Adventist Church. Today Seventh-day Adventists in many places still enjoy camp meeting and God continues to bless His people as they gather to hear His Word.

Rachel Oaks Preston (1809-1868)

Washington, New Hampshire, church

Rachel Oaks (1809-1868)

Rachel Oaks Preston was born in Vernon, Vermont. Her maiden name was Rachel Harris. At the age of 17 she was converted and joined the Methodist Church. After her marriage to Amory Oaks in 1824, they moved to Verona in central New York, where at the age of 25 she became an observer of the seventh-day Sabbath. "The Methodist minister, her pastor, did what he could to turn her from the Sabbath, but finally told her she might keep it if she would not leave them. But she was faithful to her convictions of duty and united with the first Seventh-day Baptist church of Verona. . . . She and her daughter, Delight Oaks, were members of the first Verona church at the time of their removal to Washington, N.H."[7] Her husband, Amory, died in 1835, the same year she joined the Seventh Day Baptist Church.

The Verona church was serious about taking care of their widow, Rachel Oaks. Still a young woman at 26, with a 10-year-old daughter, she received help from Seventh Day Baptist men in settling her late husband's estate. It seems a Samuel Marsh had not paid $10 in rent that was due Rachel. This disagreement split the Verona church for a period of years, until finally Marsh was removed from membership. In 1859 he agreed to pay the $10 and was readmitted to the congregation.[8] In Verona, Rachel was remembered as a widowed schoolteacher with some property. The November 23, 1835, New York state census lists Rachel Oaks as a landowner

with 12 acres but as having no livestock.[9] According to local memories she taught in various places, among them Stacy Basin, which was about two miles west from the Verona Seventh Day Baptist Church. Rachel's daughter also became a schoolteacher, and according to Verona Seventh Day Baptist recollections she went to teach in Washington, New Hampshire, where her mother joined her about Thanksgiving time 1843.[10] Thus Rachel was in her mid-30s and her daughter was about 18 when Rachel attempted to introduce the Sabbath to the little Christian church in Washington.

A curious note in the Verona Seventh Day Baptist records indicates that in early 1845 Rachel and her daughter requested that their names be dropped from membership. Presumably this was because of their faith in the Second Advent message. The minutes of March 20, 1845, record, "The requests of sister Rachel Oakes and Delight Oakes were laid before the church after some remarks thereto it was[:] Resolved that the clerk write and inform them that the Church cannot consistently grant them their request while they walk by faith and in obedience to the laws of God."[11] One explanation for this denial is that Rachel's brother was the clerk at the meeting. Both women remained listed as members of the Verona congregation until it was noted that they were "deceased."

Graves of Cyrus Farnsworth and Rachel Delight Oaks

Another interesting sidelight is that Delight married Cyrus K. Farnsworth—younger brother of William Farnsworth—on June 14, 1847, and so Rachel Oaks became a member of the Farnsworth family (see Farnsworth family below).

At some point Rachel Oaks married Nathan Preston and moved back to Vernon, Vermont, where she is buried. Shortly before her death she heard of the 1867 Christmastime revival in Washington and rejoiced.

Seventh Day Baptist Influence

During the early 1840s there was a special effort by Seventh Day Baptists to promote the Sabbath among other Christian denominations. Historically Seventh Day Baptists were quite passive in promoting the Sabbath. In 1841 the Seventh Day Baptist General Conference acknowledged that God "required" them to share the Sabbath. The next year a tract society was formed, and special days of fasting and prayer were called between 1843 and 1845.[12] The local Verona congregation joined in the evangelistic fervor. The church minutes of

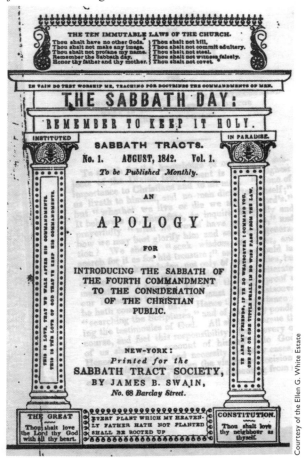

1842 Seventh Day Baptist evangelistic tract on the Sabbath

Courtesy of the Ellen G. White Estate

October 1, 1843, read: "Resolved that we approve the resolution of the General Conference in relation to a day of fasting and prayer that the efforts which are being made in relation to the Sabbath may have the divine blessing."

Seventh Day Baptists were disappointed when other Christian denominations rejected their evangelistic efforts on behalf of the Bible Sabbath. There was one noted exception. Millerite Adventists responded more positively. The *Sabbath Recorder* in June 1844 reported: "We learn, from several sections, that considerable numbers of those who are looking for the speedy appearance of Christ have embraced the seventh day, and commenced observing it as the Sabbath."[13]

In Millerite publications there is evidence that Sabbathkeeping became an active issue in various locations, though none of the prominent Millerite leaders became Sabbatarian. Millerite and Seventh Day Baptist literature suggests that there were people in a number of other locations besides Washington that adopted the Sabbath as a result of Seventh Day Baptist efforts. Like conditionalism, the Sabbath was an active minority view within the movement.[14]

When Rachel Oaks relocated to Washington, New Hampshire, she brought recently published tracts on the Sabbath from the Seventh Day Baptist General Conference with her. These she shared with any who would listen. While Frederick Wheeler responded to Rachel's appeals, it seems that the rest of the Adventists in Washington were not interested. S. N. Haskell recalled, "She [Rachel Oaks] told me that she was much disappointed because the people were so deeply interested in the coming of the Lord that they would not listen to her. She thought after the time when they expected the Lord to come had passed, they certainly would read her [Seventh Day Baptist] publications; but even then they did not seem to be interested. Because of this lack of interest, she felt sad indeed."[15] After the 1844 disappointment William and Cyrus Farnsworth were among the first of many within the Washington congregation to adopt the seventh-day Sabbath.

The Farnsworth Family in Washington

William Farnsworth and his father, Daniel (1782-1864), were among the founders of the Washington Christian Church in April 1842.[16] Captain Daniel Farnsworth accepted the Advent message and gave everything he had to the Advent cause. "Once when there was a church squabble, Captain Farnsworth said,

William Farnsworth (1807-1888)

Cyrus K. Farnsworth (1823-1899)

'A little less straight testimony and a little more straight living will be better for all of us.'"[17] William was the eldest son of Daniel. A history book on Washington, New Hampshire, said of him, "He has always [resided] in [Washington], and is universally respected."[18]

The Farnsworth family recollections generally agree that William accepted the Sabbath after the October 1844 disappointment. D. E. Robinson, grandson of William Farnsworth, was told that in the autumn of 1844 William kept the Sabbath and then went out on Sunday with his son John to work on the road. John told Robinson that this happened in November 1844.[19] Eugene W. Farnsworth wrote the following: "Mother

began to keep the Sabbath the same day that Father began; and an uncle of mine [Cyrus Farnsworth], with his wife [Rachel Delight Oaks], began the next Sabbath. Very soon there was a company in Washington of some fifteen or eighteen keeping the Sabbath."[20]

William's family was truly a clan. He had a total of 22 surviving children. His first wife bore him 11 children before her death, and his second wife did the same. A story is told that Eugene, ninth child of William, was awakened in the middle of the night by his father and told to get dressed, hitch the horse, and go to Marlow for the doctor. But when Eugene heard that his stepmother was ready to give birth to another baby, he

William Farnsworth homestead

Cyrus Farnsworth home
8 Millen Pond Road, Washington, New Hampshire

didn't want to go. William asked his son why and was told in no uncertain terms that there were already too many children in the family. Quoting Scripture, William said: "Remember, son, the Bible says, 'increase and multiply and replenish the earth.'" To this Eugene retorted, "Yes, but He didn't tell you to do it all!"

William Farnsworth's home is no longer standing, but pictures of it reveal that it was remarkably small for such a large family. The children slept mostly in the attic in a very crowded condition. Little wonder that Eugene was not interested in having more siblings. To his credit, many of William's children made significant contributions to the work of the Seventh-day Adventist Church.

Cyrus Farnsworth lived for many years in a commodious brick home on Millen Pond. It was by this home under the trees by the lake that Joseph Bates, Frederick Wheeler, Cyrus Farnsworth, and maybe his brother William studied the Sabbath and helped settle Bates' decision to be a Sabbatarian. Baptisms were also performed at various times in Millen Pond by this home.

The 1867 Revival

In the years following its 1862 organization the Washington congregation experienced a spiritual decline. This was also true of a number of churches in Maine. There was an anti-organizational attitude in the northern New England states. Many were watching for any discipline or rebuke from Battle Creek as an excuse to rebel. D. M. Canright and J. N. Andrews had worked in New England between 1865 and 1867 with limited success. In Washington the spiritual state had declined to the point that they had closed up the church. Even William Farnsworth had secretly returned to chewing tobacco. The rancor of the members, and particularly Worcester Ball, brought a judgmentalism and bitterness that poisoned relationships. The most serious casualties of this spiritual neglect and backsliding were the children and youth of the church.

Unfortunately, Frederick Wheeler was no longer available to give spiritual counsel and encouragement. He had moved to New York State in 1857 and settled in West Monroe in 1861.

Eugene Farnsworth remembered J. N. Andrews coming to visit him when he was a teenager, probably in 1865 or 1866. Here is the story in Eugene's words:

When Elder Andrews came, I was out in the field hoeing corn. I looked up and saw him coming. I was rather timid those days, and I never got near enough to a preacher

Cynthia Farnsworth (1830-1917)

Cyrus Farnsworth home and pond
GPS: N 43°09.779' W 072°07.655'

Millen Pond, near Cyrus Farnsworth's home

to let him speak to me. When one came to the house, I found my place out in the barn among the cattle and sheep. As Elder Andrews came toward me, he took a hoe off the gate near where I was working, and I said to myself, "What in the world will that fellow do now?" He came along and began to hoe corn. Boy that I was, I could see that he didn't know a thing about hoeing corn. . . .

Finally he said, "Eugene, what is your purpose in life?"

I liked his frank way of speaking, and I said, "Elder Andrews, I am going to be a lawyer."

"Well, sir," he said, "you might do a good deal worse." . . . If he had something directly against my plans, my opposition would have been up. "But," he continued, "what are you going to do before you are a lawyer?"

"I am going to go to school until I get an education."

"What will you do then?"

"I am going to study law."

"Yes, and what next?" he said.

"Well," I said, "I hope I will practice."

"And what next?"

"I hope to earn some money and get a competency, get a home, and have a family."

Eugene W. Farnsworth (1847-1935)

"Yes, and what next?"

I began to grow nervous. I didn't like the way he was crowding me into that corner, for I saw that he was. . . . "Well," I said, "I suppose I shall die."

And again he said, "What next?"

I tell you that great good man had driven me to the end of my chain. Those words stuck in my memory. Then, with his great blue eyes looking straight through me, he said, "My boy, you take hold of something that will help you to span the chasm, something that will land your feet safely on the other side, where you will be safe for eternity." I have honored Elder Andrews all the days of my life.[21]

Hoping to bring revival, James and Ellen White and J. N. Andrews came to New Hampshire just before Christmas of 1867. Arriving previous to Sabbath on December 20, they stayed in the home of Cyrus Farnsworth. Over the next several days they held nine meetings. At first it was very difficult work.

Worcester Ball had become a bitter antagonist to Ellen White and had abandoned some tenets of the Seventh-day Adventist faith. He even went a step further and corresponded with Miles Grant and the *World's Crisis*, J. V. Himes' paper, *Voice of the West*, and the anti-Seventh-day Adventist periodical, *Hope of Israel*. Ball was somewhat of a thorny character even when faithful to the message. He served for a period of years as the church clerk. One of Cyrus Farnsworth's descendants described him thus: "This man used to bear testimonies at every opportunity in our church services. He brought and read every testimony published, and used them for a club to use on them that failed to follow the writings of Sister White." One Sabbath he was criticizing a sister's dress. Hosea Dodge spoke up and said, "Worcester, have you never read where it says, 'Thou shalt not rebuke the daughter of my people'?" The next week Worcester came to Dodge and said that during the past week he had gone all through his Bible but had not been able to find the text. Hosea got a twinkle in his eye as he replied, "Worcester, I didn't say it was in the Bible; I just asked you, 'Have you never read?'"[22]

Ellen White's prophetic responsibility often led her to share testimonies received in vision. Imagine the intensity of feeling for those who received a direct message of encouragement, rebuke, or guidance from God.

Worcester Ball (1825-1902)

Ellen White revealed her own feelings and the circumstances surrounding a strong testimony she shared at an 1880 camp meeting. "I have had many individual testimonies to write which has been quite a heavy burden on me in addition to my labors in talking the truth."[23] "Friday night I bore my testimony with great power. It seemed to cut everything before it that night. Brother Stone was nearly all night in prayer in the grove, and Sabbath morning he made a most humble confession. I assure you there was a break in the camp. . . . I had some very bad, bad jobs to perform. I took Brother Bean and wife and talked to them very plain. They did not rise up against it. I cried myself, could not help it."[24]

The 1867 meetings at Washington, New Hampshire, were similarly intense. The straight testimony began with Ball. James White described it thus: "The truth, theoretical and practical, was spoken with great plainness, and was having its influence upon all. Mrs. [White] faithfully, yet tenderly, appealed to Bro. [Ball]. Bro. Andrews set forth his great wrong with weeping. He was called upon to state his difficulties. He did so, and was faithfully and kindly replied to." And thus it continued. Finally, "he began to see that he had been fighting against God, and cruelly wounding His people.

Washington, New Hampshire, church

Cemetery next to the Washington, New Hampshire, church as seen through a window of the church

Washington, New Hampshire, Church Cemetery

William Farnsworth

Worcester W. Ball

Lydia A. Ball

John Ball

Sarah Mead Farnsworth

Hosea Dodge

Newell Mead

Daniel Farnsworth

Patty Farnsworth

Washington, New Hampshire, church and cemetery

The scene was most touching. Our erring brother was returning with weeping and mourning, and all present seemed to be reaching out their glad hands to receive him."[25] Ball's was perhaps the most impressive return to the faith. But there were other testimonies.

Another remarkable meeting was held in the Farnsworth home, located near Millen Pond. It is said to have continued for more than five hours. During this time Ellen White addressed one person after another. There were varied issues. James White mentions Newell Mead and his wife. Newell had received a severe injury in a fall from a ladder, and Mrs. Mead had "a severe run of fever, which left her almost helpless." They were in financial difficulties because of these health problems, even though Newell was a "successful teacher of penmanship and music."[26] Discouragement had taken them in their many troubles, and they were not attending the meetings. James White sent for them to come. Ellen White had comforting words for them and assured them that "God loved them and if they would only trust their ways to Him He would bring them forth from the furnace of affliction purified."[27] There were some other straight words for them spoken in love. James White commented that "we all wept together for very joy, and Bro. Mead seemed comforted." Newell then made a further appeal to Ball and to the children and youth to give their hearts to God. The immediate result was that the hired girl who was helping the Mead family and the two Mead children, ages 9 and 14, stood to accept Jesus.[28] Person after person received testimonies from Ellen White.

The elderly Brother Stowell was using tobacco and "acted a part of deception." She spoke directly to him and encouraged him to "accomplish the work of purification of the flesh and spirit." Then she turned to Stowell's daughter-in-law, who was also Brother Mead's sister. This woman was suffering under the controlling hand of her husband in "servile bondage." She was exhorted to "remember that her marriage does not destroy her individuality." She was further urged not to yield "her conscience to an overbearing, tyrannical man."[29]

Then there were words for another young girl and her mother. The girl was becoming indifferent to spiritual things, and the mother was vacillating and indecisive. They were both urged to be faithful, and it would have a good effect on their unbelieving father and husband.

James Farnsworth and his wife had been excluded from the church. She then said that "God who seeth

hearts has been better pleased with the life and deportment of Brother James than some of those who were united with the church." James's wife was urged not to "look at the failures and wrongs of those who profess better things."

As these testimonies were being given, young Eugene Farnsworth was present, and it occurred to him that if Ellen White was a true prophet she would know about his own father's problem with chewing tobacco. He had seen his father discreetly spit while working out in the snow and then cover it up with his shoe. As if in answer to his thought, she gave a testimony for William Farnsworth about his use of pork and tobacco while at the same time taking a "position as a defender of the visions." She stated that he had been a "greater hindrance" to the "cause of God in Washington" than Worcester Ball, because he "professed to know the truth" but was not "sanctified through the truth."[30] William confessed his sins and made a public turn in his life.

As the children saw their parents confessing it had a profound effect on them. At a meeting on Wednesday, Christmas Day, 13 of the children and youth arose and expressed a desire to be Christians. W. C. White visited with one of those children, Orville O. Farnsworth, in 1937 and was told: "I went with some of my brothers to exchange Christmas gifts with our cousins Fred and Rose Mead. Because of the meetings the previous evening, we were delayed one day in giving our humble presents to each other. Fred had been a rather wild boy, but he was present in the morning meeting, and he with his sister had taken their stand for Christ. Now they felt a burden for souls, and we were invited into Fred's room, where, after an earnest appeal, we knelt together by his bed, and I gave my heart to the Lord."[31]

Four more children besides Orville, who were not at the Christmas meeting, also gave their lives to Christ for a total of 18. Of those 18, nine became workers in the Seventh-day Adventist Church. One of these was Eugene Farnsworth, who is mentioned above.

The Story of Stephen Smith

Stephen Smith's conversion is intimately intertwined with Washington, New Hampshire, and the Seventh-day Adventist Church. It is the story of a lifetime of spiritual struggle with a final decision for the right.

Stephen (1806-1889) and Matilda (1809-1891) Smith lived in Washington, New Hampshire, until 1841, when they moved to Lempster and finally settled in Unity. Stephen became an Adventist about 1842 through the efforts of J. V. Himes. He helped the pre-1844 movement with his money and influence. Smith accepted the Sabbath through the influence of Joseph Bates during the late 1840s.[32] He pointed Bates to various friends and acquaintances who also responded to the message. In 1852 Smith became involved with spiritualizing views of the Second Coming and was briefly separated from the Washington church.[33] In the fall of 1853 James and Ellen White along with J. N. Andrews and Frederick Wheeler held a successful conference in Washington. At that time the "Christian meeting-house" was filled, with more than 100 present. "Cheering testimonies" were given, including one by Stephen Smith, and six were baptized.[34]

About 1854 Smith became involved in the Advent Christian time-setting expectation. When the Sabbath-keeping Adventists in Washington rejected the idea, he became "hard and some saucy." Once again he was out of harmony with the movement.[35] He supported the Messenger Party when it arose. But then again in 1857, he came back to the Sabbatarian Adventist position with the new emphasis on the Laodicean message.[36] His earnestness led him to walk the 12 miles or so through the snow from his home in Unity to Washington to confess his errors.[37]

But this revival did not last. By the next year he received a testimony from Ellen White.[38] Ernest Farnsworth, a son of William Farnsworth, recalled: "When I was a lad he used to come to the Washington church to blow off steam. As he put it, to rap on the hive and hear the bees hum. He was so loud and vicious in his talks that we youngsters were afraid of him. But in a testimony meeting, everyone was permitted to speak and so [he did]."[39] Eugene Farnsworth remembered that he had "the most withering, blighting tongue of any man I ever heard" and "could say the meanest things in the meanest, most cutting way of any man I ever met."[40]

Eugene told a story of the 1885 revival and evangelistic meetings shortly after it happened. It seems that Stephen Smith had read an article by Ellen White in the *Review and Herald* about a year before the meetings and liked it. Perhaps his wife, Matilda, who was a "godly woman," had arranged for the paper to be lying conveniently near his chair.

When Eugene came to Washington, Stephen decided to attend. The first Sabbath the sermon was on Revelation 7 and the rise of the Advent movement. At the conclusion Stephen was on his feet, and all "expected a perfect blast." But to everyone's surprise he instead said, "I don't want you to be afraid of me, brethren, for

Stephen Smith (1806-1889)

Courtesy of the Ellen G. White Estate

I have not come to criticize you. I have quit that kind of business." He then reviewed how he had opposed church organization and sympathized with the Messenger Party and Marion Party. Then he concluded that all of these had come to confusion, but the church had continued to grow.

> Facts . . . are stubborn things, but the facts are that those who have opposed this work have come to naught, while those who had been in sympathy with it have prospered—had grown better, more devoted, and godlike. Those who have opposed it have only learned to fight and debate, they have lost all of their religion. . . . No honest man can help but see that God is with them, and against us. I want to be in fellowship with this people in heart and in the church.[41]

During the next week Stephen remembered the testimony he had received from Ellen White, perhaps the one she wrote in 1858. Retrieving it, he attended the next Sabbath meeting, which was on spiritual gifts. Again there was a rustle in the audience, and old Stephen Smith struggled to his feet and said the following (as quoted by Eugene Farnsworth):

> I received a testimony myself [25 to] 28 years ago, took it home, locked it up in my trunk, and never read it until last Thursday.[42]

He indicated that he was afraid to read it for fear of getting mad, but said that he was "mad all the time nearly" anyway. Old Stephen then said:

> Brethren, *every word of the testimony for me is true,* and I accept it. And I have come to that (place) where I firmly believe they are *all* of God, and if I had heeded the one God sent to me as well as the rest, it would have changed the whole course of my life and I should have been a very different man. Any man that is honest must say, . . . that they lead a man toward God and the Bible always. If he is honest, he will say that; if he won't say that, he is not honest.[43]

Smith concluded his testimony with these compelling words: "Brethren, . . . I'm too old to undo what I've done. I'm too feeble to get out to our large meetings, but I want you to tell our people everywhere that another rebel has surrendered."[44] Eugene remarked that "his heart was as tender as a child's and he wept constantly as well as nearly the whole congregation."[45]

Smith died in 1889 and his obituary, written by one of his daughters, read: "During his last sickness, he felt to regret that he had not always cherished a Christian spirit toward those from whom he conscientiously felt called to differ, and he desired their forgiveness. His sickness was short, and his end peaceful."[46]

Notes

[1] Joshua Goodwin, "Letter From Joshua Goodwin," *Signs of the Times*, Feb. 1, 1843, p. 158.

[2] Frederick Wheeler, "A Message From Our Most Aged Minister," *Review and Herald*, Oct. 4, 1906, p. 9.

[3] C. E. Eldridge, "An interview Held at the Home of George Wheeler," West Monroe, New York, May 5, 1934 (Silver Spring, Md.: Ellen G. White Estate).

[4] Frederick Wheeler, "A Message From Our Most Aged Minister"; W. A. Spicer, "Fulfilling the Word," *Review and Herald*, Nov. 24, 1910, p. 10.

[5] W. A. Spicer, "Our First Minister," *Review and Herald*, Feb. 15, 1940, p. 8.

[6] S. N. Haskell, "Obituary Notices," *Review and Herald*, Mar. 3, 1868, p. 190.

[7] J. N. Andrews, *History of the Sabbath and First Day of the Week*, 2nd ed. (Battle Creek, Mich.: Seventh-day Adventist Publishing, 1873), p. 501.

[8] Surrogate Court Minutes and Orders, 1830-1836, Oneida County, New York, pp. 362, 363; see various entries in the *1st Verona Seventh Day Baptist Church Record* for the July 27, 1838, to Sept. 27, 1839, and 1859 in Seventh Day Baptist headquarters, Janesville, Wisconsin.

[9] State of New York, census of the state for the year 1835, town of Verona, county of Oneida, book 1, p. 33. The record also lists one male death (probably Amory, her husband). There were three males and three females living in the home, all between 16 and 45 years of age.

[10] John C. Reichert (unpublished manuscript, Seventh Day Baptist records, Janesville, Wisconsin).

[11] Verona Seventh Day Baptist Church records (Seventh Day Baptist records, Janesville, Wisconsin).

[12] James Bailey, *History of the Seventh-Day Baptist General Conference: From Its Origin, September 1802, to Its Fifty-third Session, September 1865* (Toledo, Ohio: S. Bailey & Co., Publishers, 1866), pp. 245, 246.

[13] George B. Utter, "The Second Advent and the Sabbath," *Sabbath Recorder*, June 13, 1844, p. 2.

[14] Merlin D. Burt, "The Historical Background, Interconnected Development, and Integration of the Doctrines of the Sanctuary, the Sabbath, and Ellen G. White's Role in Sabbatarian Adventism From 1844 to 1849" (Ph.D. diss., Andrews University, 2002), pp. 45-55.

[15] S. N. Haskell, "Our First Meeting-House," *General Conference Bulletin*, June 2, 1909, p. 290.

[16] See constitution and early papers of the Washington, New Hampshire, First Christian Society (Silver Spring, Md.: Ellen G. White Estate).

[17] Eldridge, "An Interview Held at the Home of George Wheeler."

[18] *History of Washington, New Hampshire, From the First Settlement to the Present Time. 1768-1886* (Claremont, N.H.: Claremont Manufacturing Co., 1886), p. 398.

[19] D. E. Robinson, "Sabbath-keeping in Washington" (Loma Linda, Calif.: Archives and Special Collections, Loma Linda University).

[20] E. W. Farnsworth, "Symposium of Pioneers," *Review and Herald*, June 4, 1926, p. 1.

[21] *Ibid.*, p. 2.

[22] Harold Farnsworth to James R. Nix, February 1988, quoted in Mark Ford, *The Church at Washington, New Hampshire* (Hagerstown, Md.: Review and Herald, 2002), p. 86.

[23] Ellen G. White to Willie and Mary White and S. N. Haskell, Sept. 16, 1880 (letter 41, 1880) (Silver Spring, Md.: Ellen G. White Estate).

[24] Ellen G. White to William and Mary White, Sept. 22, 1880 (letter 42, 1880) (Silver Spring, Md.: Ellen G. White Estate).

[25] James White, "Eastern Tour," *Review and Herald*, Jan. 28, 1868, p. 104.

[26] *Ibid.*

[27] Ellen G. White, manuscript 2, 1868, p. 12 (Silver Spring, Md.: Ellen G. White Estate). This Testimony was copied from a handwritten testimony lent to J. L. McElhany by one of the Farnsworth family around 1945. It was apparently left with Cyrus Farnsworth after the revival meetings. Ellen White asked him to return a copy to her. The written testimony perhaps had more details than her oral message, and Cyrus was asked to read it discreetly to members of the church.

[28] James White, "Eastern Tour," p. 105.

[29] Ellen G. White, manuscript 2, 1868, pp. 14, 15.

[30] *Ibid.*, pp. 11, 12, 17, 18; letter from Mrs. E. W. Farnsworth to her nephew Guy C. Jorgensen, Dec. 1, 1921 (Berrien Springs, Mich.: Center for Adventist Research).

[31] W. C. White, "Sketches and Memories of James and Ellen G. White: XLIV," *Review and Herald*, Feb. 11, 1937, p. 8.

[32] Lanora Jones, "Smith," *Review and Herald*, Jan. 28, 1890, p. 63.

[33] [James White], "Bro. Stephen Smith," *Review and Herald*, Nov. 25, 1852, p. 112.

[34] James White, "Eastern Tour," *Review and Herald*, Nov. 8, 1853, p. 140.

[35] [James White], "Bro. J. Stowell," *Review and Herald*, Apr. 18, 1854, p. 102.

[36] Stephen Smith, "Returning to the Ranks," *Review and Herald*, Feb. 19, 1857, p. 126.

[37] A. S. Hutchins, "Communication From Bro. Hutchins," *Review and Herald*, Mar. 12, 1857, p. 152; John Stowell, "Extracts From Letters," *Review and Herald*, Mar. 19, 1857, p. 159.

[38] Ellen G. White, manuscript 2, 1858 (Silver Spring, Md.: Ellen G. White Estate).

[39] Ernest Farnsworth to Arthur L. White, Feb. 26, 1971, quoted in Ford, p. 79.

[40] Eugene W. Farnsworth to E. G. White, July 15, 1885 (Silver Spring, Md.: Ellen G. White Estate); see also Arthur L. White, "The Story of Stephen Smith and the Unread Testimony," *Review and Herald*, Aug. 6, 1953, pp.16-18.

[41] *Ibid.*

[42] *Ibid.*

[43] *Ibid.*

[44] Arthur L. White, "The Story of Stephen Smith and the Unread Testimony."

[45] Eugene W. Farnsworth to Ellen G. White, July 15, 1885.

[46] Lanora Jones, "Obituary Notices," *Review and Herald*, Jan. 28, 1890, p. 63.

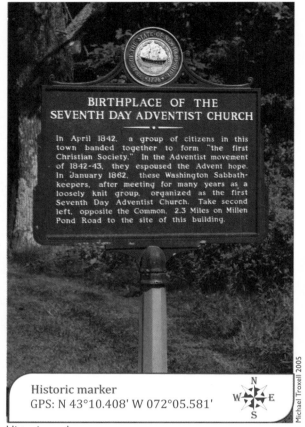

Historic marker
GPS: N 43°10.408' W 072°05.581'

Michael Troxell 2005

Historic marker

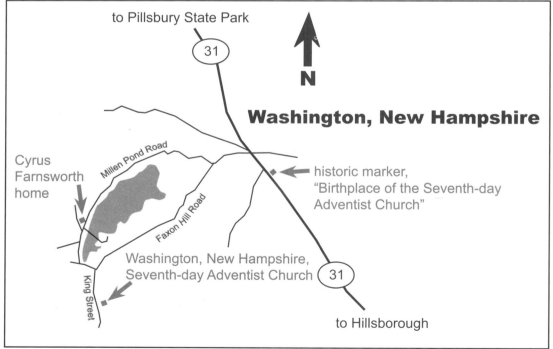

Adventist historic sites, Washington, New Hampshire

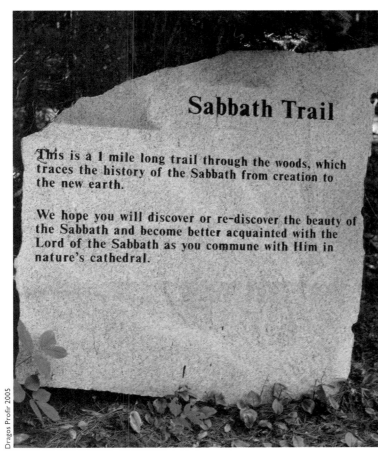

Sabbath Trail

This is a 1 mile long trail through the woods, which traces the history of the Sabbath from creation to the new earth.

We hope you will discover or re-discover the beauty of the Sabbath and become better acquainted with the Lord of the Sabbath as you commune with Him in nature's cathedral.

Sabbath -
At Sinai Mountain

At Sinai mountain, God at first reminded His children of their special relation to Him and that He had saved them. Next He gave them the ten laws which list the principles of His government and describe His character. He asked His people to live according to these principles. Exodus 20:1-17.

Uriah Smith (1832-1903)

Sketch of West Wilton, New Hampshire, by Uriah Smith (1847)

West Wilton, New Hampshire

Uriah and Annie Smith Sites

West Wilton, New Hampshire, is the natal town of Annie and Uriah Smith. Both were remarkably talented young people who played important roles in early Adventist experience. Sadly, Annie died on July 26, 1855, of tuberculosis, or consumption, as it was then called. Annie was a talented poet, editor, and artist. Seventh-day Adventists still have three hymns written by her in their official hymnal. Annie and her parents, other siblings, and family members are buried in the South Yard Cemetery in Wilton Center.

Not far off Highway 101 is the large brick tavern where both Annie and her four-years-younger brother, Uriah Smith, were born. Their father and mother, Samuel and Rebekah Smith, were owners and proprietors of the tavern and store until April 1, 1836, when it was sold to Thomas Spaulding for $2,200. The railroad came to Wilton in December 1851, and the tavern remained a prosperous business because the stage was required to take rail passengers on to the next station. There was a schoolhouse just up the road from the tavern that is currently integrated into a home. At least Annie likely attended this school for a time. In 1835 her father sold the land with the schoolhouse.

Though the Smiths sold the tavern, it seems they continued to live in and operate the tavern until at least 1850. It is even possible that Rebekah continued to live there after her husband died in 1852. It was not until 1858 to 1860 that Samuel W. Smith, another of Rebekah's sons, bought his own property. The 1860 fed-

eral census lists Rebekah and Samuel's invalid brother John as living with him. Samuel finally married in 1864. It is still not clear where his home was located.[1]

Annie and Uriah's father, Samuel Smith, worked as a civil engineer, road builder, and contractor. He built the fitted stone bridge, without mortar, that is located across the road from the tavern. Samuel's father, Uriah Smith, operated a button factory and other industries down the river from where the Smith tavern was located. Those who visit the Wilton Historical Society museum can see a display of these buttons as well as a wallet that belonged to Uriah Smith, Sr.

Annie Smith

Annie was born on March 16, 1828, the only daughter of Samuel and Rebekah Smith. She was four years older than Uriah and four months younger than Ellen G. White. At 10 she was converted and became a Baptist, but left that faith to accept the Advent message before 1844. With the disappointment came disillusionment. As a result, Annie left her home to attend Charlestown Female Seminary across the Charles River from Boston, Massachusetts. The school provided a broad classical liberal arts education. She spent six terms at the school. Rebekah mentions that Annie studied French and oil painting. During Annie's last term at the seminary in 1850, she was enrolled in an art course. One day while sketching a picture of Boston from Prospect Hill in Somerville, she strained her eyes and for eight months could hardly see. She was unable to accept a coveted position at a school in Hancock, New Hampshire.[2] She did, however, continue to write for the *Ladies' Wreath* and other literary magazines.

Probably in 1851 Joseph Bates visited Rebekah Smith in West Wilton. Rebekah urged Bates to visit Annie while he was in Boston. She then wrote Annie regarding a meeting to be held in Elizabeth Temple's home. The night before the meeting both Bates and Annie had dreams. They dreamed of a meeting in which only one seat was available near the door and Annie arrived late. When the dream happened for both of them, it deeply impressed Annie. Bates presented the heavenly sanctuary explanation for the disappointment of 1844 and shared with her about the Sabbath. Within a month Annie wrote a poem for the *Review and Herald*, titled "Fear Not, Little Flock." It was published on September 16, 1851. James White recognized Annie's talent and invited her to join the publishing effort. She assisted for a short time in Saratoga Springs, New York, and then relocated to Rochester with the Whites. James White was not always an easy employer. He was demanding and sometimes even harsh in expecting editorial perfection. Annie vented some of her frustration while also revealing her literary talent in this extract from "The Proof-Reader's Lament":

Charlestown Female Seminary, which Annie Smith attended

What news is this falls on my ear?
What next will to my sight appear?
My brain doth whirl, my heart doth quake—
Oh, that egregious mistake!

"Too bad! too bad!!" I hear them cry,
"You might have seen with half an eye!
Strange! passing strange!! how could you make
So plain, so blunderous a mistake!"

Smith Tavern
GPS: N 42°49.844' W 071°48.330'

Birthplace of Annie and Uriah Smith, West End Highway, Wilton, New Hampshire

Guilty, condemned, I trembling stand,
With pressing cares on every hand,
Without one single plea to make,
For leaving such a bad *mistake.*

If right, no meed [reward] of praise is won,
No more than duty *then is done;*
If wrong, then censure I partake,
Deserving such a gross mistake.

How long shall I o'er this bewail?
"The best," 'tis said, "will sometimes fail;"
Must it then peace *forever break—*
Summed up, 'tis only a mistake.[3]

Annie is known as the premier early Sabbatarian Adventist hymn writer. The 1941 *Church Hymnal* has 10 songs written by her. A well-known song is "I Saw One Weary." It traces the blessed hope of such Adventist pioneers as Joseph Bates, James White, and perhaps Annie herself. Other songs include "How Far From Home" and "Long Upon the Mountains."

It is probable that while living in Rochester, Annie developed a romantic attraction for J. N. Andrews. She thought he shared her feelings, but to her great sorrow he turned instead to his childhood sweetheart, Angeline Stevens. Angeline's sister, Harriet, married Uriah Smith. This made J. N. Andrews and Uriah Smith brothers-in-law through their wives.

Sadly, Annie contracted tuberculosis, probably from exposure to James White's brother Nathaniel and sister Anna. As the illness progressed, James White provided $75 for Annie to receive medical treatment. This was to no avail. In November 1854 Annie returned home to West Wilton, and with her mother and Uriah's help she completed her book of poems, *Home Here, and Home in Heaven*, just 10 days before her death on July 26, 1855. Uriah made a woodcut of a peony flower for the title page.[4] Rebekah provided further information about her daughter, including some additional poems, in a later publication.[5] Besides her poems and hymns, Annie left several beautiful works of art, including what is believed to be a self-portrait.

Uriah Smith (1832-1903)

Like his older sister, Uriah Smith was also very talented. He attended school in Hancock, New Hampshire, in the autumn of 1845 and during 1846. He then continued his education for three years, from August 1848 to August 1851, at the prestigious Phillips Exeter

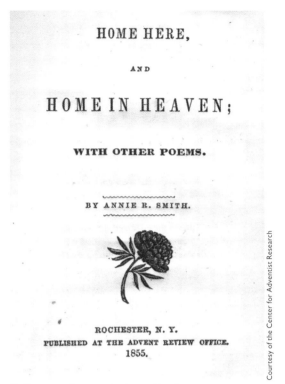

HOME HERE,

AND

HOME IN HEAVEN;

WITH OTHER POEMS.

BY ANNIE R. SMITH.

ROCHESTER, N. Y.
PUBLISHED AT THE ADVENT REVIEW OFFICE.
1855.

Collection of poems by Annie Smith

Academy in Exeter, New Hampshire. The academy is one of the "oldest nurseries of classical education in America." While Uriah was a student at the school, Gideon L. Soule was the principal. From him Uriah learned not only the various branches of secular learning but also "good manners, sound morality, and pure religion." Although nonsectarian, the academy was Protestant in orientation.[6] After completing his training, Uriah became a public school teacher.

All of Uriah's educational work was completed with a physical disability. As a child he had developed an infection in his left leg that caused it to atrophy. In 1844, when Uriah was 12, further infections required its amputation. Amos Twitchell, a surgeon from nearby Keene, took it off quickly on the kitchen table in about 20 minutes without the use of an anesthetic. The best doctors in those days were known for their speed.

Uriah was a talented artist. He drew detailed bird's-eye views of his hometown and other surrounding villages. His sketch of West Wilton remains the town's earliest lithographic representation.[7] He was also responsible for the first illustrations in the *Review and Herald* and the first illustration in a Sabbatarian Adventist published book.

Uriah Smith

Annie Smith, thought to be a self-portrait (1828-1855)

South Yard Cemetery, Wilton Center

Smith family burial site

Annie Smith

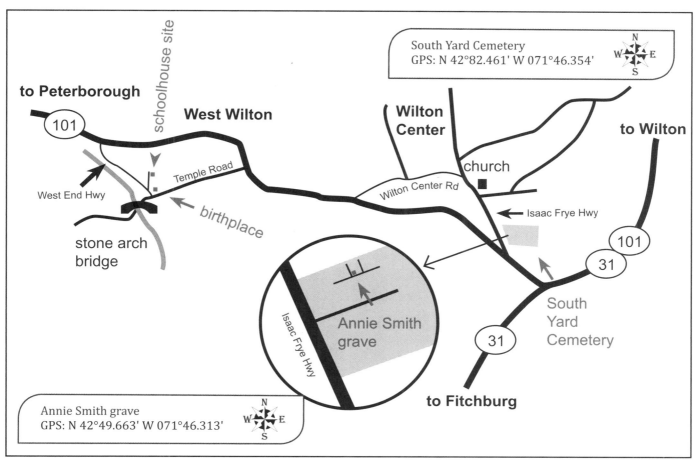

Adventist historic sites, West Wilton, New Hampshire

Smith Tavern, West Wilton, New Hampshire

While working as a teacher, Uriah attended a Sabbatarian Adventist conference in Washington, New Hampshire, September 10-12, 1852. The Smiths had accepted the Millerite message in 1843 and 1844. Uriah now accepted the Sabbath and the third angel's message. Within six months he joined the Review and Herald office newly established in Rochester, New York; later in 1855 he transferred to Battle Creek, Michigan. He remained connected with that office throughout almost all the rest of his life. Uriah Smith is best known as editor of the *Review and Herald* and for his popular book that remains in print to this day—*Thoughts on Daniel and the Revelation*. Uriah Smith was also known for his humor and literary talent.[8]

In a very real sense Uriah Smith was the pastor for thousands of nineteenth-century Seventh-day Adventists scattered in small communities around the United States. His editorials in response to letters provided continuing guidance and encouragement. Though he had a period of spiritual backsliding during the 1880s, he repented and remained a humble and faithful worker. He wrote some 4,000 *Review and Herald* editorials and articles and more than 20 major books and tracts.[9]

His creative genius was revealed in the design of a new flexible prosthetic leg. He patented it in 1863 and made a modest royalty.[10] But most important, he was able to improve his own life. Those who observed him walking in later life could not tell that he had an artificial leg. The flexibility of the artificial limb allowed Uriah to go to one knee in prayer with his brothers and sisters in faith. Smith also improved the design of the classic school desk and again received royalty income. He enjoyed woodworking as a hobby and made furniture, including several desks.

Notes

[1] The various details in this paragraph are drawn from deed, census, and town record research by the author.

[2] Ron Graybill, "The Life and Love of Annie Smith," *Adventist Heritage* 2, no. 1 (Summer 1975): 15.

[3] Quoted from Graybill, p. 17.

[4] Annie R. Smith, *Home Here, and Home in Heaven, With Other Poems* (Rochester, N.Y.: Advent Review Office, 1855).

[5] Rebekah Smith, *Poems: With a Sketch of the Life and Experiences of Annie R. Smith* (Manchester, N.H.: John B. Clarke, 1871).

[6] "Phillips Exeter Academy," *The Granite Monthly: A New Hampshire Magazine, Devoted to Literature, History, and State Progress*, April 1877, pp. 12-16.

[7] View of Wilton, West Village, N.H., 1847. Original sketch hangs in the museum of the Wilton Historical Society.

[8] Eugene F. Durand, "Uriah's Merry Medicine," *Adventist Review*, Feb. 3, 1983, pp. 4-6.

[9] A. G. Daniells, "Uriah Smith: A Sketch Read at the Funeral of Uriah Smith, March 8, 1903" (Loma Linda, Calif.: Ellen G. White Estate Branch Office).

[10] United States Patent Office, Patent Number 39362, dated July 28, 1863.

Courtesy of the Center for Adventist Research

Stone bridge built by Samuel Smith, father of Annie and Uriah

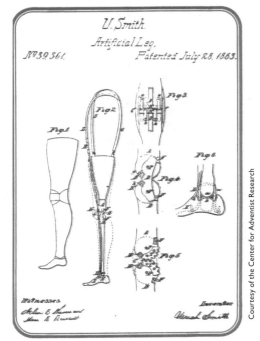

Courtesy of the Center for Adventist Research

Uriah Smith patent: flexible prosthetic leg (1863)

ADVENTIST PIONEER PLACES

NEW YORK

Volney
West Monroe
Low Hampton
Rochester
Roosevelt
Port Gibson

Katy Wolfer 2008

William Miller chapel, in Low Hampton, New York

Erie Canal, Rochester, New York

Erie Canal and Across New York

The Erie Canal spans the state of New York from Albany in the east to Buffalo in the west. Finished in 1825, the canal took seven-plus years to construct and was considered the engineering marvel of its day. It cut through 363 miles of wilderness and featured 18 aqueducts and 83 locks, with an elevation change of 568 feet between the Hudson River and Lake Erie. The waterway opened the way to the "West." The population of New York State grew dramatically from 1.4 million to 3.1 million in the 30 years from 1820 to 1850.[1]

There were three types of canal boats that traversed the shallow and narrow canal of the late 1840s: freight barges, line boats, and packets. Usually there were three mules providing the forward momentum. Packets—in contrast to barges or lines—were designed exclusively to carry passengers rapidly between the west and east. Generally, "mule speed" was between two and three miles per hour. Sometimes packets seeking to speed passengers to their destination were known to travel up to seven miles per hour. Such speeds were considered reckless, and if caught, the captain was subject to a fine. For the packet captain, speed was the primary goal. By being the fastest, he could attract more passengers and thus greater revenues. This effort for speed caused captains to be quite inconsiderate of other boats on the canal.

Once on board, passengers could sit on top of the packet and breathe fresh air or go below to the cabin, where blue cigar smoke hung heavy in the air. Hazards awaited in either case. For those sitting on the roof alertness was a necessity. Frequent low bridges were encountered along the way. A popular folk song of the day was "Low Bridge, Everybody Down." Passengers found it necessary to prostrate themselves on the deck whenever the cry went up that a bridge was coming. Those who went below—especially at night—faced significant challenges. The cabin was transformed into a crowded sleeping room. Women slept to the front and men to the rear. "The bunks were arranged so that three or four men might sleep on top the other, and sleep or suffer through the night from the nearness of the neighbors in bunks above and below. But 'bunks' might be too grand a word—they were nothing but wooden frames with canvas tacked to them. These were attached to the hull on one side and suspended from overhead on the other side by chains or ropes. When a rope broke or the canvas ripped, a special form of comedy ensued." A German traveler named Frederick Gerstaecker immortalized himself by writing about how it felt to be a "ripped-canvas" victim:

> I awoke with a dreadful feeling of suffocation; cold perspiration stood on my forehead, and I could hardly draw any breath; there was a weight like lead on my stomach and chest. I attempted to cry out—in vain; I lay almost without consciousness. The weight remained immovable; above me

Erie Canal, Rochester, New York (circa 1900)

was a noise like distant thunder. It was my companion of the upper story, who lay snoring over my head; and that the weight which pressed on my chest was caused by his body no longer remained a doubtful point. I endeavored to move the Colossus—impossible. I tried to push, to cry out—in vain. He lay like a rock on my chest and seemed to have no more feeling.

"When Gerstaecker finally resorted to the ultimate solution and jabbed his cravat pin into the interloper's backside, that individual instantly came alive, yelling 'Help! Murder!' and leaping high enough for Gerstaecker to slide out from beneath him. Only then, in

the dim light of the cabin, was the German able to see the ripped ruins of the bunk above and to understand what had happened."[2]

The Whites and Joseph Bates doubtless faced similar challenges. They were particularly vexed by the continual presence of tobacco smoke and the brown slurry of pouch tobacco. Still, the canal was a vast improvement over the dusty and bumpy stagecoach.

After the 1848 Sabbath Conference held in Port Gibson at Hiram Edson's home, James and Ellen White, together with Joseph Bates, traveled back across New York via the canal. On Wednesday, August 30, 1848, the group left Hiram Edson's home intending to reach New York City by Sabbath. Ellen White wrote,

> We were too late for the packet, so we took a line boat, designing to change when the next packet came along. As we saw the packet approaching, we commenced making preparations to step aboard. . . . Bro. Bates was holding the money in his hand, saying to the men on the line boat, 'Here, take your pay.' As he saw the boat moving off he sprang to get aboard, but his foot struck the edge of the boat, and he fell back into the water. Bro. Bates commenced swimming to the boat. His pocket-book was in one hand, and a dollar bill in the other. His hat came off, and in saving it lost the bill, but held

Packet boat typical of the Erie Canal

"Our Home on the Hillside" Sanitarium, Dansville, New York (about 1865)

fast his pocket-book. The packet halted for him to get aboard. We were near Centerport, and called at Bro. Harris' to put Bro. Bates' clothes in order. Our visit proved a benefit to that family.[3]

America and Adventism Along the Way Through New York

The New York State Thruway (Interstate 90) follows roughly the path of the Erie Canal. Occasionally one can see some parts of the canal from the road. As one travels from Rochester going east, Dansville is located to the south. It is where Dr. James C. Jackson operated his sanitarium. James and Ellen White and other Adventists had been patients in the years before the 1866 Health Reform Institute was established in Battle Creek. Also to the south of the canal and interstate is the town of Canandaigua, where Dr. Franklin B. Hahn (1809-1866) lived and where O.R.L. Crosier edited the *Day-Dawn* between 1845 and 1847. Canandaigua is situated at the north end of one of the finger lakes, which extend north to south through much of central New York.

In the same region, but to the north of Canandaigua, is Port Gibson and the farm of Hiram Edson (see the

chapter on Port Gibson, New York). About three miles from Hiram Edson's farm in a direct line is Hill Cumorah, and not far from there is the site of Joseph Smith's boyhood home. In Palmyra is a well-restored printshop that is operated as an evangelistic ministry site of the Mormon Church. It was in this shop that the *Book of Mormon* was first printed in 1830.

Franklin B. Hahn grave, West Avenue Cemetery, Canandaigua, New York (located on the north side of West Avenue)

James C. Jackson (1811-1895)

One more interesting site in west-central New York is the home of the Fox sisters. In 1847 John and Margaret Fox and two of their daughters, Margaret (1833-1893) and Kate (1836-1892), settled in Hydesville. The original home is gone, but one can still see a monument and building covering the original foundation of the home. In the spring of 1848 the girls reported mysterious rappings in their bedrooms. They eventually held séances, and their activities led to the formation of Spiritualist organizations.

East of Syracuse is Oneida, an area where John Humphrey Noyes in 1848 established his free-love utopian society. His community believed that the millennial kingdom had arrived and that complex marriage was to be practiced by men and women in the community. The communal society had strict rules of conduct that included male continence.

A few miles east and north of Oneida is the town of Verona, where Rachel Oaks lived. She was the Seventh Day Baptist widow who traveled to Washington, New Hampshire, and presented the Sabbath to the Adventist congregation there.

About 20 to 25 miles north of Albany are the towns of Ballston Spa and Saratoga Springs, where the *Review and Herald* was published during 1851 and 1852.

Many other interesting sites could be mentioned in New York. For a time in the early 1850s this state contained the largest number of Sabbatarian Adven-

tists. Western New York has been aptly described as the "burned-over district" because it had so many new and unique reform movements during the first half of the nineteenth century.[4] Seventh-day Adventists have long observed that Satan often presents counterfeits to obscure or confuse the true working of God's Spirit. Around the time of William Miller and the rise of Sabbatarian Adventism, there were many other groups vying for people's attention. Most of the groups have disappeared, becoming mere historical curiosities. Today the Church of Jesus Christ of Latter-Day Saints and the various spiritualistic organizations exist as theological polarities or counterpoints to the Seventh-day Adventist Church.

Notes

[1] George T. Ferris, ed., *Our Native Land: or, Glances at American Scenery and Places With Sketches of Life and Character* (New York: D. Appleton, 1889), pp. 608, 609. Appendix contains census compilations for the United States between 1790 and 1880.

[2] Russell Bourne, *Floating America West: The Erie and Other American Canals* (New York: W. W. Norton & Co., 1992), p. 167.

[3] Ellen G. White, *Spiritual Gifts*, vol. 2, pp. 99, 100.

[4] Whitney R. Cross, *The Burned-over District: The Social and Intellectual History of Enthusiastic Religion in Western New York, 1800-1850* (New York: Harper & Row, 1965).

Three mule rigs used on the Erie Canal

Courtesy of Jim Howe and the Adventist Heritage Ministry 2007

Aerial view of William Miller home, chapel, and Ascension Rock in Low Hampton, New York

Low Hampton, New York

William Miller Farm

The Miller farm and chapel is a place of spiritual renewal and commitment for many Adventists and a place of historical interest for many others. Located in Low Hampton, New York, it is just across the border from Vermont. As one crosses the bridge from Vermont into New York on Highway 4 there is a road immediately to the right. A little more than a half mile up the road you come to the cemetery where William Miller is buried. His gravestone is in the center of the cemetery, a bit to the left from the entrance. The stone is nearly six feet tall with a scroll-type design on the top. Continuing on the road to the T, you will see a home and land on the southwest side of the road. This is the site of William Miller's parents' homestead. His mother lived there during the years Miller was a farmer in Low Hampton. Continuing from the T to the left, you come to the Miller home and then the chapel on the left. The home was purchased by Adventist Heritage Ministries in 1984 and is partially restored. Various outbuildings, including a large barn, are on the property. William Miller built the chapel in 1848. It is owned by the Advent Christian Church, but is jointly operated with Seventh-day Adventists. There is no regular congregation meeting

there; rather the chapel serves as a historical and spiritual monument to the Advent faith. Between the home and the chapel is "Ascension Rock," overlooking the valley. It is composed of a form of gray limestone that is marked by glacial striations. As you walk the path from the chapel to the Miller home, you pass Ascension Rock and come to the grove of maple trees where Miller wrestled with God before accepting the call to become an Advent preacher. As you continue down the decline, the home and other buildings come into view.

When you visit the Miller home, be sure to look at the interesting exhibits. There are several original pieces of furniture and other artifacts that belonged to William Miller. The bed and a few chairs are original, as are two paintings—one of William (in the bedroom) and the other of Lucy (in the parlor). An original 1843 prophetic chart also hangs in Miller's bedroom. The furniture in the parlor belonged to William Miller's daughter Lucy Bartholomew. In the exhibit area, be sure to see the small oval painting on ivory of William Miller, with a lock of his auburn hair. This image was probably made about the time Miller entered military service. There are several other original items that have been donated by descendants of William Miller.

William Miller farm
GPS: N 43°59.484' W 073°31.093'

William Miller home, 1614 County Route 11, Whitehall (Low Hampton), New York

William Miller's Life and Faith[1]

William Miller was born on February 15, 1782, in Pittsfield, Massachusetts, the eldest of 16 children. His father, Captain William Miller, was an officer in the Revolutionary War. His mother, Paulina, was the daughter of Elnathan Phelps, a Baptist minister.[2] In 1786 the family moved to Low Hampton, New York, where "our" William was reared.

Though Miller's education was typical for his day, he had an unusual passion to learn. His mother taught him to read using the family's only books—the Bible, a Psalter, and an old hymnbook. In addition, each year from the age of 9 to 14 he attended school for about three months. By borrowing books from neighbors and reading by firelight at night, Miller was able to expand his knowledge further.[3] Miller's father, anxious that he not overtax himself and thus become less helpful in working the family farm, forbade his son to study so late at night. A perusal of Miller's diary from 1798 to 1803 reveals that he did in fact keep busy planting, tending, and harvesting.[4] But in spite of the pressure of earning a living, Miller developed a talent for prose and poetry and distinguished himself by writing "verse"

for hand-decorated cards. He was jokingly dubbed the "scribbler-general."[5]

After his marriage to Lucy P. Smith on June 29, 1803, the couple settled in Lucy's hometown of Poultney, Vermont. Lucy's parents, Ebenezer Smith and Lucy Stearns, had come to Poultney from Canaan, Connecticut, about 1785. They were among the earliest settlers.[6] Lucy understood her husband's passion for learning and supported his use of the Poultney library.[7] Together they had 10 children, of whom eight survived—six sons and two daughters.[8]

Miller's life in Poultney, compared with his later years in Low Hampton, was a spiritual wilderness. Confused by what he considered a blind, unreasonable Christian faith, Miller turned to deism. Many of the community leaders in Poultney were deists. He remained a deist from about 1804 until 1816. During his agnostic years, as he socialized with his "infidel" friends, he would sometimes mimic the mannerisms of preachers he had seen. Little did he know that one day he would himself be the subject of derision and mockery by many throughout New England.

Miller's talent as a writer of patriotic verse brought him popularity in Poultney and the surrounding region. By 1809 he was appointed a constable and subsequently served as a sheriff and justice of the peace. Except during his time in military service, he continued in these capacities until 1834.[9]

In 1810 Miller was commissioned as a lieutenant in the Vermont state militia. Two years later, at the commencement of the war with Great Britain, he received a captain's commission in the volunteer militia. In due course he was transferred to the regular army of the United States as a lieutenant, and, after gathering recruits in Rutland, Vermont, was elevated to the rank of captain. In 1814 he and his soldiers were at Plattsburgh, New York, beside Lake Champlain. During the first 11 days of September they participated in the decisive engagement with the British that helped bring the war to an end. The Battle of Plattsburgh itself lasted only a few hours on September 11, 1814.[10]

In 1815 Miller established his comfortable home and farm in Low Hampton. It became his Bethel. Here he became a Christian and Bible student. It was in Low Hampton that he discovered the prophecies on the second coming of Jesus and began to share his views. It was from here that began a revival and preaching ministry that dramatically impacted New England.

William Miller was ripe for conversion in 1815. Fresh from the battlefield, he questioned whether deism could provide answers to life's deepest questions. The realization "that deism was inseparably connected with, and did tend to, the denial of a future existence" led him to choose "the heaven and hell of the Scriptures."[11] The second anniversary of the Battle of Plattsburgh in September 1816 was an exciting time. But the celebrations in nearby Fair Haven were tempered by the spiritual influence of a sermon heard by Miller and his friends.

Miller's home was located on the road between his mother's home to the east and the Baptist meetinghouse to the west. Miller regularly attended the Baptist services. His mother, Paulina, observed that when the local deacon read the sermon, William was not present. She therefore arranged for him to read the sermon in the absence of the preacher. On one occasion soon after the anniversary festivities, Miller was so affected by Alexander Proudfit's sermon on parental duties that he ended his reading before he could finish.

With eloquent words he later described his state of mind:

"Annihilation was a cold and chilling thought, and accountability was sure destruction to all. The heavens were as brass over

Painting on ivory miniature thought to be of William Miller, with a lock of his auburn hair (circa 1812)

William Miller

Courtesy of James R. Nix

my head, and the earth as iron under my feet. *Eternity!—what was it? And death—why was it?* The more I reasoned, the further I was from demonstration. The more I thought, the more scattered were my conclusions. I tried to stop thinking, but my thoughts would not be controlled. I was truly wretched, but did not understand *the cause.* I murmured and complained, but knew not of whom. I knew that there was a wrong, but knew not how or where to find the right. I mourned, but without hope."[12]

During this time of spiritual struggle "the character of a Savior was vividly impressed" upon his mind.[13] He began to study the Bible and was surprised by the relevance of the plan of salvation. It provided the perfect answer to human need. He wrote of his conversion thus:

I saw that the Bible did bring to view just such a Savior as I needed; and I was perplexed to find how an uninspired book should develop principles so perfectly adapted to the wants of a fallen world. I was constrained to admit that the Scriptures must be a revelation from God. They became my

delight; and in Jesus I found a friend. The Savior became to me the chiefest among ten thousand. . . . The Bible now became my chief study, and I can truly say, I searched it with great delight.[14]

Two foundations of the Millerite movement were rooted in Miller's own conversion. They were the *Bible as a revelation from God* and *Jesus as Savior and Friend.* This was the foundation that made the second coming of Jesus so precious. The veracity of the Bible made it a certainty, and the loving Savior made it the "blessed hope."

For the next two years William Miller carefully studied the Bible using only his Cruden's concordance to determine if the Bible was internally consistent and whether it provided reasonable answers to deistic criticisms. During these years, based on his study of the prophecies of Daniel, Miller came "to the solemn conclusion, that in about twenty-five years from that time all the affairs of our present state would be wound up."[15] Around 1832 Miller began to share his views with his friends and associates. His ability to organize ideas and express them eloquently, together with his position as a respected public servant and war veteran, opened opportunities. Members of the clergy and community leaders were the recipients of his correspondence. His passion and eloquence are demonstrated in correspondence with a Baptist minister: "Where your hearers are not well indoctrinated, you must preach *Bible*; you must prove all things by *Bible*; you must talk *Bible*; you must exhort *Bible*; you must pray *Bible*, and love *Bible*; and do all in your power to make others love *Bible*, too."[16] Writing again to the same minister about the second coming of Jesus, he wrote powerfully:

Behold, the heavens grow black with clouds; the sun has veiled himself; the moon, pale and forsaken, hangs in middle air; the hail descends; the seven thunders utter loud their voices; the lightnings send their vivid gleams of sulphurous flame abroad; and the great city of the nations falls to rise no more forever and forever! At this dread moment, look! look!—O, look and see! What means that ray of light? The clouds have burst asunder; the heavens appear; the great white throne is in sight! Amazement fills the universe with awe! He comes!—he comes! Behold, the Savior comes! Lift up your heads, ye saints—he comes! he comes!—he comes![17]

It is unclear just when Miller began his public speaking career. Bliss's *Memoirs* states that it was in

Early sketch of William Miller's home

Courtesy of the Center for Adventist Research

1831.[18] Yet in separate recollections, Miller clearly remembered first speaking in public on the prophecies "in the year 1832."[19] In 1845 he recollected that during the summer of 1833 he had a remarkable experience. The first Saturday morning in August, he promised the Lord that if he received an invitation to speak, he would consider it a sign that he should begin a preaching career. To his amazement and chagrin, within a half hour his nephew Irving Guilford arrived from Dresden, New York, with the invitation to speak on Sunday.[20] Miller left Irving at the door and went into the maple grove, where he wrestled with God until he found peace. His daughter Lucy remembered observing the gestures of intensity by her father during his time in the grove. Miller was still a farmer in his own thinking when he went into the grove, but he came out a preacher.

A brief overview of Miller's public work can be summarized as follows. He worked for a number of years on a personal level to convince people of his views. Then in May 1832 he wrote a series of 16 articles for the *Vermont Telegraph* and gave several lectures during the early part of 1832.[21] After his experience in the maple grove during the summer of 1833, he decided to lay aside his secular pursuits and become a full-time minister of the gospel. On September 14, 1833, Miller received a license to preach from the Baptist church where he was a member.[22] An examination of Miller's justice of the peace records shows that he continued his work as a justice until the summer of 1833, then did little until a final brief session in February 1834.[23] By 1836 he was carrying a certificate with the signatures of between 70 and 80 ministers who supported his preaching.[24] In the same year his 16-lecture series was published by Isaac Westcott in Troy, New York, titled *Evidence From Scirpture* [*sic*] *and History of the Second Coming of Christ About the Year 1843: Exhibited in a Course of Lectures*.[25]

During 1838 and 1839 Miller's influence continued to expand, though his impact on New England remained modest. In March 1838 Charles Fitch, a prominent abolitionist and holiness preacher, accepted Miller's views after reading *Evidence From Scripture*. Then Josiah Litch, a well-known Methodist minister, accepted Miller's prophetic chronology and immediately began to publish the message.[26] Miller made his most important convert, Joshua V. Himes, in November 1839 at Exeter, New Hampshire. As pastor of the Chardon Street Christian chapel in Boston, Massachusetts, Himes was an active temperance reformer and abolitionist.

By March 1840 Himes began publication of the *Signs of the Times*, later called the *Advent Herald*.

Lucy Miller, wife of William Miller

Courtesy of James R. Nix

With his considerable skills as a publicist, the movement rapidly gained momentum. During the year and a half from October 1839 to April 1841 Miller traveled more than 4,500 miles and gave 627 lectures in dozens of churches throughout the Northeast and Quebec.[27] "Infidels, Deists, Universalists and sectarians were all chained to their seats, in perfect silence, for hours—yes, days—to hear the old stammering man talk about the second coming of Christ."[28] A correspondent of Miller's remarked that he had "never witnessed so powerful an effect in any place, as in this, on all who heard." He believed that at least "one hundred persons, who held infidel sentiments," were brought to "believe the Bible."[29] In place after place where Miller preached, people were either converted or "quickened" to new spiritual life.

By the summer of 1842, however, public sentiment turned aggressively against Miller. The negative reaction, combined with the ever-larger crowds of interested hearers, led to open meetings in tents more than town meetings in churches. It was at a campground in East Kingston, New Hampshire, in early July 1842 that the decision was made to purchase a large tent that seated more than 3,000 people. By August the tent was in use, with capacity crowds in attendance.[30]

With the dawn of 1843 attention was focused on the time of the Second Advent. Miller's conflict with ministers and the public press became sharp and frequent. Because some were saying that Miller believed Jesus would come in April 1843, he decided to quell the agitation by giving a range of time rather than a specific month.[31] He wrote to Himes on February 4, 1844, "Jesus Christ will come again to this earth, cleanse, purify, and take possession of the same, with all his saints, some time between March 21, 1843, and March 21, 1844. I have never, for the space of more than twenty-three years, had *any other time preached or published by me*; I have never fixed on any month, day, or hour, during that period."[32] He, with other Adventists, was disappointed when Jesus did not come in the spring of 1844.

While Miller accepted the October 22, 1844, date, he did not lead out in its promotion. On that day only a few were gathered at Miller's home. Though some perhaps went out to Ascension Rock as they waited, it was not a dramatic gathering. Bliss observed that the October date was the "*only* specific *day* which was regarded by intelligent Adventists with any positiveness."[33]

After the spring and fall 1844 disappointments, Miller and most other active Adventists kept their faith in the soon coming of Jesus. A scribbled note in the Advent Christian library at Gordon-Conwell Theological Seminary in Hamilton, Massachusetts, attributed to the spring 1844 expectation expresses his feelings clearly:

How tedious and lonesome the hours
*   while Jesus, my Savior, delays.*
I have sought him in solitude's bowers
*   and looked for him all the long days.*
Yet he lingers—I pray tell me why
*   His chariot no sooner returns?*
To see him in clouds of the sky,
*   my soul with intensity burns.*
I long to be with him at home,
*   my heart swallowed up in his love.*
On the fields of new Eden to roam,
*   and dwell with my Savior above.*

After his disappointments Miller set a new time for the second coming of Jesus. He wrote: "I have fixed my mind on another time, and here I mean to stand until God gives me more light, and that is, *to-day*, *to-day*, and *to-day*, until he comes."[34]

As Miller's health declined after 1844, he preached on a more limited basis. By January 1848 his eyesight had dimmed so much that he was not able to read or write. Even with this disability he continued an infrequent correspondence with the help of his son and others.[35] During 1848 Miller arranged for the construction of a simple chapel near the rock protrusion to the west of his home, as he and other Adventists were no longer welcome in the local Baptist church.

Toward the end of his life a visitor described him as "much swollen by dropsy," or edema.[36] Yet until the last, his mind remained clear. His final exhortation was: "Tell them (the brethren) we are right. The coming of the Lord draweth nigh; but they must be patient, and wait for him."[37] Miller died on Thursday, December 20, 1849, and was buried near his home in the Low Hampton Cemetery. A memorial service was held at the Congregational church in Fair Haven.[38] His gravestone appropriately contains quotations from Daniel 8:14, 7:12, and 12:13. The last text reads: "But go thou thy way till the end be, for thou shalt rest, and stand in thy lot at the end of the days."

Though William Miller never accepted distinctive Seventh-day Adventist doctrines such as the Sabbath, conditional immortality, or the heavenly sanctuary explanation for the 1844 disappointment, Ellen White wrote positively of his faith. She observed that "angels watch the precious dust of this servant of God, and he will come forth at the sound of the last trump."[39]

The Millerite movement impacted a large number of Americans. It has been estimated by historians that as many as 200,000 accepted Miller's views, with 1 million or more brought under the influence of the movement.[40] Miller placed the number of true believers at "some fifty thousand" in about 1,000 different locations.[41] In 1845 he knew of about 200 ministers in the United States and Canada who taught his views, with perhaps a total of 500 "public lecturers" on prophecy.[42] He also reported that he had given some 4,500 lectures over 12 years to about 500,000 individuals.[43] He numbered his personal converts at some 6,000, of which about 700 were former "infidels."[44] These numbers are significant considering that in 1840 the total population (free and slave) of the United States stood at a little more than 17 million. Since Miller was a northerner, where abolitionist sentiment was strong, the real population base of his labors was closer to 10 million.[45] Thus he spoke to perhaps one in 20 in the northeastern United States. When the other Millerite ministers and lecturers are added to the equation, it is easy to understand how dramatically the movement impacted America.

Miller was led by God to establish a movement of prophecy that prepared the way for a worldwide church that today numbers in the many millions. Seventh-day

Low Hampton Cemetery

Lucy Miller

William Miller

Adventists still cherish a hope in the soon coming of Jesus. Though never setting upon a day, they understand that Bible prophecy reveals that these are the last days, and that Jesus is soon to come. "Lift up the trumpet, and loud let it ring: Jesus is coming again!"

Notes

1 Much of this sketch is drawn from Merlin D. Burt's "Historical Introduction to Sylvester Bliss," in *Memoirs of William Miller*, Adventist Classic Library (Berrien Springs, Mich: Andrews University Press, 2005), pp. vii-xv.

2 Sylvester Bliss, *Memoirs of William Miller, Generally Known as a Lecturer on the Prophecies, and the Second Coming of Christ* (Boston: Joshua V. Himes, 1853), p. 4.

3 Joshua V. Himes, *Views of the Prophecies and Prophetic Chronology, Selected From Manuscripts of William Miller; With a Memoir of His Life* (Boston: Moses A. Dow, 1841), p. 7.

4 William Miller diary, 1798-1803, Vermont Historical Society, Barre, Vermont.

5 Bliss, p. 16.

6 H. Buckley, "Obituary," *Advent Herald*, July 22, 1854, p. 231.

7 Bliss, p. 19.

8 Lucy Bartholomew Bible and Miller Family Bible, Hazel Stannard, Fairhaven, Vermont; H. Buckley, "Obituary," *Advent Herald*, July 22, 1854, p. 231.

9 William Miller, Justice of the Peace Records (Silver Spring, Md.: Ellen G. White Estate).

10 Bliss, pp. 52, 53.

11 *Ibid.*, p. 55.

12 In Bliss, p. 65.

13 William Miller, *Apology and Defence* (Boston: Joshua V. Himes, 1845), p. 5.

14 Bliss, p. 67.

15 *Ibid.*, p. 76.

16 *Ibid.*, p. 101.

17 *Ibid.*, p. 102.

18 *Ibid.*, p. 98.

19 *Ibid.*, p. 254; Himes, *Views of the Prophecies*, p. 12; William Miller, "Letter From Mr. Miller—No. 1," *Signs of the Times*, Mar. 20, 1840, p. 8.

20 Miller, *Apology and Defence*, pp. 17, 18. Those who argue for the 1831 date (Bliss, Nichol, Maxwell), correctly observe that Miller did not mention his experience in the maple grove in a letter written on August 9, 1831, to Hendryx. They thus conclude that Miller's experience happened on the second Sabbath in August 1831. This tour book suggests that an 1833 date is more consistent with the primary sources. Miller could then be correct that his experience happened the first weekend of 1833.

21 David Rowe has correctly observed that Miller wrote on March 27, 1832, to Joseph and Anna Atwood, that he had "lectured on it [1843] in a number of places this winter." See David L. Rowe, *God's Strange Work: William Miller and the End of the World* (Grand Rapids: William B. Eerdmans, 2008), pp. 98, 99.

22 Bliss, p. 108.

Ascension Rock near William Miller's home

Katy Wolfer 2009

[23] Miller, *Justice of the Peace Records*.

[24] Bliss, pp. 121, 122; Miller, *Apology and Defence*, 19, 20.

[25] William Miller, *Evidence From Scripture and History of the Second Coming of Christ About the Year 1843: Exhibited in a Course of Lectures* (Troy, N.Y.: Kemble & Hooper, 1836), p. 2.

[26] Josiah Litch, *The Probability of the Second Coming of Christ About A.D. 1843* (Boston: David H. Ela, 1838).

[27] Bliss, p. 157.

[28] *Ibid.,* p. 125.

[29] *Ibid.,* p. 127.

[30] [A. Hale], "Concord Second Advent Meeting," *Signs of the Times*, Aug. 17, 1842, p. 157; Francis D. Nichol, *The Midnight Cry: A Defense of William Miller and the Millerites* (Washington, D.C.: Review and Herald, 1944), pp. 114-125.

[31] William Miller, "Synopsis of Miller's Views," *Signs of the Times*, Jan. 25, 1843, pp. 147.

[32] Bliss, pp. 180, 181.

[33] *Ibid.,* p. 276.

[34] *Ibid.,* p. 278.

[35] *Ibid.,* p. 366

[36] *Ibid.,* p. 375.

[37] J. V. Himes, "Visit to Father Miller," *Advent Herald*, Dec. 29, 1849, p. 176.

[38] J.V. Himes, "Funeral of Father Miller," *Advent Herald*, Jan. 5, 1850, p. 184.

[39] Ellen G. White, *Early Writings*, p. 258.

[40] George R. Knight, *Millennial Fever and the End of the World* (Boise, Idaho: Pacific Press, 1993), p. 213; Whitney R. Cross, *The Burned-over District,* p. 287.

[41] Miller, *Apology and Defence*, p. 22.

[42] *Ibid.*

[43] William Miller, "Address to Second Advent Believers," *Signs of the Times*, Jan. 31, 1844, p. 196.

[44] Miller, *Apology and Defence*, p. 23.

[45] John Marshall, *Brookes's Universal Gazetteer, Re-modelled and Brought Down to the Present Time* (Philadelphia: E. H. Butler, 1843), p. lvii (United States Census statistics).

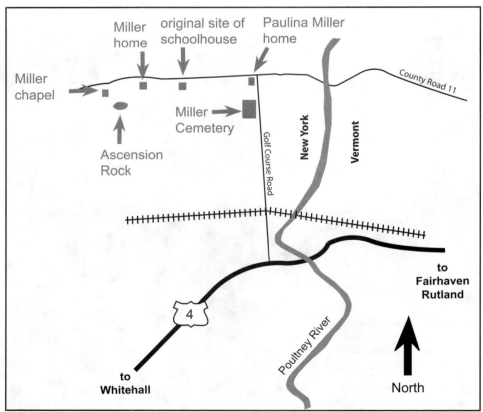

William Miller sites, Low Hampton, New York

On the sign:

WILLIAM MILLER CHAPEL

BUILT IN 1848 BY ADVENTIST
FOUNDER WILLIAM MILLER.
THIS CHAPEL WAS PLACED ON
NATIONAL REGISTER, CA. 1975

BY W.C.H.S. 2000

William Miller chapel, Low Hampton, New York

Hiram Edson farm
GPS: N 43°00.028' W 077°08.511'

Luther Edson's restored barn, relocated at Hiram Edson farm, 780 Field Street, Clifton Springs (Port Gibson), New York

Port Gibson, New York

Theological Birthplace of the Seventh-day Adventist Church

The Hiram Edson farm in Port Gibson, New York, is rightly called the theological birthplace of the Seventh-day Adventist Church. It was in Port Gibson that the Sabbath and sanctuary doctrines came together in 1846. This farm is also one of the places where O.R.L. Crosier studied and received spiritual and relational support as he was writing material on the sanctuary. After the October 1844 disappointment Edson had an experience of enlightenment that pointed his and Crosier's eyes to the heavenly sanctuary ministry of Jesus as the answer to the disappointment.

On January 26, 1989, Adventist Heritage Ministry purchased 17.5 acres of the Hiram Edson farm. The exact location of Edson's barn is not known. Though the original house and barn were gone, a similar vintage barn belonging to Edson's father, Luther Edson, was reconstructed and restored on the site. The barn was dedicated on October 23, 1994. On August 21, 2010, a newly constructed visitor center with caretaker quarters was dedicated.

Port Gibson was an Erie Canal station and thus was a part of the great westward expansion in America during the first half of the nineteenth century. It was in western and central New York that several American religious movements found their origin. Only a couple of miles west of Edson's farm are Hill Cumorah, Joseph Smith's boyhood homes, and the birthplace of the Mormon faith.

The Edson farm is where Hiram Edson and his family, along with some other friends, experienced disappointment in October 1844. It is the place where, passing through a cornfield, Edson had an insight that encouraged his faith. He realized that the heavenly sanctuary and the high-priestly ministry of Jesus held the key to their disappointment. O.R.L. Crosier, a schoolteacher and Millerite minister, and Dr. Franklin B. Hahn, a prominent physician from nearby Canandaigua, New York, cooperated together to develop the idea further.

In March 1845 Crosier wrote and Hahn published the first issue of the *Day-Dawn,* which suggested an extended atonement by Jesus in the Most Holy Place of the heavenly sanctuary. This explained the delay of Jesus' coming after October 1844, and preserved the prophetic historicist framework of Daniel 8 and 9. The conclusion of the 2300 days on October 22, 1844, became a baseline marker for the investigative judgment. The judgment determines the identity of the redeemed of the ages and closes human probation.

It was at Port Gibson on Edson's farm that Joseph Bates shared the seventh-day Sabbath truth in the late fall of 1846. As Bates was reading his tract, Edson jumped to his feet and exclaimed: "Brother Bates, this is light and truth! The seventh day is the Sabbath, and I am with you to keep it!"[1] Hahn and Crosier also accepted the Sabbath, and the initial linking of those in western New York presenting the sanctuary and those in New England teaching the Sabbath was accomplished.

It is not entirely clear where Bates connected the Sabbath to the heavenly sanctuary, but immediately after his trip to western New York and the Edson farm he published a second edition to his Sabbath tract, *The Seventh Day Sabbath: A Perpetual Sign*. The first edition of this tract, published in August 1846, had convinced the newlyweds James and Ellen White to become Sabbathkeepers. It contained solid biblical arguments for the perpetuity of the Sabbath based on Creation and the Ten Commandments. The second edition, published in January 1847, added a critical component that gave the Sabbath end-time eschatologi-

Owen Russell Loomis Crosier (1820-1913)

Photo found in *The Founders of the Seventh day Adventist Denomination*, by Richard Conradi (1939)

cal importance. Bates pointed to Revelation 11:19 and the seventh trumpet, which read:

> And the temple of God was opened in heaven, and there was seen in his temple the ark of his testament: and there were light-

Cornfield by Hiram Edson's farm

Ken Olin 2005

nings, and voices, and thunderings, and an earthquake, and great hail.

Bates and other early Sabbatarian Adventists came to understand that Jesus was ministering in the Most Holy Place of the heavenly sanctuary before the ark of the covenant, which contained the Ten Commandments. The fourth commandment is the only one that identifies God as the Creator and requires rest from human endeavor. It links obedience and grace, law and gospel, and provides an end-time framework for the proclamation of the everlasting gospel as described in the three angels' messages, of Revelation 14:6-12. For Joseph Bates and James and Ellen White the Sabbath was "present truth" and the bridge to receiving the seal of God. It became integral to the conclusion of human probation. The Holy Spirit's work of sealing the human heart is tied to the blessing of righteousness by faith, as demonstrated in the Sabbath.

This is the theological heart and core of Sabbatarian Adventist theology. It remains core to the mission of the Seventh-day Adventist Church. The integration of the Sabbath, righteousness by faith, and eschatology has driven Adventists' worldwide proclamation of the gospel.

Hiram Edson and the 1844 Disappointment

There is another practical message that encourages our faith as we think of Edson's simple farm. It answers the cry of our heart, "God, where are You?" and "When will You come?" Those were the key thoughts for disappointed Millerite Adventists on October 22 and 23, 1844. They had studied their Bibles, and Jesus had become their Savior and Friend. The prophecies of Daniel 2, 7, 8, and 9, but particularly Daniel 8:14 and the 2300 days, pointed to the Second Coming. It was not an abstract idea—it was a practical reality. Hiram Edson poignantly recalled their experience when Jesus did not come in 1844.

Our fondest hopes and expectations were blasted, and such a spirit of weeping came over us as I never experienced before. It seemed that the loss of all earthly friends could have been no comparison. We wept, and wept, till the day dawn.[2]

At that moment Edson had a crisis of faith. He wondered if everything he had believed was a lie. He wrote:

I mused in my own heart, saying, My advent experience has been the richest and brightest of all my Christian experience. If this had proved a failure, what was the rest of my Christian experience worth? Has the Bible proved a failure? Is there no God, no heavens, no golden home city, no paradise? Is all this but a cunningly devised fable? Is there no reality to our fondest hope and expectation of these things? And thus we had something to grieve and weep over, if all our fond hopes were lost. And as I said, we wept till the day dawn.[3]

At his dark moment he found the assurance of a living God who answers prayer. Here is how Edson described what happened next.

A second glance over past experience, and the lessons learned, and how when brought into strait places where light and help was needed by seeking the Lord He had answered by a voice and other ways, I began to feel there might be light and help for us in our present distress. I said to some of my brethren, "Let us go to the barn." We entered the granary, shut the doors about us and bowed before the Lord. We prayed earnestly; for we felt our necessity. We continued in earnest prayer until the witness of the Spirit was given that our prayer was accepted, and that light should be given, our disappointment be explained, and made clear and satisfactory.[4]

God is always with those who in sincerity and trust seek His presence and the answers to perplexity. With some measure of peace Edson and those with him went to have breakfast. Edson described what happened next:

After breakfast I said to one of my brethren, "Let us go and see, and encourage some of our [brethren]." We started, and while passing through a large field I was stopped about midway of the field. Heaven seemed open to my view, and I saw distinctly, and clearly, that instead of our High Priest coming out of the Most Holy of the heavenly sanctuary to come to this earth on the tenth day of the seventh month, at the end of the 2300 days, that He for the first time entered on that day the second apartment of that sanctuary; and that He had a work to perform in the Most Holy before coming to this earth.

Field near Hiram Edson's farm in Port Gibson, New York

Katy Wolfer 2008

no mention of Edson's experience by any other Adventist pioneer. It seems best to conclude that what happened for Edson was a personal answer to prayer. It inspired him and those with him, including O.R.L. Crosier, to study their Bibles again. This led to the publication of the idea of an end-time extended atonement by Jesus in the Most Holy Place of the heavenly sanctuary.[6]

Edson's experience is an assurance to us that God does answer prayer and that He can be trusted to keep His word. Though the Second Coming seems long delayed, God's plans and purposes have no delay. Like the first coming of Jesus, the certainty of the promise will be fulfilled, and the fulfillment of the prophecies of Daniel and Revelation in connection with 1844 is an encouraging marker that confirms that we are living just before the second coming of Jesus. Everything points to the fulfillment of the blessed hope. The history of the Advent movement; the fulfillment of prophecy; the proclamation of the gospel in all the world; the signs in the earth; and the global changes of human interactions and technology all tell us that Jesus is coming soon!

The 1848 Evangelistic Sabbath Conference

Edson's farm was the site of an early evangelistic Sabbath Conference. The 1848 Sabbath Conferences launched the Sabbatarian Adventist movement that became the Seventh-day Adventist Church. The meeting in Edson's barn occurred on Sunday and Monday, August 27 and 28, 1848. Ellen White described it in 1860:

> There were those present who loved the truth, and those who were listening to and cherishing error, and were opposed to the truth. But the Lord wrought for us in power before the close of that meeting. I was again shown in vision the importance of brethren in Western New York laying their differences aside, and uniting upon Bible truth.[7]

The 1848 Sabbath Conferences had a powerful effect in promoting the Sabbath. They gathered scattered Adventists into unity with the new theological framework of the Sabbath and the heavenly sanctuary. As the Whites and Bates returned to the east from New York they considered the Sabbath and the seal of God. Their study continued in Rocky Hill, Connecticut; Topsham, Maine; and Dorchester, Massachusetts, during September and October. This led to the publication of the *Present Truth,* beginning in 1849. Then in 1850 James White launched the *Review and Herald.* A movement

That He came to the marriage at that time; in other words, to the Ancient of days, to receive a kingdom, dominion, and glory; and we must wait for his return *from the wedding;* and my mind was directed to the tenth ch. of Rev. where I could see the vision had spoken and did not lie; the seventh angel had began [*sic*] to sound; we had eaten the littl [*sic*] book; it had been sweet in our mouth, and it had now become bitter in our belly, embittering our whole being. That we must prophesy again, etc., and that when the seventh angel began to sound, the temple of God was opened in heaven, and there was seen in his temple the ark of his testament, etc.[5]

For Edson this was the answer to his prayer that "light would be given." This recollection describes him having more understanding than was presented in either the first issue of the *Day-Dawn* of March 1845 or the *Day-Star* Extra of February 7, 1846. This type of redaction is understandable when someone looks back on his or her experience as Edson did in this manuscript fragment. The bottom line, though, for Edson was that there was a biblical explanation for the 1844 disappointment and it was linked to the work of Jesus in the heavenly sanctuary. Did Edson have a vision? It is not definitive from this description. It certainly was at least a particularly direct flash of insight. During the twentieth century Seventh-day Adventists gave more emphasis to the importance of Edson's experience than is probably warranted. Until the description of the manuscript by A. W. Spalding in the early twentieth century, there is was born that now encircles the globe and includes many millions of people. Edson sold his farm in 1850 and received the balance of a loan on the property in 1852. These resources assisted in the purchase of the Washington hand press used to publish the *Review and Herald* and Adventist publications in Rochester, New York.

Notes

[1] W. A. Spicer, *Pioneer Days of the Advent Movement,* p. 62.

[2] [Hiram Edson], manuscript fragment, autograph (Berrien Springs, Mich.: Center for Adventist Research, Andrews University), p. 8a.

[3] *Ibid.,* pp. 8a, 9.

[4] *Ibid.,* pp. 9, 9a.

[5] *Ibid.* pp. 9a, 10.

[6] See Merlin D. Burt, "The Historical Background, Interconnected Development, and Integration of the Doctrines of the Sanctuary, the Sabbath, and Ellen G. White's Role in Sabbatarian Adventism From 1844 to 1849," pp. 250-254; James R. Nix, "The Life and Work of Hiram Edson" (research paper, Andrews University, 1971).

[7] Ellen G. White, *Spiritual Gifts,* vol. 2, pp. 99.

Courtesy of Loma Linda University

Hiram Edson (1806-1882)

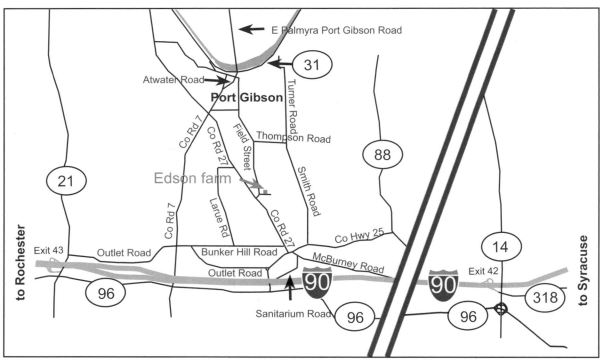

Hiram Edson farm, Port Gibson, New York

Andrews graves, Mount Hope Cemetery, Rochester, New York

Rochester, New York

Background

Rochester, along with Cincinnati, Ohio, was an important western Millerite Adventist center both before and after 1844. It was in this city that Joseph Marsh published the *Voice of Truth*, which in 1846 was renamed the *Advent Harbinger and Bible Advocate*. It was also the location of the first Sabbatarian Adventist printing press and headquarters of James and Ellen White for the incipient Seventh-day Adventist Church. The Whites lived here for three and a half years between 1852 and 1855. They gathered around them a group of generally competent helpers, including such individuals as George Amadon, Warren Bacheller, Stephen Belden, Annie Smith, Uriah Smith, Oswald Stowell, and Anna White.[1] Some continued with the Review and Herald office through most of their careers. They hired a non-Adventist who, as a skilled printer, could superintend the operation of the press. His name was Lumen V. Masten. He had previously been employed by Davison Printing Company, which had printed the *Review and Herald* in Saratoga Springs. Most of these people were in their teens or early 20s.

Rochester was the longtime home of J. N. Andrews and his family. When the Review and Herald office moved to Battle Creek in 1855, Andrews continued to live in Rochester. He found the university library and other research resources in Rochester, better than those in Battle Creek. Other Adventists, such as the Lamsons and Ortons, also remained in Rochester, and the town remained a place of influence within the Seventh-day Adventist Church through the 1860s.

In the early 1850s Rochester was still a new city. A city directory of 1844 stated: "Where now stands a mighty city, peopled by tens of thousands of inhabitants, thirty-three years ago was naught but primeval forests."[2] Flour production was the major industry during the early days of the city, with more than a score of mills. The waterfalls of the Genesee River provided much

Rochester, 1843

Rochester aqueduct, 1878

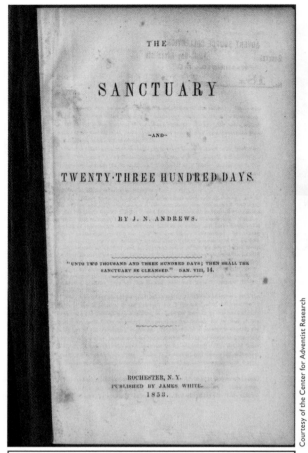

Original Washington hand press

124 Mount Hope Avenue, Rochester, New York, from an 1880 bird's-eye view

of the power for these operations. Vital to the growth of this city was the Erie Canal. An 800-foot limestone aqueduct built by masons was completed in 1842 after six years of labor. Seven 52-foot Roman-style arches and three piers, along with other structures, presented an imposing view to visitor or resident. The masonry

was particularly fine, with the joints having a space of only one sixteenth of an inch. The lower arches of the structure remain, though the present-day bridge is no longer an aqueduct.

The *Review and Herald* Moves From Eastern New York to the West

The *Advent Review and Sabbath Herald* began publication in Paris Hill, Maine, in November 1850. In August 1851 James White relocated to Saratoga Springs, New York, where volume 2 of the paper was job-printed by G. M. Davison. James White continued to publish the *Review and Herald* in Saratoga Springs until March 1852.

In the February 17, 1852, issue of the *Review and Herald*, James White wrote: "We think the time has come when a press should be owned by Sabbath-keepers. Now our work is being done on the Sabbath, which is very unpleasant and inconvenient. It also costs much more than it would if we had an office of our own."[3] On March 12, 1852, an important conference was held in the home of Jesse Thompson, two miles from Ballston Spa, New York.[4] At the conference it was decided to purchase a printing press and shift the publishing headquarters of the movement to Rochester, New York. Ballston Spa was an important town in Saratoga County, located six and a half miles southwest of Saratoga Springs. The towns were in proximity to the Hudson River and abounded in streams and springs. Roughly a score of springs were discovered in the region, and it was popularly believed that they had heal-ing properties. Various hotels were established, "some of them truly elegant." The establishment of a rail line from Albany made Saratoga Springs and the surrounding towns a popular tourist destination and a "summer resort of thousands."[5]

With generous donations from Hiram Edson and others, a Washington hand press was purchased, and the fledgling printing operation was established in Rochester. May 6, 1852, was an auspicious date. For the first time the *Review and Herald* was printed on an Adventist press operated by Sabbatarian Adventist workers. The printing operation continued in Rochester until October 30, 1855, when the press and headquarters were again relocated, this time to Battle Creek, Michigan.

J. N. Loughborough described the simple operation of the Review and Herald office during 1853. One book printed on the Washington hand press was an 80-page work by J. N. Andrews entitled *The Sanctuary*. "The office had no stitching or trimming machine. Elder White, anxious to send copies to all the brethren, called a 'bee' of the Rochester members, who folded the signatures for 100 books. I perforated them with a shoemaker's pegging awl, the sisters stitched them with needle and thread, Mary Patten put on the covers, and Uriah Smith trimmed them with his pocket knife and straight edge. Sister White wrapped them, and Elder White addressed them for the mail. We were a happy company together, for we were getting off the first book printed on a press owned by Seventh-day Adventists."[6]

John N. Loughborough (1832-1924)

James and Ellen White, 1857

James and Ellen White in Rochester

James and Ellen White lived in Rochester for just three and a half years (spring 1852 to autumn 1855). It was a time of financial, physical, and spiritual hardship. The Whites established the press in their home on 124

Courtesy of the Center for Adventist Research

Angeline (1824-1872) and John Andrews (1829-1883)

Mount Hope Avenue (renumbered to 491 Mount Hope). They were extremely poor. To "furnish" the home, they purchased two old bedsteads for 25 cents, six chairs for a dollar, and four more chairs that were without seating for 62 cents. They could not afford potatoes, so they ate turnips. Butter was expensive, so they used fruit sauce provided by an Advent believer. Besides the turnips and sauce, there was very limited and simple fare. Uriah Smith joined the Review and Herald in March 1853 and was provided only room and board. After Smith had been eating in the Whites' home for a few weeks, "he remarked to a comrade, that though he had no objection to eating beans 365 times in succession, yet when it came to making them a regular diet, he should protest!"[7]

Soon there were more than a dozen workers and others living with the Whites. By June 1853 the *Review and Herald* was being published semimonthly at South St. Paul Street, Stone's Block, No. 21, third floor. In August the publishing moved to room number 23 and remained at that location until the Review and Herald office removed to Michigan in the fall of 1855. At some point the Whites moved to 111 Monroe Street. The home next door at 109 Monroe Street was also used for Sabbath worship services and conferences. The Whites may have lived there for a time as well.[8]

After the Whites moved to Rochester, the *Review and Herald* had an increasing influence, and the message spread rapidly. It was the practice of James White and the publishing committee to print large numbers of each issue. About 2,000 copies were published and mailed to 1,600 homes. In August 1852 the *Youth's Instructor* began, with a circulation of about 1,000. This broad distribution had a significant evangelistic effect. The printing size of tracts ranged from 2,000 to 4,000.[9] This, though, led to even greater hardship for the Sabbatarian Adventist workers in Rochester, as subscription receipts did not keep pace with expenses. James White recollected, "The autumn of 1855 found me much reduced in strength, in consequence of incessant toil and care, editing, publishing, journeying and preaching. Very many gave me over to die of consumption. A change seemed necessary. Heavy debts were upon me, in consequence of printing large editions of our publications."[10]

Even with financial difficulties the movement expanded rapidly during the Rochester days. In 1853 the first regular Sabbath school classes were organized. The distribution of the *Review and Herald* and other publications greatly increased. "The *Review* alone," wrote James White, "with the blessing of God, has brought many to the keeping of the Sabbath."[11] A growing number of ministers spread the message. J. N. Andrews was an effective writer and speaker. J. H. Waggoner worked extensively in Wisconsin, and M. E. Cornell and others had success in Michigan. Joseph Bates was particularly blessed in doing Bible study work in various states and in Canada.[12] Of course, the work in New York also continued to expand. James White noted that during the summer of 1854 "tent meetings" were employed to gather larger audiences. First held in Battle Creek, Michigan, June 10 and 11, 1854, they were later conducted in several other states.[13]

Around August 1852 a cholera epidemic laid Rochester low and little 3-year-old Edson White was afflicted. Ellen took her son in her arms, prayed for him,

Nathaniel White
Anna White   Mary F. Andrews   Angeline S. Andrews   Carrie M. Andrews   Orton family

Mount Hope Cemetery, Rochester, New York
1133 Mount Hope Avenue
Rochester, New York

GPS coordinates:
N 43°07.773'
W 077°36.950'

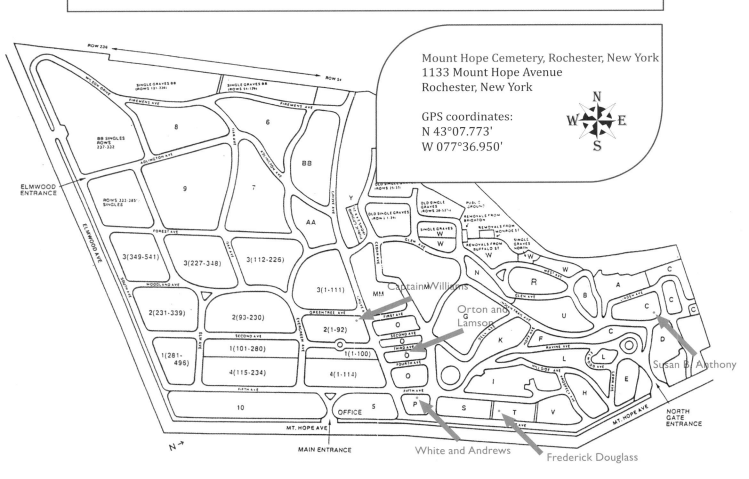

139

William Clarence White, 1857

Courtesy of the Ellen G. White Estate

and rebuked the disease, resulting in immediate relief. When another woman began to pray for his healing, the little boy looked up and said, "They need not pray any more, for the Lord has healed me." The same cholera epidemic afflicted the non-Adventist printer, Lumen V. Masten, who was expected to die. He recovered and through the process became a Christian and a Sabbatarian Adventist. Sadly, he died of tuberculosis about a year and a half later on March 1, 1854.[14]

Cholera was not the only affliction Adventists faced in Rochester. The Whites received news that Ellen's brother Robert was dying so they made an emergency visit to Gorham, Maine. Nathaniel and Anna White, siblings of James White, died in Rochester of tuberculosis. Additionally, Ellen White contracted a heart condition that led to a stroke. To their many financial and physical hardships were added the vicious attacks by the Messenger Party in Jackson, Michigan. The critics in Michigan fragmented soon after the Whites moved to Battle Creek, but while James and Ellen were in Rochester they remained a real challenge.

"Trials thickened around us," wrote Ellen White. "We had much care. The Office hands boarded with us, and our family numbered from fifteen to twenty. The large conference and the Sabbath meetings were held at our house. We had no quiet Sabbaths, for some of the sisters generally tarried all day with their children."[15] In summing up their experience at Rochester, she wrote: "From the time we moved to Battle Creek, the Lord began to turn our captivity. We found sympathizing friends in Michigan who were ready to share our burdens, and supply our wants."[16]

Besides the Lord's continued blessing in the expansion of the movement, the Whites experienced the joy of adding another little boy to their family on August

29, 1854. William Clarence, usually called "Willie," joined Henry and Edson as the Whites' third son.

Mount Hope Cemetery

Mount Hope Cemetery was considered a landmark even before James and Ellen White moved to Rochester. It currently contains 196 acres, with more than 14 miles of roads and paths. Two of James White's siblings are buried here. Nathaniel and Anna White may have brought "consumption," as tuberculosis was called in the nineteenth century, to the White home. Before he died on May 6, 1853, Nathaniel, who had been indifferent to religion, was won to Christ by the family worships. He accepted the Sabbath, but died soon after. Anna White, an accomplished organizer and writer, became editor of the *Youth's Instructor* and edited the first

Annie Smith, likely a self-portrait

Courtesy of the Ellen G. White Estate

Mary Frances Andrews (1861-1878)

Adventist hymnal for children. She died on November 30, 1854, and is buried beside her brother. It was not until 1980 that monuments were erected on their graves. This was made possible by the fund-raising efforts of the Rochester Seventh-day Adventist Church, the General Conference, and the White family. Annie Smith, sister of Uriah Smith, probably contracted tuberculosis from Nathaniel or Anna White. She returned to be with her mother in West Wilton, New Hampshire, where she died on July 28, 1855, and was buried.

Annie wrote a poem on the occasion of Nathaniel's death. Below are three of the five verses.

Gone to thy rest, brother! Peaceful thy sleep;
While o'er thy grave bending in sorrow we weep,
For the loved and the cherished, in life's early bloom,
Borne from our number to the cold, silent tomb.

Sweet be thy slumber! In quiet repose;
Beneath the green turf, and the blossoming rose;
O, soft is thy pillow, and lowly thy bed;
Mournful the cypress that waves o'er the dead.

Not long will earth's bosom his precious form hide,
And death's gloomy portals from kindred divide;
For swiftly approaching, we see the bright day,
That brings the glad summons, Arise! Come away!

J. N. Andrews' wife, Angeline, and their two daughters, Mary and Carrie, are buried next to Nathaniel and Anna White. J. N. Andrews is buried in Switzerland, and his son, Charles, is buried in Washington, D.C. Angeline Stevens was a sister to Harriet, Uriah Smith's

wife. Thus J. N. Andrews and Uriah Smith were brothers-in-law. John and Angeline had a very tender and loving relationship. It was a great trial for both of them to have John traveling so often. When Angeline died in 1872, John relocated from Rochester to North Lancaster, Massachusetts, so that he could continue work on a new edition of his *History of the Sabbath*. In September 1865, while John was traveling in New England, his daughter Carrie Matilda died of dysentery. He was not present for the funeral, which was conducted in the Andrews home on Main Street by Uriah Smith. At the time Uriah was in Dansville, New York, with the Whites, who were patients of Dr. James C. Jackson.

The story of Mary Frances Andrews is particularly touching. She contracted tuberculosis while in Europe. Her father brought her home to Battle Creek, where she was treated by Dr. J. H. Kellogg. There was nothing that could be done, and she passed away after a brief illness. The Center for Adventist Research has a very touching series of letters from J. N. Andrews, recorded by Charles, that were written while Mary was a patient at Battle Creek Sanitarium. She expressed a desire to recover and return to Europe and help her father. One day after a particularly difficult coughing spell, her grandmother said, "We must believe," to which Mary replied, "I do believe." Her last words were "Pray, father." Elder Andrews brought Mary back to Rochester for burial. She was tremendously talented, and her death was a great blow to Elder Andrews. The current marker was erected in 1986.

Another Adventist burial site in Mount Hope Cemetery attracts our attention. These are the graves of Jon-

Frederick Douglass (1818-1895)

Susan B. Anthony (1820-1906)

Two other graves in Mount Hope Cemetery are worth mentioning, though they are not directly related to Adventists. Just up the road from the White and Andrews graves is the burial place of Frederick Douglass, an escaped slave who became a renowned leader of the abolitionist movement. His famous newspaper, *The North Star,* was published in Rochester. Also buried in Mount Hope Cemetery is Susan B. Anthony. After Anthony was prohibited from speaking at a temperance rally in Albany in 1852 because of her gender, she spent the rest of her life seeking equality for women. She proposed the Nineteenth Amendment to the U.S. Constitution. Known as the Anthony Amendment, it gave voting rights to women and was finally adopted in 1920. In recent years a $1 coin was minted with her picture in honor of her contributions.

athan and Caroline Orton. Jonathan and Caroline were among those who earnestly prayed in December 1865 for James White's recovery. It was in the home of their daughter Drusilla and son-in-law J. Bradley Lamson that Ellen White had her Christmas Day 1865 vision that led to the first Seventh-day Adventist health institution that would eventually become world-famous as the Battle Creek Sanitarium. The Lamson farm was located near the northwestern edge of Rochester on Lake Avenue. The exact location of the Lamson home remains uncertain. After Bradley's death from typhoid fever in 1870, Drusilla lived near J. N. Andrews in Rochester and later worked at the Battle Creek, Michigan, and Clifton Springs, New York, sanitariums. She died in Rochester in 1919. Both Bradley and Drusilla are buried near the Ortons in Mount Hope Cemetery.

Jonathan Orton was a hackman and would often meet Adventist ministers who came through town and provide them a room in his home. In the early days his home on Union Street was often used for church services. Tragically, Jonathan was bludgeoned to death in March 1866 by an ex-convict. This shocking murder became a local sensation. J. N. Loughborough recalled that Ellen White's December 25, 1865, vision had included a warning to Mr. Orton that he live very close to the Lord. Orton's death was a terrible blow to his wife, and she never fully recovered emotionally or spiritually.

The Ortons' home on Union Street (where they lived for about 30 years) was a short distance from the Monroe Street home of James and Ellen White (where they lived during 1854 and 1855).

Captain Edward C. Williams' grave in Mount Hope Cemetery is located opposite 1st Street. Captain Williams was an "extensive tent and sail maker" in Rochester during the mid-nineteenth century. He became a believer in the soon coming of Jesus, and Loughborough reported that he invited William Miller and J. V. Himes to come to Rochester to hold meetings.[17]

The Millerite movement received a strong boost in the Rochester area during the spring and summer of 1843. A resolution at the New York Conference in May 1843 called for the establishment of a weekly paper in Rochester and the opening of a book room.[18] On June

Lamson grave monument, Mount Hope Cemetery

7 it was announced that the paper would begin on June 20 and be entitled *The Glad Tidings of the Kingdom at Hand*.[19] The great Millerite tent was moved to Rochester, and meetings were held between June 23 and July 7, 1843. J. V. Himes, along with T. F. Berry and Charles Fitch, spoke to large crowds. On June 24 the tent collapsed during a major storm while a meeting was in progress. It is supposed that Edward Williams, the tent and sail maker, assisted with the repair of the tent and its reerection.[20] After the meetings in the great tent ended, Fitch and Barry continued to hold meetings in Tolman Hall.[21] On November 12-19, 1843, William Miller followed up on the successful summer meetings and "gave his first course of lectures in the city of Rochester."[22]

In May 1854 M. E. Cornell, with $200 in hand, first went to Detroit, Michigan, and then Rochester, New York, in search of a tent to be used for the first Sabbatarian Adventist tent meetings. He found a used tent offered by E. C. Williams' "sail loft" for a bargain price of $160. It was a 60-foot-diameter round tent that included a "nice bunting flag 15 feet in length, with the motto on it 'What Is Truth?'"[23] Williams was at the time an "earnest First-day Adventist." The tent was quickly sent to Battle Creek, Michigan, where it was erected on a "vacant lot, directly across the street east of where now [in 1910] stands the Nichol's Hospital."[24] The *Review and Herald* included a notice from Loughborough and Cornell that the meetings would be held June 9-11, 1854.[25] Loughborough was the first speaker in that tent, and in those days he noted that listeners could hear him up to a half mile away.[26] Thus began tent evangelism by the future Seventh-day Adventist Church.

Thus Edward C. Williams played a role in establishing the Millerite message in Rochester and in launching a new method of evangelistic outreach for Sabbatarian Adventists that has impacted the Seventh-day Adventist Church to this day.

Captain Edward C. Williams (1815-1868) grave

J. T. and Caroline Orton (on Lamson monument)

Captain Edward C. Williams gravestone

143

Site of James and Ellen White home, 491 Mount Hope Avenue

Site of home of James and Ellen White, 228/230 Monroe Street

Site of Jonathan and Caroline Orton home (part of home may be original), 120 S. Union Street

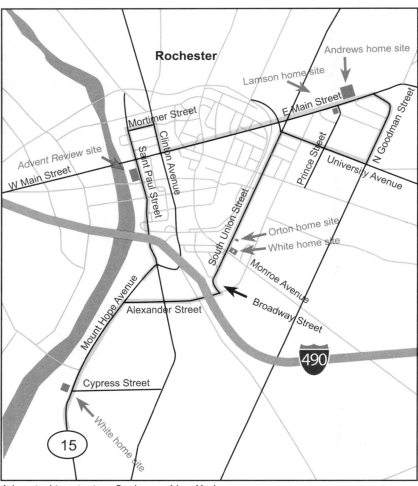

Adventist historic sites, Rochester, New York

Site of Andrews home, 964 E. Main Street, where Angeline died

Site of Drusilla Lamson home, 59 Prince Street; she lived here at the same time that the Andrews lived around the corner

Driving by Adventist sites in downtown Rochester

There are no remaining Adventist-related sites standing in Rochester except for the Tolman Building. To pass by the original locations, proceed north on Mount Hope Avenue. On the left just before Ford Street and the bridge across the Genesee River is "505 Episcopal Church Home." This is the site of the original location of James and Ellen White's first home in Rochester. It is located on the west side of the road between Cypress Street and Sanford Street. The original street number was 124 Mount Hope Avenue, but today it corresponds to 491 Mount Hope Avenue, which is a part of the Episcopal Church Home complex.

Continue north on Mount Hope Avenue and turn right on Alexander Street. Cross over I-490 and immediately turn left onto Broadway. In half a block, keep right on the Y onto Union. The location of James and Ellen White's home on Monroe Street is on the northeast corner of the intersection. The homes were located on the site of the market and restaurant corresponding to 228 and 230 Monroe Street (originally 109 and 111).

Continue on Union Street past Monroe Street. Less than a block from the site of the Whites' homes was the home of Jonathan and Caroline Orton. The home was on the location of 120 S. Union. Further research is needed to determine if any part of the current building dates to the 1850s.

Take Union Street to University and turn right. Then turn left on N. Goodman Street. Turn left on Maine Street toward downtown Rochester. Almost immediately on the right is 962 Maine Street and Rochester Steel Treating Works, Inc. J. N. Andrews' home was near the railroad tracks corresponding to the parking lot to the right of the building. It was in this home that is no longer standing that John and Angeline Andrews lived.

Not far from the Andrews home was the home of Drusilla Orton Lamson on Prince Street just off Main Street. Her home originally stood in the parking lot almost across from College Street. Drusilla moved here after the death of her husband in 1870.

Continue toward downtown on Main Street. There is no left turn allowed on St. Paul Street. Therefore turn right on Clinton Avenue and left on Mortimer Street, which dead-ends into St. Paul Street. Turn left and continue past Main Street. On your right is the large gray convention center building. The location of the Review and Herald printing press was toward the far end of the

Site (near lamppost) of the *Advent Review* office, 31/33 South Saint Paul, while the Whites lived on Monroe Street

building on your right. From this location you can go straight and return to Mount Hope Avenue or take the on-ramp to I-490.

If you wish to drive by the Tolman Building, where Millerite meetings were held, turn right off Main Street to Clinton Avenue. Turn left on Andrews Street. Take the bridge over the river and turn left on State Street. The Tolman Building is an older multistory building on Main Street on the southeast side of the street (the opposite side of Main Street), where State Street turns into Exchange Street. Turn left on Broad Street and then right onto South Street and return to Mount Hope Avenue or I-490.

John N. Andrews and his family had moved to their home on 213 Main Street by 1866, but perhaps as early as 1864. In correspondence with James White in 1864, Andrews described living near the university in Rochester. His home on Main Street was not far from the university. He purchased his Main Street home on October 14, 1869, for $1,000. It was in this home that his beloved wife, Angeline, died on March 19, 1872, at the age of 48. She had suffered a stroke on February 17, 1872, from which she had largely recovered. On March 18 a second stroke occurred from which she did not recover. The funeral was conducted in the Main Street home with C. B. Reynolds as the officiating minister. Andrews wrote of his loss: "What sorrow and anguish have been mine during these days no words can express. Yet with the terrible bitterness of the cup has been such sweetness and such blessing from God as exceeds everything that I have ever before experienced. . . . During the entire period of our married life no unkind word ever passed between us, and no vexed feeling ever existed in our hearts."[27]

Elder Andrews moved to North Lancaster soon after the death of his wife and left the sale of his home in the hands of his uncle, Edward L. Pottle, who was an attorney in Rochester. In describing the property, J. N.

Andrews mentioned the many fruit trees, grapevines, and berries. During 1872-1874 he wrote regularly from North Lancaster and other places hoping the Rochester property would sell. At first he hoped it would sell for $8,000 or even $10,000. He apparently did not have any indebtedness, and so was willing to wait to get the best price. As the decision was made for him to go to Switzerland, he seemed to become more urgent and came at various times to Rochester to try to find a buyer. Finally on August 3, 1874, he sold the home and property for $5,000.[28]

View of Rochester, New York 1880

Sites of the Andrews home on Main Street and Rochester University as they appeared in 1880

Notes

[1] *Dewey's Rochester City Directory for 1855-'56* (Rochester, N.Y.: D. M. Dewey, 1855), pp. 90, 94, 100, 277.

[2] James L. Elwood and Dellon M. Dewey, *A Directory and Gazetteer of the City of Rochester for 1844* (Rochester, N.Y.: Canfield & Warren, 1844), p. 5.

[3] S. W. Rhodes and James White, "The Paper," *Review and Herald*, Feb. 17, 1852, p. 96.

[4] S. W. Rhodes and James White, "Conference," *Review and Herald*, Mar. 2, 1852, p. 104.

[5] John W. Barber and Henry Howe, *Historical Collections of the State of New York* (New York: S. Tuttle, 1842), pp. 491-499.

[6] J. N. Loughborough, *Miracles in My Life: Autobiography of Adventist Pioneer J. N. Loughborough* (Payson, Ariz.: Leaves-of-Autumn Books, 1999), p. 27.

[7] W. C. White, "Sketches and Memories of James and Ellen G. White: XIV. Beginnings in Rochester," *Review and Herald*, June 13, 1935, p. 10.

[8] *Dewey's Rochester City Directory*, p. 307; "Meetings on the Sabbath," *Review and Herald*, June 23, 1853, p. 24; "Appointments," *Review and Herald*, July 7, 1853, p. 32.

[9] J. N. Loughborough, *Rise and Progress of the Seventh-day Adventists,* pp. 168, 179; W. C. White, "Sketches and Memories of James and Ellen G. White: XVI," *Review and Herald*, June 27, 1935, p. 5.

[10] James White, *Life Incidents,* p. 297.

[11] [James White], "The Review," *Review and Herald*, Aug. 4, 1853, p. 48.

[12] James White, *Life Incidents*, pp. 293, 294.

[13] *Ibid.,* pp. 296, 297.

[14] W. C. White, "Sketches and Memories," *Review and Herald*, June 13, 1935, p. 11; L. V. Masten, "Experience of Bro. Masten," *Review and Herald*, Sept. 30, 1852, p. 86; "Obituary," *Review and Herald*, Mar. 14, 1854, p. 63.

[15] Ellen G. White, *Spiritual Gifts*, vol. 2, pp. 191, 192.

[16] *Ibid.,* p. 203.

[17] J. N. Loughborough, *The Great Second Advent Movement,* pp. 132, 133; J. N. Loughborough, *Last Day Tokens* (Mountain View, Calif.: Pacific Press, 1904), pp. 153, 154.

[18] "New York Conference," *Signs of the Times*, May 17, 1843, p. 85.

[19] "Advent Depot at Rochester, N. Y.," *Signs of the Times*, June 7, 1843, p. 105.

[20] [J. V. Himes], "The Cause in Rochester," *Signs of the Times*, July 12, 1843, p. 152.

[21] Joshua V. Himes, "The Tent Meeting at Rochester," *Signs of the Times*, July 19, 1843, p. 156.

[22] Sylvester Bliss, *Memoirs of William Miller,* p. 246.

[23] Loughborough, *Miracles in My Life*, p. 39.

[24] J. N. Loughborough, "Sketches of the Past, No. 94," *Pacific Union Recorder*, Apr. 14, 1910, p. 2.

[25] M. E. Cornell and J. N. Loughborough, "Tent Meeting at Battle Creek, Mich.," *Review and Herald*, May 30, 1854, p. 152.

[26] J. N. Loughborough, "Sketches of the Past, No. 94."

[27] J. N. Andrews, "Death of Sister Andrews," *Review and Herald*, Apr. 2, 1872, p. 124.

[28] Correspondence from J. N. Andrews to E. L. Pottle (Berrien Springs, Mich.: Center for Adventist Research, Andrews University); property deeds, Monroe County, New York; "Died," Rochester *Daily Union and Advertiser*, Mar. 20, 1872, p. 3.

Sacrificing for God's Cause

Mary, John, Charles, and Angeline Andrews

John N. Andrews was the first official Seventh-day Adventist foreign missionary, as well as the author of scholarly books and tracts. Stories of his dedication and sacrifice still move people's hearts today. Yet we must not overlook the sacrifice made by his spouse, Angeline. Loma Linda University holds a diary dated from 1859 to 1865, written by her in Rochester, New York. The diary reveals the tenderness and deep love the couple shared and her willingness to accept his absence for the sake of God's dear cause. Adventist ministers at that time were not settled in a local parish but rather traveled to establish new churches and "strengthen the work."

The following excerpts from Angeline's diary express her feelings. "I miss my dear husband very much—seems as though I could not endure the idea of his being away several months longer [June 2, 1860]." "Received a letter from my dear husband, also his picture. I can hardly be reconciled to his long absence. How my heart would love to meet him again. He is one of the kindest and best of husbands. It is a great sacrifice to us both to be thus separated [June 6, 1860]." After a two-and-a-half-month separation she wrote: "My dear husband returned about 5:00 p.m. Most glad were we to see him [September 16, 1861]." One particularly poignant entry reveals that John had been away from home so much that his 17-month-old daughter hardly

knew him and was afraid to sit by him. About the same time Angeline noted that she had not attended a meeting with her husband for eight or nine months.

John Andrews was gone for about two weeks in May 1863 to attend the first General Conference session in Battle Creek and then returned home for only two days before leaving on another extended trip. The diary entries breathe both her willingness to sacrifice and her tender feelings. "My dear husband left us this noon. . . . I believe the Lord calls him to labor in His service and [I] mean to cheerfully submit to the necessary separation [May 18, 1863]." "About 12 [midnight] Friday night my husband arrived at home. I was awakened by his calling my name at our bedroom window. O how my heart leaped with joy at the sound of his dear voice [May 31, 1863]." "My dear husband left about 9 this morning. It is a sacrifice to have him thus leave home. I miss him much, but it is for the Lord's work and I will do it cheerfully [June 2, 1863]."

It was a love for Jesus and a commitment to the end-time mission of the Seventh-day Adventist Church that motivated such pioneer spouses as Angeline Andrews to willingly sacrifice.

Carrie Matilda Andrews (Aug. 9, 1864-Sept. 24, 1865)

Roosevelt Seventh-day Adventist Church
GPS: N 43°18.481' W 076°15.325'

Katy Wolfer 2008

Roosevelt Seventh-day Adventist Church, 4456 State Route 49, Fulton (Roosevelt), New York

Roosevelt, New York, Seventh-day Adventist Church

The Roosevelt, New York, Seventh-day Adventist Church is located in Oswego County and was built during the summer and fall of 1858 and dedicated on June 17, 1859. The deed indicates that the property was purchased for $36 and owned by Lyman Drake and Alexander Ross. In the days before church organization, individuals held church property.

The original orientation of the church was different from today. While the pulpit is original, the front of the church was between the entrance doors. Those who came in and out of the sanctuary passed the platform. Other churches had this orientation during the nineteenth century. An example is the restored Parkville, Michigan, Seventh-day Adventist Church, which has been relocated to the Historic Adventist Village in Battle Creek, Michigan. In October 1862 the New York Conference was organized in the Roosevelt church.

Ellen White visited the church a few months after it was dedicated and described it thus: "They have a

neat little meetinghouse. It was filled and crowded and many could not get in at all. In the afternoon they were obliged to give it up to the women and infirm and aged men. They drew up the wagons to the windows and the men filled them full."[1]

In 1848 an early Sabbath Conference was held north of Roosevelt in Volney, with David Arnold's barn or carriage house serving as the meeting location. Also located not far from the Roosevelt church is the grave of Frederick Wheeler. He is buried in West Monroe. Wheeler moved to New York in 1857 and worked as a part-time farmer/preacher until his death in 1910 at 99 years of age.

On October 26 and 27, 1867, James and Ellen White, together with J. N. Andrews, passed through Roosevelt on their way to Massachusetts, Maine, and New Hampshire. This is the trip that included a Christmas visit to the Washington, New Hampshire, Seventh-day Adventist Church, where God brought a wonderful

Interior of Roosevelt Seventh-day Adventist Church showing original pulpit and pews

revival. Ellen White wrote of their visit to Roosevelt thus: "This meeting was one of hard labor, in which pointed testimonies were given. Confessions were made, followed by a general turning to the Lord on the part of backsliders and sinners."[2]

Ellen White's Second Civil War Vision

Perhaps the most significant event to happen at the Roosevelt church was Ellen White's second Civil War vision, which she received here on August 3, 1861. Her first Civil War vision had been given at Parkville, Michigan, on Sabbath afternoon, January 12, 1861. J. N. Loughborough recalled the events of that day. In the Parkville vision she was shown that though people were casual or indifferent about the pending war, it would in fact be a "terrible war." Looking pensively at the congregation, she said, "There are men in this house who will lose sons in that war."[3]

These two visions, nearly seven months apart, show the interface between political and social developments and the moral responsibility of God's people. The second vision in particular identified the moral issues connected to the Civil War. The sin of slavery was the particular focus of the vision. When Ellen White presented her vision, it was to a politically mixed audience. The Roosevelt church was split in their loyalties

between the North and the South. A key leader in the church, Alexander Ross, was a Southern sympathizer. It is not clear how many stood with him in this view. God directly confronted this man through His messenger. Thankfully, Ross eventually accepted the testimony.

James and Ellen White and their third son, William, were at the Roosevelt church over the weekend of August 3 and 4, 1861. James White spoke on sanctification and wrote that the meeting was a "refreshing season." It was at this time that 7-year-old Willie saw his mother in vision for the first time. W. C. White gave his recollection in a 1905 talk:

Father had given a short talk. Mother had given a short talk. Father prayed, Mother prayed, and as she was praying, I heard that shout, "Glory." There is nothing like it—that musical, deep shout of "Glory." She fell backward. My father put his arm under her. In a little while her strength came to her. She stood up in an attitude of one seeing wonderful things in the distance, her face illuminated, sometimes bright and joyous. She would speak with that musical voice, making short comments upon what she saw. Then as she saw darkness in the world, there were sad expressions as she spoke [about] what she saw. This continued [for] ten or fifteen minutes. Then she caught her breath, and breathed several times deeply, and then, after a little season of rest, probably five or ten minutes, during which time Father spoke to the people, she arose, and related to the congregation some of the things that had been presented to her.[4]

August 3, 1861, was only two weeks after the Battle of Manassas, Virginia, which is sometimes called the Battle of Bull Run. This was the first major military action of the Civil War. To the surprise of everyone, the Union forces were defeated. Ellen White's vision pulled back the curtain to reveal the unseen principalities and powers. She was shown the "sin of slavery" that had long been a "curse to this nation. The fugitive slave law was calculated to crush out of man every noble, generous feeling of sympathy that should arise in his heart for the oppressed and suffering slave. It was in direct opposition to the teaching of Christ. God's scourge is now upon the North, because they have so long submitted to the advances of the slave power. The sin of the Northern proslavery men is great."[5] She then described the battle at Manassas. As the "Northern army was moving on with triumph," "an angel descended and waved his hand backward. Instantly there was confusion in the ranks. It appeared to the Northern men that their troops were retreating, when

it was not so in reality, and a precipitate retreat commenced."[6]

The net effect of the battle, according to Ellen White, was that both sides were seriously bloodied. The North was rebuked for their sins, yet the South was kept from triumphing because of the Northern losses. God wouldn't allow the North to win until slavery had been abolished.

Alexander Ross

Most Adventists in the North were strongly opposed to slavery, but Alexander Ross was an exception. As mentioned, he also happened to be a prominent leader in the Roosevelt church. His words and influence were having a morally detrimental effect. Ellen White was shown his condition in the same vision. She wrote:

> Satan was the first great leader in rebellion. God is punishing the North, that they have so long suffered the accursed sin of slavery to exist; for in the sight of heaven it is a sin of the darkest dye. God is not with the South, and He will punish them dreadfully in the end. Satan is the instigator of all rebellion. I saw that you, Brother A [Alex-

Roosevelt Cemetery

Hiram and Esther Edson

Alexander Ross

ander Ross], have permitted your political principles to destroy your judgment and your love for the truth. They are eating out true godliness from your heart. You have never looked upon slavery in the right light, and your views of this matter have thrown you on the side of the Rebellion, which was stirred up by Satan and his host. Your views of slavery cannot harmonize with the sacred, important truths for this time. You must yield your views or the truth. Both cannot be cherished in the same heart, for they are at war with each other.[7]

Ross's letter of confession was published in the *Review and Herald* nearly two years later. One can only wonder what happened during the intervening time between the testimony and the confession. His confession is reproduced in part:

It is a little over nineteen years since the sound of the everlasting gospel saluted my ears, and found a welcome place in my poor heart. . . . But for a few years in the past, during the great political excitement, the enemy of all righteousness has well nigh destroyed me, by stirring up old preconceived political opinions, so that I became a blind apologist for slavery, and a sympathizer with the rebellion, which I feel assured is a great sin in the sight of heaven.

I had at times convictions of the wrong course I was pursuing, in using language that was unbecoming one professing godliness, and even sinful, until I finally found myself in the lamentable situation as described in Testimony No. 9, which I do fully endorse. . . . I do thank the Lord, and also Sr. White, for the testimony, and the kindness of the closing remarks of the letter.

Dear Bro. Andrews is with us at Roosevelt, and the Lord is with him. With the help of the Lord and the brethren, whose good counsel I have too often rejected, I will make amends. I feel that my whole being is faced about, and I am resolved to be an overcomer by the word of my testimony, and through the blood of the Lamb. I do humbly crave pardon of all my brethren and sisters in the Lord. Pray for me.[8]

Alexander Ross is buried in the cemetery across the road from the Roosevelt church. Also buried there are Hiram Edson and his second wife, Esther Persons.

Hiram Edson's Life and Contribution

Hiram Edson was a Methodist farmer when he married Effa Chrisler on December 2, 1830. In 1835 they bought a 56-acre farm near Port Gibson, New York. Effa died in May of 1839, leaving Edson with three children—George, 8; Susan, 6; and Belinda, 4. He remarried in October 1839. His second wife, Esther Persons, was a youthful 23 years of age. Edson and Esther's first child, Viah Ophelia, born on June 5, 1841, died within a year, and they had a second child on June 2, 1843, which they gave the same name. Their third and last child, Lucy Jane, was born 13 years later on July 30, 1856.[9]

Edson probably accepted the Advent message during 1843, when the "great tent" was brought to central New York. His daughter Viah had heard that her parents had accepted the message from William Miller himself. There were meetings held in Rochester beginning in June 1843, and during November Miller spent 10 days lecturing in the city.

For many years Edson served as the example of a lay pastor. He played an important role in reclaiming and supporting ministers. In 1849 he helped reclaim Samuel Rhodes. In 1850 he laid hands on Clarissa Bonfoey, and she was healed. Edson dedicated long weeks and even months to take evangelistic trips in New York and even into Canada. He traveled both alone and with others such as Joseph Bates, J. N. Andrews, G. W. Holt, and Frederick Wheeler. J. N. Loughborough received support and training in ministerial work with Edson.

Edson farmed to support his family, but lived to share the sanctuary and the Sabbath. In those days there was no organization to issue licenses or pay salaries; but this did not deter Spirit-filled men such as Edson. He was eventually ordained as a minister. Official records report he was granted ministerial credentials between September 28, 1866, and September 9, 1875.

Over the years Edson generously and sacrificially supplied funds to support the Adventist movement. He and his wife sold their family silverware to raise funds to publish Crosier's exposition of the sanctuary doctrine. The Port Gibson farm was sold in 1850, and the proceeds were used two years later to assist in the purchase of the Seventh-day Adventist press in Rochester. At another time Edson provided funds ". . . to hire a man to go and do Elder J. N. Andrews' work, so that Andrews would be free to do evangelistic work with a tent."

By the mid-1870s Edson had begun slowing down. He spent more time at home, and wrote a manuscript for publication presenting theological speculations and ideas that Ellen White recommended should not be published. She used his case as a reason for having a book committee review manuscripts for publication. Ellen White commented regarding his manuscript, "The matter which he had brought together was . . . not meat in due season for the flock of God. It . . . would bear fruit in dissension and discord."[10] The whole manuscript was never published.

Edson became somewhat cantankerous in his old age, and may have stayed away from church for a few years in the late 1870s. His daughter wrote that Edson and his family were "firm believers in the cause of

truth to the close of their lives, and were true to the message." Hiram Edson is buried in the cemetery just across the road from the historic Roosevelt, New York, Seventh-day Adventist Church.

(For more on Edson and the distinctive theological framework of the Seventh-day Adventist Church, see the chapter on Port Gibson, New York.)

Notes

[1] Ellen G. White, manuscript 7, 1859 (Silver Spring, Md.: Ellen G. White Estate).

[2] Ellen G. White, *Life Sketches* (1915), p. 178.

[3] J. N. Loughborough, "Sketches of the Past—No. 121," *Pacific Union Recorder*, Mar. 7, 1912, pp. 1, 2.

[4] W. C. White, "The Visions of Ellen G. White: Remarks in Takoma Hall, December 17, 1905" (Silver Spring, Md.: Ellen G. White Estate), p. 1.

[5] Ellen G. White, *Testimonies for the Church*, vol. 1, p. 264.

[6] *Ibid.,* pp. 266, 267.

[7] *Ibid.,* p. 359.

[8] Alexander Ross, "From Bro. Ross," *Review and Herald*, Apr. 21, 1863, p. 167.

[9] Genealogical information is from the Hiram Edson family record found in the Edson Bible (Loma Linda, Calif.: Archives and Special Collections, Loma Linda University).

[10] Ellen G. White to W. H. Littlejohn, Aug. 3, 1894 (letter 49, 1894) (Silver Spring, Md.: Ellen G. White Estate).

Hiram Edson grave
GPS: N 43°18.444'
W 076°15.325'

Alexander Ross grave
GPS: N 43°18.465'
W 076°15.313'

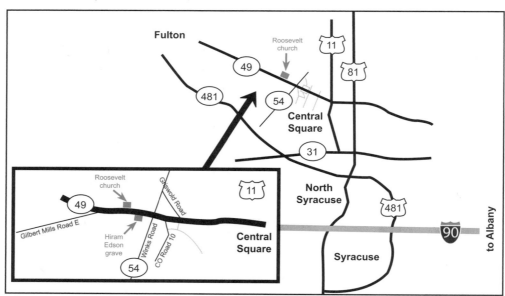

Adventist historic sites, Fulton, New York

Historic Sites in Oswego County

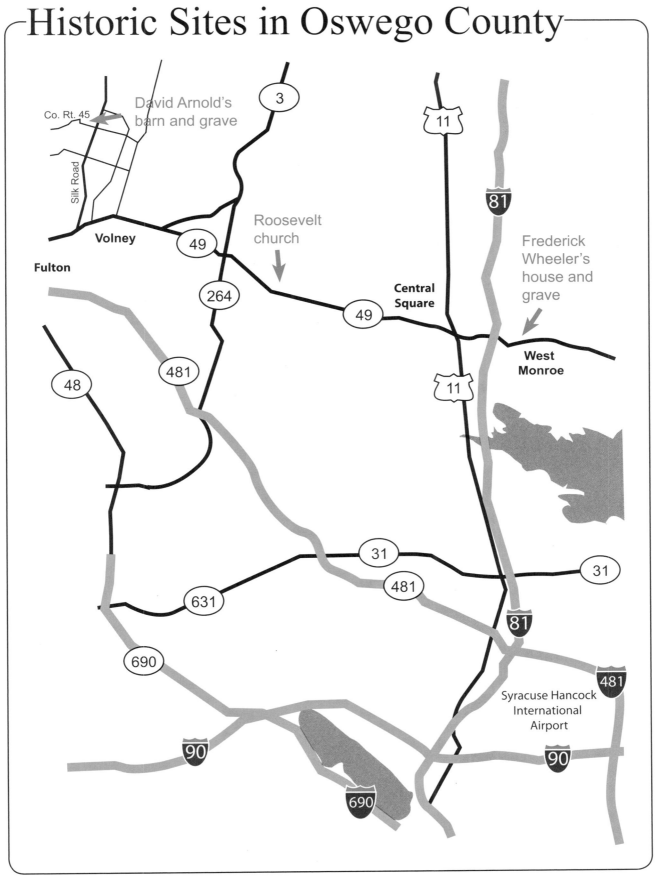

David Arnold barn
GPS: N 43°23.135' W 076°22.430'

Merlin D. Burt 2009

David Arnold's barn, 27 Mount Pleasant-Palermo Road (County Road 45), Volney, New York, as it appeared in 2010

Volney and West Monroe

Oswego County, New York, is the location of many early Sabbatarian Adventist and Seventh-day Adventist developments. The county is centrally located in the state and is divided by the Oswego River. Adventist-related sites in the county are located mostly east of the river on what was part of "Scriba's patent." Significant sites include the Roosevelt Seventh-day Adventist Church, David Arnold's barn, the town of Oswego, and the site of Frederick Wheeler's home and grave in West Monroe.

Volney, New York, Sabbath and Sanctuary Conference in David Arnold's Barn

The first significant Sabbatarian Adventist event in central New York was the August 18-20, 1848, Sabbath and Sanctuary Conference held in the barn of David Arnold in Volney, New York. Hiram Edson organized the conference.[1] A previous major conference had been held in Rocky Hill, Connecticut, in the home of Albert Belden in April. Various regional conferences were also held within traveling distance to Rocky Hill between

April and August. Significant is the effort James White put into raising money for the trip. During the summer of 1848 he went into a hayfield with a scythe and earned $40.[2]

James and Ellen White, together with Joseph Bates and E.L.H. Chamberlain, traveled west via canal boat to Oswego, where they met Heman Gurney, and then traveled on to Arnold's home in Volney.[3] James White described the meeting: "Friday P. M. the brethren came in to our meeting in Volney. There were 30 or 40 who met with us. Brother Bates preached the Sabbath to them with strong argument, much boldness and power. My principal message was on Matt. 25:1-11."[4] This meeting was without question an evangelistic meeting. At first there was confusion and debate. White recollected:

A spirit of discussion and contention for points not important prevailed, so that we who had come so far could hardly have [a] chance to give our message, and the meeting would have proved a failure, and the good brethren would have separated in confu-

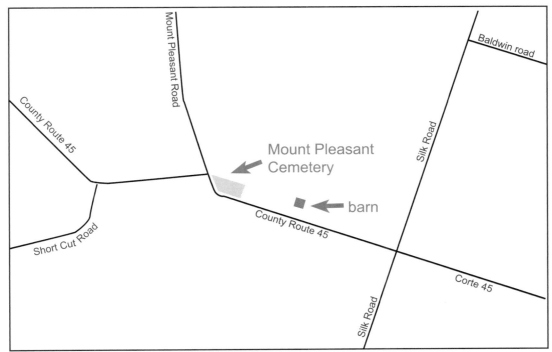

David Arnold barn and cemetery, Volney, New York

Historic marker near the grave of David Arnold in Volney, New York

Gravestone of David Arnold

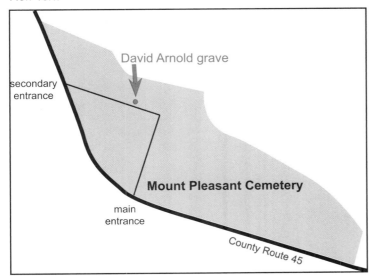

Mount Pleasant Cemetery

David Arnold's barn in Oswego County, New York

David Arnold's barn as seen from the road

Frederick Wheeler (1811-1910)

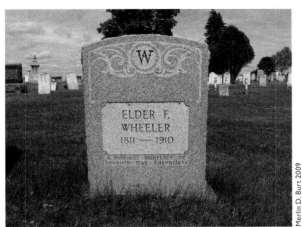

Frederick Wheeler grave in West Monroe, New York

sion and trial, had not the Lord worked in a special manner. His Spirit rested upon Mrs. [White], and she was taken off in vision. The entire congregation believed that it was the work of God, and were deeply affected.[5]

In 1860 Ellen White gave a similar recollection and showed their evangelistic purpose: "There were hardly two agreed. Each was strenuous for his views, declaring that they were according to the Bible. All were anxious for an opportunity to advance their sentiments, or to preach to us. They were told that we had not come so great a distance to hear them, but had come to teach them the truth."[6] David Arnold had become a post-millennialist, believing that the 144,000 were those resurrected after Jesus rose from the dead following His crucifixion, and that the Communion service was an extension of the Passover and should be observed only once a year.[7] Arnold also believed that Michael stood up (Daniel 12:1) in October 1844 and that the 1260, 1290, and 1335 days in Daniel were literal days extending to the end.[8] The teaching and preaching of Bates and James White together with Ellen White's compelling prophetic testimony corrected these and other divergent views and brought unity to the group.

The success of the Volney meeting resulted in an invitation to hold a second general meeting on Hiram Edson's farm in Port Gibson. On the way they stopped in the village of Hanable at the home of "Brother Snow." The traveling group included the Whites, Bates, Edson and his wife, and Simmons.

By 2009 David Arnold's barn had collapsed from neglect and will likely be removed. The current home located by the historic barn is believed to have been built since the time of David Arnold. The location has been confirmed by deeds and maps found in the county records office. David and Lucretia had one daughter, Julia, who was about 14 at the time of the 1848 conference described above.[9] Arnold purchased the property in 1831 and sold parts of it during the 1850s. He and his wife, Lucretia, lost their home through legal action in 1877.[10] Arnold died on June 11, 1889, and is buried just up the road from his home in Mount Pleasant Cemetery on the right-hand side of the road. Enter the main gate and proceed down the lane until it meets the larger lane. Turn left toward the second entrance. The grave is on the right side close to the lane. (See attached map.)[11]

Frederick Wheeler Home Site and Grave

Frederick Wheeler was the first ordained minister in the United States who was both an Adventist and a Sabbathkeeper. See chapters on Fairhaven, Massachusetts, and Washington, New Hampshire, for more information on Wheeler. In 1857 he moved from New Hampshire, and began ministerial work and farming in New York, and in 1861 he and his family moved to West Monroe, New York.[12] He had assisted in building up the Seventh-day Adventist church there that was organized in 1859.[13] In 1867 Wheeler purchased a modest home in West Monroe for $600. He required a $300 mortgage on the property, which indicates his limited resources. Both Frederick and his son George Wheeler lived for many years in the same locations, and to this day the street where their homes were located is called Wheeler Road. Frederick Wheeler's home is no longer standing, but was located on the west side of the road about midway down the street. The location of the home is now part of a wildlife refuge and is near Todd Harbor Swamp on the north side of Oneida Lake. The only remaining evidence of human activity at the location of Wheeler's home is the layout of the land and a large pile of rocks.

Wheeler and his wife, Lydia P., and another grave with the name Lydia Ann, are in the West Monroe Cemetery. Frederick was born on March 12, 1811, and died in his hundredth year on October 11, 1910.[14] Lydia died on March 11, 1886, and is buried by his side. Also buried in the cemetery are Wheeler's son George C. Wheeler (1834-1936); his wife, Sarah E. Shattuck (1839-1924); and two children, Flora V. (1860-1894) and Willie H. (1865-1879). George Wheeler had helpful recollections of his father that he shared later in life. Though not a Seventh-day Adventist, he was a Sabbath-keeper.

Notes

[1] James White to My Dear Brother, July 2, 1848 (Silver Spring, Md.: Ellen G. White Estate).

[2] Ellen G. White, *Spiritual Gifts*, vol. 2, p. 94.

[3] Joseph Bates to Brother and Sister Hastings, Aug.7, 1848. (Silver Spring, Md.: Ellen G. White Estate). James White to Brother and Sister Hastings, Aug. 26, 1848 (Silver Spring, Md.: Ellen G. White Estate).

[4] James White to Brother and Sister Hastings, Aug. 26, 1848.

[5] James White, *Life Incidents,* p. 274; see also Ellen G. White, *Spiritual Gifts*, vol. 2, pp. 97-99.

[6] Ellen G. White, *Spiritual Gifts*, vol. 2, pp. 97, 98.

[7] *Ibid.,* p. 98.

[8] David Arnold, "Letter From Bro. Arnold," *Girdle of Truth, and Advent Review*, Aug. 14, 1848, pp. 52-54.

[9] 1850 U. S. Federal Census, Volney, Oswego County, New York, Oct. 9, 1850, p. 351.

[10] Oswego County, New York, records, vol. 156, pp. 7, 8.

[11] A. E. Place, "Arnold," *Review and Herald*, July 23, 1889, p. 479; Mount Pleasant Cemetery register, Oswego Historical Society, Oswego, N.Y.

[12] C. E. Eldridge, "Interview With George Wheeler," May 5, 1934 (Silver Spring, Md.: Ellen G. White Estate).

[13] James White, "Eastern Tour," *Review and Herald*, Dec. 1, 1859, p. 13.

[14] "The Oldest Minister," *Review and Herald*, Oct. 27, 1910, p. 24.

Frederick Wheeler grave
GPS: N 43°17.092' W 076°06.248'

Merlin D. Burt 2009

West Monroe Cemetery in West Monroe, New York

Site of Frederick Wheeler home
GPS: N 43°26.799' W 076°05.494'

Merlin D. Burt 2010

Site of the home of Frederick Wheeler is located on Wheeler Road, West Monroe, New York

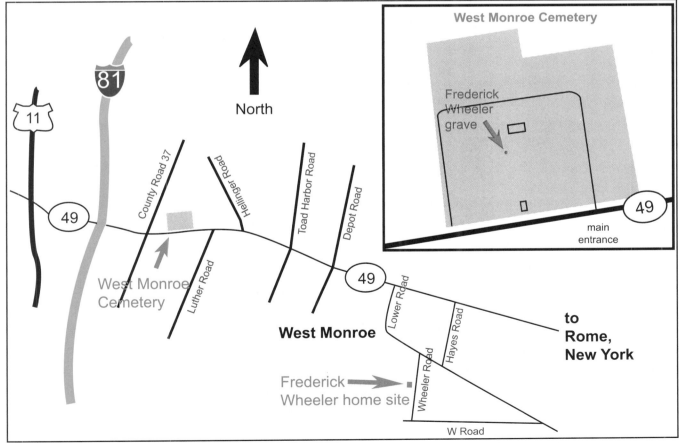

West Monroe Cemetery

Frederick Wheeler grave

main entrance

North

81

11

49

County Road 37

Hellinger Road

Toad Harbor Road

Depot Road

West Monroe Cemetery

Luther Road

49

West Monroe

Lower Road

Hayes Road

Wheeler Road

to Rome, New York

Frederick Wheeler home site

W Road

Frederick Wheeler sites, West Monroe, New York

ADVENTIST PIONEER PLACES

VERMONT

Vernon

Tyler (Sunset) Cemetery, Vernon, Vermont

Merlin D. Burt 2009

Pond Road chapel, built in 1860 by the Second Advent Society, and attended by Rachel Oaks Preston

Merlin D. Burt 2009

Vernon, Vermont

Rachel Oaks Preston in Vernon, Vermont

Vernon, Vermont, located near the border of New Hampshire, was the hometown of Rachel Oaks Preston, Sabbath pioneer for the Seventh-day Adventist Church. Rachel was the middle child of five born to Sylvanus and Nancy Harris on February 22, 1809.[1] Rachel "experienced religion" at the age of 17 and joined the Methodist Church. In 1837 at the age of 28 she was convinced of the seventh-day Sabbath, left the Methodist Church, and joined the Verona, New York, Seventh Day Baptist Church.[2] Rachel's parents continued to live in Vernon, Vermont, through the remainder of their lives. Probably in the late 1850s Rachel and her second husband, Nathan Preston, moved from Washington, New Hampshire, back to Rachel's hometown of Vernon.

Neither Nathan nor Rachel owned any property in Vernon. The traditional site for her home in Vernon is 630 Pond Road, but this home was owned by Rachel's sister Ardelia Ray until her death in 1896.[3] An interview with the owners of the property on Pond Street in 2009

revealed a long tradition in the community that the back part of the house was originally built for Rachel Preston. The owner indicated that his family had lived on Pond Road since the 1850s. The home is located off Highway 142 along with two other sites of interest, the Pond Road chapel and Tyler (Sunset) Cemetery.

Not far from the traditional site of Rachel Oaks' home is a well-preserved historic Advent Christian chapel. Joshua V. Himes dedicated it in 1860. Dwight L. Moody, who lived nearby, preached in it on a number of occasions. In addition, Ira D. Sankey sang in the chapel several times. It is probable that Rachel attended this chapel, as it is only .2 miles from her home and she did not join the Seventh-day Adventist Church until the last year of her life. The restored structure is now called the Pond Road chapel and is maintained by the local historical society with authentic furnishings and a wood stove with a lengthy stovepipe. It looks similar to the William Miller chapel in Low Hampton, New York.

Interior of Pond Road chapel, Vernon, Vermont

Merlin D. Burt 2009

Rachel Oaks Preston's grave is located 1.2 miles south of the Pond Road chapel in Tyler (Sunset) Cemetery. She died on February 2, 1868. She is buried near the corner of the cemetery on the right side of the road as you come from the chapel (the northwest corner). Her grave is close to the first gate as you enter the graveyard. The General Conference has placed a bronze marker directly behind the original marker. Buried next to her is her second husband, Nathan T. Preston, who died on January 19, 1871, at the age of 57.

According to the obituary notice written by S. N. Haskell, Rachel remained unwilling to join the Seventh-day Adventist Church for a number of years, "hearing much said against Bro. and Sr. White, at different times, by individuals who were disaffected in consequence of reproof which they needed, and who sought to relieve their minds by poisoning others [possibly a reference to Stephen Smith and/or Worcester Ball], she became cold in religion, and prejudiced to some extent against the Testimonies, having never seen Bro. and Sr. White."[4] Toward the end of October 1867 *Testimony for the Church,* No. 13, by Ellen G. White, was published. This tract dealt largely with the hard spirit that had been manifested against James White. It also included a testimony of reproof by Ellen White for her husband on the subject. James White's sorrow for his failings was clearly evident. After reading *Testimony* No. 13, which an unknown friend sent her, Rachel Preston changed

her mind about James and Ellen White. Shortly before her death she also heard of the 1867 Christmastime revival in Washington, New Hampshire, and rejoiced. She died in harmony with the Seventh-day Adventist Church and looked for the soon coming of Jesus.[5]

Notes

[1] *Vernon Town Records, Deeds, and Vital Records, 1774-1825,* vol. 1, p. 506. The Rachel Oaks grave marker in Tyler (Sunset) Cemetery in Vernon, Vermont, reads, "In Memory of Rachel, Wife of Nathan T. Preston, Daughter of Sylvanus Harris, died Feb. 2, 1868, Age 58 years 11 mos." In the same cemetery are gravestones that probably belong to Rachel's grandparents. "Mr. Sylvenus [*sic*] Harris, died Feb. 23, 1826, AE 82." His wife was Mary Pond, born in Wrentham, Massachusetts, died Nov. 24, 1838.

[2] S. N. Haskell, "Obituary Notices," *Review and Herald,* Mar. 3, 1868, p. 190; J. N. Andrews, *History of the Sabbath and First Day of the Week,* 2nd ed. enl. (Battle Creek, Mich: Seventh-day Adventist Pub. Assn., 1873), p. 501.

[3] Ardelia Ray probate records, Probate Office records, Brattleboro, Vermont.

[4] Haskell, "Obituary Notices," p. 190.

[5] *Ibid.*

Rachel Oaks Preston home
GPS: N 42°44.831' W 072°30.672'

Merlin D. Burt 2009

Home owned by Rachel's sister Ardelia Ray. The back portion of the house was reportedly built for Rachel.

Merlin D. Burt 2009

Likely home of Rachel Oaks Preston in Vernon, Vermont. The portion of the house where she probably lived.

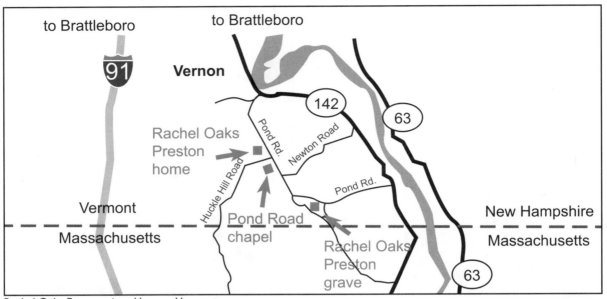

Rachel Oaks Preston sites, Vernon, Vermont

Tyler (Sunset) Cemetery 1796

Rachel Harris

Sylvanus Harris, Jr.

Charles Harris

Mary Pond

Sylvanus Harris

Rachel Harris Oaks Preston

Rachel Harris Oaks Preston historic marker

Tyler (Sunset) Cemetery

Rachel Oaks Preston grave
GPS: N 42°44.095' W 072°29.833'

Preston graves, Tyler (Sunset) Cemetery

Index

C

Canaan, Connecticut 121
Canandaigua, New York 118, 130
Canright, D. M. 98
Cape Elizabeth, Maine ii, xii, 30, 42
Casco Street Christian Church, Portland, Maine 4, 8, 30, 35-41
Centerville, Maryland 66
Central Cemetery, New Ipswich, New Hampshire 90
Central Hall, Portland, Maine 53
Chamberlain, E.L.H. 49, 154
Chardon Street chapel, Boston, Massachusetts 52, 53, 124
Charlestown Female Seminary, Charlestown, Massachusetts 109, 110
Chestnut Street Methodist Church, Portland, Maine 8, 10, 30, 35, 39-42
Chrisler, Effa 151
Christian Connexion or Christian Church 2, 13, 53, 60, 61, 63, 65
Christian Experience of William E. Foy 42, 54
Church Hymnal 111
Church of Jesus Christ of Latter-Day Saints 119
Cincinnati, Ohio 135
Clifton Springs, New York 130, 142
Concord, New Hampshire 80
Congregational Church 13
Congregationalist Bulfinch Church, Lancaster, Massachusetts 77
Cornell, M. E. 138, 143
Cox, Gershom F. 40
Crosier, O.R.L. 69, 118, 130-133, 151
Curtis, Mercy 46, 48
Curtis, Robert 46
Curtis, Silas 3

D

Dansville, New York 118, 141
Darden, Genevieve 58
Darden, Hugh 58
Davison, G. M. 137
Davison Printing Company 135
Day-Dawn 118, 130, 133
Day-Star 30, 133
Deering, Henry 31
Deering, Nathaniel 31
Deering Oaks Park, Portland, Maine 9, 31
Detroit, Michigan 143
Dodge, Hosea 100, 102
Dorchester, Massachusetts 26, 48, 49, 52, 133
Douglass, Frederick 142
Drake, Lyman 148
Dresden, New York 124

Drew, Mr. 70

E

East Kingston, New Hampshire xiv, 53, 80-83, 125
East Poland, Maine 42
East Sullivan, Maine xii, 2-5, 42, 53, 72
Edson, Belinda 151
Edson, Esther 150, 151, 157
Edson, George 151
Edson, Hiram 69, 94, 117, 118, 130-134, 137, 150-154, 157
Edson, Lucy Jane 151
Edson, Luther 130
Edson, Susan 151
Edson, Viah Ophelia 151
1843 prophetic chart 76
1863 prophetic chart 50
1834 Portland Directory 32
Elmwood Cemetery, Haverhill, Massachusetts 72, 73
Emmanuel Missionary College, Berrien Springs, Michigan 76
Erie Canal 116-119, 130, 136
Evidence From Scirpture [*sic*] 124
Exeter, New Hampshire xiv, 52, 80, 83-88, 111, 124

F

Fair Haven, Vermont 122, 126
Fairhaven, Massachusetts xiii, 57-61, 157
Fairhaven Academy, Fairhaven, Massachusetts 57, 59, 63
Fairhaven High School, Fairhaven, Massachusetts 57
Faneuil Hall, Boston, Massachusetts 54
Farnsworth, Cyrus 68, 95-100
Farnsworth, Daniel 96, 97, 102
Farnsworth, Delight 96
Farnsworth, Ernest 104
Farnsworth, Eugene 97, 99, 100, 103, 104
Farnsworth, James 103
Farnsworth, John 97
Farnsworth, Orville O. 103
Farnsworth, Patty 102
Farnsworth, William 96-98, 102-104
Farrington, William 10, 40
First Christian church, Boston, Massachusetts 52, 53
Fitch, Charles 124, 143
Fitchburg, Massachusetts 90
Fleming, Lorenzo Dow 37, 39
Fort Hill Cemetery, Gorham, Maine 8
Foss, Hazen 2, 27, 42, 72, 73
Foss, Mary 24, 25, 27, 40, 72
Foss, Samuel 24, 25, 27, 40, 72
Foster, Gideon 40
Fox, John and Margaret 119

Jordan, Sarah 28

K

Keene, New Hampshire 111
Kellogg, J. H. 141
Knowles, Merlin 93

L

Ladies' Wreath 110
Lake Champlain, New York 122
Lamson, Drusilla 135, 142, 144, 145
Lamson, J. Bradley 135, 142
Lancaster, Massachusetts 77
Lempster, New Hampshire 93, 104
Lincoln, Abraham 86
Lincoln, Todd 86
Lindsey, Benjamin 70
Litch, Josiah 124
Loma Linda University, Loma Linda, California 147
Longfellow, Henry Wadsworth 30, 42-45
Loughborough, J. N. 5, 26, 27, 32, 70, 137, 142, 143, 149, 151
Low Hampton, New York xvi, 120-129, 161
Low Hampton Cemetery, Low Hampton, New York 126

M

Maine Historical Society, Portland, Maine 19, 30
Manassas, Virginia 150
Marion Party 104
Marlboro chapel, Boston, Massachusetts 52, 55
Marlboro Hotel, Boston, Massachusetts 55
Marlow, New Hampshire 93, 98
Marsh, Joseph 135
Marsh, Samuel 95
Masten, Lumen V. 135, 140
McCann, Harriet 24
Mead, Fred 103
Mead, Newell 102, 103
Mead, Rose 103
Mead, Sarah 102
Megquier, Hannah 25
Megquier, John 24-27
Melodeon, Boston, Massachusetts 53, 55
Memphis, Michigan 69
Messenger Party 104
Methodist Episcopal church, Fairhaven, Massachusetts 64
Middle Range Pond, Poland, Maine 25
Middletown, Connecticut 49
Milbridge, Maine 2
Millen Pond, Washington, New Hampshire 68, 92, 93, 98, 99, 103

Millennial Harp 47, 66, 67
Miller, Lucy 76, 120, 125, 126
Miller, Paulina 121, 122
Miller, William 3, 8, 14, 26, 30, 37-41, 52-54, 57, 63, 65, 68, 76, 80, 83, 84, 119-129, 142, 143, 151
Miller, William, Sr. 121
Millicent Library, Fairhaven, Massachusetts 57
Moody, Dwight L. 161
Mount Hope Cemetery, Rochester, New York 139-143
Mount Pleasant Cemetery, Volney, New York 155, 157

N

New Bedford, Massachusetts 2, 57, 60, 68-70
New Bedford Academy, New Bedford, Massachusetts 59
New Bedford North Christian Church, New Bedford, Massachusetts 65
New Bedford Whaling Museum, New Bedford, Massachusetts 57, 64
New Ipswich, New Hampshire xiv, 89-91
Newman, Robert 54
New York City 90, 117
Nichols, Otis 26, 48, 52
North Lancaster, Massachusetts xiv, 77, 78, 141, 145, 146
Northeast Maritime Institute, Fairhaven, Massachusetts 63
North Star, The 142
Nye, Deborah 57

O

Oak Hill Cemetery, Battle Creek, Michigan 49
Oaks, Amory 95
Oaks, Rachel 94-96, 119, 161-165
Oaks, Rachel Delight 95, 97. *See also* Farnsworth, Delight
Old Sturbridge Village, Massachusetts xiv, 51, 74
Oneida, New York 119
Oneida Lake, New York 158
Orton, Caroline 135, 139, 141-145
Orton, Jonathan 135, 139, 141-145
Oswego, New York 154
Otter Creek, Maine 2
"Our Home on the Hillside" Sanitarium, Dansville, New York 118

P

Pacific Union College, Angwin, California 76
Palmyra, Maine xii, 13-16
Palmyra, New York 118
Paris, Maine 19, 21
Paris Hill, Maine xii, 1, 18-22, 137
Park Street church, Boston, Massachusetts 54